At the End of Darwin Road

A Memoir

Fiona Kidman

16pt

Copyright Page from the Original Book

A catalogue record for this book is available from the National Library of New Zealand

A VINTAGE BOOK
published by
Random House New Zealand
18 Poland Road, Glenfield, Auckland, New Zealand
www.randomhouse.co.nz

Random House International
Random House
20 Vauxhall Bridge Road
London, SW1V 2SA
United Kingdom

Random House Australia (Pty) Ltd
20 Alfred Street, Milsons Point, Sydney,
New South Wales 2061, Australia

Random House South Africa Pty Ltd
Isle of Houghton
Corner Boundary Road and Carse O'Gowrie
Houghton 2198, South Africa

Random House Publishers India Private Ltd
301 World Trade Tower, Hotel Intercontinental Grand Complex,
Barakhamba Lane, New Delhi 110 001, India

First published 2008

© 2008 Fiona Kidman

The moral rights of the author have been asserted

ISBN 978 1 86941 944 8

This book is copyright. Except for the purposes of fair reviewing no part of this publication may be reproduced or transmitted in any form or by any means, electronic or mechanical, including photocopying, recording or any information storage and retrieval system, without permission in writing from the publisher.

Text design: Anna Seabrook
Cover illustration: Ian Kidman, Te Kaha, 1964
Cover design: Katy Yiakmis
Printed in Australia by Griffin Press

TABLE OF CONTENTS

Preface	vii
Chapter 1	1
Chapter 2	10
Chapter 3	34
Chapter 4	50
Chapter 5	62
Chapter 6	81
Chapter 7	109
Chapter 8	134
Chapter 9	169
Chapter 10	201
Chapter 11	236
Chapter 12	272
Chapter 13	300
Chapter 14	344
Chapter 15	376
Chapter 16	406
Chapter 17	435
Chapter 18	469
Chapter 19	488
Chapter 20	507
Chapter 21	528
Works by the author quoted in this volume	551
Other works quoted in this volume	553
Acknowledgements	555

Fiona Kidman has written more than 20 books, mainly novels and collections of short stories. Her most recent novel, *The Captive Wife,* was a joint winner of the Readers' Choice Award and a finalist for the Deutz Medal for Fiction at the 2006 Montana New Zealand Book Awards. *The Book of Secrets* won the fiction category of the awards in 1986, and several other of her books have been short-listed. She has been awarded a number of prizes and fellowships, including the Mobil Short Story Award, the Victoria Writers Fellowship, and the OBE for services to literature. In 2006 she was the Meridian Energy Katherine Mansfield Fellow in Menton, France, and toured France as part of *Les Belles*

Etrangères, sponsored by the French government.

Fiona Kidman is a Dame Commander of the New Zealand Order of Merit and lives in Wellington.

Other works by Fiona Kidman

Novels
A Breed of Women (1979)
Mandarin Summer (1981)
Paddy's Puzzle (1983, also published as
 In the Clear Light)
The Book of Secrets (1987)
True Stars (1990)
Ricochet Baby (1996)
Songs from the Violet Café (2003)
The Captive Wife (2005)

Short story collections (as author)
Mrs Dixon and Friend (1982)
Unsuitable Friends (1988)
The Foreign Woman (1993)
The House Within (1997)
*The Best of Fiona Kidman's Short
 Stories* (1998)
A Needle in the Heart (2002)

Short story collections (as editor)
*New Zealand Love Stories: An Oxford
 Anthology* (1999)
The Best New Zealand Fiction 1 (2004)
The Best New Zealand Fiction 2 (2005)

The Best New Zealand Fiction 3 (2006)

Non-fiction
Gone North (1984)
Wellington (1989)
Palm Prints (1994)

Poetry
Honey and Bitters (1975)
On the Tightrope (1978)
Going to the Chathams (1985)
Wakeful Nights (1991)

Play
Search for Sister Blue (1975)

Dedicated to Hugh and Flora Eakin, who lived with me at the end of Darwin Road

I could not endure to keep so many large classes of facts all floating loose in my mind without some thread of connection to tie them together...
Charles Darwin, *More Letters*

Preface

Over the years I have been accumulating stories about my life in a fragmentary way, through dozens of short essays and articles written for magazines and periodicals. When I reread some of them, I realised that, put together, they began to form a narrative.

Some of my earlier journalism was published in a collection called *Palm Prints.* By way of introduction, I wrote a clutch of personal essays, ending them at my twenty-third birthday, when I had just become a mother and was starting to think of myself as a writer. At the time, I decided that was as far as I wanted to explore my life in public. But I have changed my mind. To be a woman writing in this country for forty-five years has been a mixed experience, but one I decided I wanted to tell people about, after all. Besides that, my life as a writer has yielded me the good fortune of meeting some fascinating people. You have only one life to draw on. Those who have read

Palm Prints may find some of the early chapters in this book familiar—but different, too.

My year in Menton, as the 2006 Meridian Energy Katherine Mansfield Fellow, offered me a unique opportunity to view my life from a distance, perhaps more so than if I had written about it here in New Zealand, to see myself more as a character and, more importantly perhaps, to see others as characters. At heart, I remain a novelist.

A few names have been changed or abbreviated. None of this alters the main narrative. There are quite enough recognisable people in it as it is.

This is the first of two books that give an account of my life.
Fiona Kidman
2007

Chapter 1

Last summer I went north to Kerikeri, where I lived when I was a child, after the end of the Second World War. I drove along Darwin Road to the patch of land my parents once owned. As I looked beyond the luxuriant tropical growth of the orchards, towards the stand of blue gum trees in the distance that formed the boundary, I heard voices of the past reaching out to me. I was overwhelmed with such a feeling of loss, and yet such a vivid sensation of memory, of the exact way things were in that odd little place, and how they shaped me as a person, that I turned away. This is all too much, I said to myself. This will be the last time I come here.

For much of my early life, I grew up surrounded by the sharp citric scent of orange groves, bright heat and, however curiously detached, the shadow of Asia. Kerikeri is a small town, so different from the rest of New Zealand, that it astonishes me how few people are aware of its post-missionary story.

They see the Old Stone Store, which symbolises New Zealand's early colonial history, and the rich new town centre, in stark contrast to other less prosperous towns in the North, but nothing of what came in between: the 'ideal city', which a group of expatriate British people who had been stationed in the Far East set out to establish in the 1920s. They came, bristling with military titles, laden with jade and precious artefacts from China, and built their houses. Some of them were little more than shacks in the dust; a few of them were grand and based on Oriental influences. Around them, they planted citrus trees and passion fruit, shaded by rapidly growing belts of gum trees and redtipped hakea hedges. The ones who had money found servants, by one means or another.

It was to one of the larger houses that my family first moved. My father had gone ahead to find a place for my mother and me to stay while he worked on a house for us on land he had bought from one of the earlier settlers. My mother thought we would be paying board and lodgings. Much to her surprise, she discovered, on the night of her arrival, that she was to be the cook.

Thus began my life as 'the servant's girl', at least until my father had fashioned a home out of a converted army hut on the piece of land he had bought at the end of Darwin Road. Some of that story forms the basis of my early novel called *Mandarin Summer*. A later short fiction, called 'All the Way to Summer', explores my life in the town.

There have been times when I have wanted to put all of this behind me. Like the day I went up Darwin Road and stood looking back towards the trees. On the spot where I stood, a green wooden gate once hung between strainer posts and a wire fence. The words 'Goathland Farm' were painted on the gate in white letters.

'What for you call your place Goatland?' one of the Dalmatian men of the neighbourhood once asked my father. (The Dalmatian gum diggers had arrived before the orchardists.) My father tried in vain to explain that it was Goathland, named for some place in Yorkshire dear to his heart. But of course that's what our place did become known as—Goatland.

That evening, I lay in the dark in the Abilene Motel, which is down and along the road a bit, and listened to summer rain on the roof, and heard the rustle of gum trees, and it occurred to me that however many times I left Kerikeri, the place would never leave me. Of course I would go back. And I did, but it's surprising how things can change in a very short time. A few weeks ago, before I left New Zealand, I went north again, and the gum trees had gone.

I am writing this story of mine from Menton, in the South of France, where I am in residence as the Katherine Mansfield Fellow. This honour, bestowed annually, allows a New Zealand writer to live in Menton and work at Villa Isola Bella, where Katherine Mansfield lived in 1920, and wrote a number of her most renowned short stories. In just three years she would be dead from tuberculosis, at the age of thirty-four. I have come here in the springtime, with my husband Ian Kidman. We live in an apartment block on a hill called Montée du Lutetia. Our apartment is shabbily genteel, with large rooms, red tiled floors, rickety white French furniture, and three balconies facing down avenue de Verdun towards the Mediterranean Sea. This town is famous for its citrus. Beneath us stands a large grove of orange trees that are just being harvested for their late crop; the streets are full of windfalls. And the air is full of the dizzying perfume of new citrus blossom; when I walk down the streets I feel as if I have been drinking quantities of Cointreau, the scent is so intense. It's like being in Crete in the springtime: you come down from the mountains into warm sun-filled valleys, and you are overpowered and languidly drowsy from its impact. Or in Kerikeri when I was a child.

If it was Mansfield who brought me to this French sojourn, it was a variety of French writers who first drew my interest towards France. Marguerite Duras, a writer I have long admired, was one. I remember hearing her on the *South Bank Show*—she died in 1992—saying that what has happened to us by the time we are sixteen or so is what will shape our impressions of the world for ever after. In essence, I think she is right, even if the age is somewhat arbitrary—it depends on what kind of a person you are, what you have already learnt about the world. I had known of Duras since I was a young woman myself when I saw her film *Hiroshima Mon Amour,* the devastation of love among the ruins, the way a shadow on a man's back makes a woman both momentarily forget barbarism, and embrace it. Not long after that, I began to read her novels about growing up young and illicitly in love in Vietnam. You would have to be French to write like that, I thought. Since then, I have followed the path of Duras's girlhood through the teeming oleander-lined streets of Ho Chi Minh City, as it is now, although hardly anybody calls it that; to those who know the city, it will always be Saigon. I have sailed along the vast coffee-brown waters of the Mekong River, on leaky barges with canopies to protect travellers from the sun, Duras's novels clutched in my travel bag, and understood how that early landscape, and what happened to her there, might have shaped the way she lived her life. However various her invention, the heat, the river, the violence and the sensuousness of a liaison behind Saigon's shuttered windows lie behind every literary decision she made. She did not say that we cannot change, or learn, or perceive the world from different angles. But there, lying at the heart of us, is the unshakeable truth of how we were made.

What I have to tell is largely a personal narrative about how I came to inhabit a fictional world, where the lines constantly blur between what happened, or people say happened, and what I think happened. Another way of putting it is to acknowledge the 'dark other' who walks beside writers, reminding us that things are never quite the way they seem. Writers have been doing this kind of explaining of themselves for a very long time, of course. In one of her essays, called 'The Black Block', Duras wrote, in effect, that when the writer sits down to write it's not translation that is going on; nor is it a matter of passing from one state to another. Rather it's deciphering something already there, something you have done 'in the sleep of your life'. Margaret Atwood comes at it another way, when she speaks of 'negotiating with the dead'. She suggests that *all* narrative writing is motivated, deep down, by a fear of and fascination with mortality—by a desire to make the risky trip to the Underworld, and to bring something or someone back from the dead. Still another approach comes from my friend, the poet and analyst Michael Harlow, who speaks of 'the sacred history', by which I understand him to be saying that each of us is entrusted with the story of who we are and where we came from. What we make of it as writers is over to us, yet it informs our every literary judgement, and a good many other judgements too.

The images I describe in my own life are as near as I can come to a kind of truth telling; the most recurring ones, like dreams, are deeply linked with real events in my life, the ones that began in childhood. It was because of Duras, not Mansfield, that I wanted to come to France. Yet Mansfield has delivered me into a landscape drenched in one of the most central sensory perceptions of my childhood: the scent of oranges.

Chapter 2

The more I think about it, the more my history has come to seem like a classy whodunit to me. I feel that I knew my parents before I was born, although I know that is a delusion based on the stories I was told. But I study photographs looking for clues. On a wall of my house in New Zealand hang heavy framed portraits of my forebears, my great-grandparents Margaret and Neil Small, whose families came to New Zealand in the 1840s. My great-grandmother was a Sutherland, the daughter of Elizabeth and Alexander Sutherland, from the village of Badbea, on the east coast of Caithness in Scotland. There is a story about my great-great-grandmother leaving Scotland that hits my heart like a hammer blow. According to the legend, her family made its way from Badbea to Brora, some eighteen miles south, accompanied by relatives who were going to bid them farewell. At Brora they would board a boat heading south to connect with ships leaving for New Zealand.

Amid a great keening as they said their goodbyes, the menfolk boarded the boat. Then Elizabeth had a sudden change of mind. She stood on the shore, clutching her youngest daughter, and refused to embark. Alexander, his face stormy, swept down the gangway and seized the baby from her arms, taking it aboard. She followed her child, as women do.

Alexander Sutherland had responded to Edward Gibbon Wakefield's call to take up land in New Zealand. Each lot comprised 100 acres of country and one town acre, and the price was £100. The site of the town was undisclosed, but it turned out to be Wellington. Elizabeth was already pregnant again when she tried to resist the journey; her next child, Katrean, was born on the *Oriental* as it sailed through the heads into Wellington Harbour, exactly one week before the Treaty of Waitangi was signed. Margaret, my great-grandmother, Elizabeth's sixth child, was born in New Zealand.

In her picture, my great-grandmother wears a gigantic hat like that of a Royal Guard, a long dress that is probably taffeta, and expensive jewellery. I often wear one of her rings. The look in her eyes is distant: perhaps she is thinking of some other home, the one her mother had found so hard to leave.

Beside these portraits are those of my grandparents, Robert Small and his wife Lizzie. They are a serious, responsible-looking Scots pair, although I am always struck by the sweet expression around my grandfather's eyes. They were not as strict a couple as many of their contemporaries. If they had been, they would never have put up with my mother's antics. In the family photographs, Flora is the hoyden, the tomboy of the family, appearing among her well-dressed and well-educated older brothers and sisters, with her tongue poking out and her mother placing a remonstrating hand on her arm.

Hold the snapshot still for a moment, and this is what I see: Margaret is the fair one with ascetic looks and glasses perched halfway down her nose, the blunt one who laughs easily, but her hidden tongue can be sharp. Roberta has a dark mop of curls and skin so transparent you could swear her blood glowed through it in the dark. The truly stylish one is Jean, her suits tailor-made, her hats perky. I see her as something of the wild card in the family; in an early photograph she wears her dark hair long and loosely scooped up, looking like a dusky Madonna, a woman who might as easily have been my mother as Flora, the *enfant terrible,* and often, it seems, wished she was.

Behind these young women stands the older brother Stewart, a dark, brooding young man, with the shadow of a clipped moustache. At the edge of the picture is Robert, the younger brother, who would try harder than anyone to please. Just a couple of years older than my mother, he shared a room with her when they were small, and at nights she heard him counting his money beneath his pillow. Most of the family had middle names reflecting their Scots ancestry—Sutherland, McKay,

Cameron (my mother's), Kirkpatrick. Roberta bore this last name, with what always seemed like a mixture of pride and embarrassment. Empress Eugenie, the wife of Napoleon III, was, I believe, a distant cousin. William Kirkpatrick of Closeburn emigrated to Spain, where he earned a living as a trader and married a Spanish noblewoman. It was his granddaughter Eugenie who became the empress. Alexander Kirkpatrick, whom I understand to be William's brother, moved to Argyllshire and married into my grandmother's family. My cousin Catherine owns the portrait of Eugenie as a young woman which has been handed down through the family.

When this photograph was taken, the family had a farm with tennis courts in the garden, and a billiard room, and good motorcars. They took holidays at the spa resorts in the central North Island, places like Rotorua and Taupo where my grandmother 'took thermal waters' for her various ailments. When they were small, the children had a plump elderly governess called Miss Adie Malcolm, who stayed on after her charges grew older. My mother caught the tail end of this bountiful life in her childhood. All my aunts went as boarders to St Cuthbert's School for Girls in Auckland, but by the time my mother's turn came, the Great Depression was making inroads into the family fortunes. So she stayed at home, on the family's sheep station, Ruakaka, in the Waiotahi Valley in the eastern Bay of Plenty. While my mother rode long distances on horseback to high school, my aunts were turning into gorgeous flappers, when they were off duty from their nursing training.

Before long my mother decided to take her place on the farm as a rouseabout in the shearing sheds, and as cook for the men who worked there. My grandmother's health was failing so, at sixteen, Flora cooked for up to a dozen people each day. My grandparents had always been generous hosts, often to those with hard luck stories, and no change in circumstance would stop the steady flow of guests who had to be catered for. Even on the farm, the woolsheds were full of passers-by at night. The Tuhoe prophet

Rua Kenana was a frequent visitor at the farm, accompanied by large groups of his wives and children. Kenana was in the process of founding an independent Maori community at Maungapohatu in the Urewera bush, which would end in grief and bloodshed.

In those days, my mother spoke Maori, although only in the shearing sheds and not at the house, where it was met with family disapproval. Yet all her life my mother retained some Maori, or a form of the language, for I doubt that by the time she was an old woman she had a real memory of what it meant. All the same, she spoke a kind of seamless and rhythmically flowing patois, always to a secret audience of children: first me, then my children—her grandchildren—and the first of her great-grandchildren. Some might say this was disrespectful of the language, not a proper way to use it. My mother would outgrow her hoyden ways as real life kicked in. She never danced, as far as I know, I rarely heard her sing, and overall she was a quiet almost shy woman, but this secret melodic hum of words in her head, this otherness from the rest of her family, was one of the things that carried her through her life. It didn't entirely protect her from her family's innate conservatism and later she sometimes found it hard to accept some of my different choices, but without those 'voices' I think she would have lacked the imaginative flair that emerged when she and I built a secret life during my childhood.

For a long time, I think, my grandparents saw themselves at the centre of their world, their prosperity beyond question. But they were not above sharing it, and their house was one to which people turned in time of trouble. I come from generations of people who expected to flourish and multiply across the land; the twist in the story is that my children and I are almost the sole survivors. I have three cousins: Stewart's daughter, born when I was almost an adult, and the two stepchildren of Margaret. Beyond us, there is no future generation except my descendants. These aunts and uncles are in my story because they have no way out of it. In time I would become the focus of all their hopes for a future on the land. That didn't happen but at least I would give them heirs. As I look back, I see there was little escape from their expectations, at least not until I grew up. For a long time, some of them would consider me 'beyond the pale'—an expression they used often—as I entered the world of a writer, so different from theirs. Some of them loved me for it, perhaps seeing in me a difference they had yearned for themselves. Others never understood what my life was about, in the same way that they did not understand my mother. But during my childhood they were important companions, in the way that brothers and sisters are—just older than me by thirty or forty years.

There is, I grant, something missing from this account of my grandparents. My experience of them was delightful but certain events unfolded that suggest hardness, even ruthlessness. My grandfather was known as unflinching, not afraid of pain, a man who would cut out his own teeth with a pocket-knife when he had toothache. I have a fragment of their history that troubles me. It is my grandmother's silver teapot, fluted halfway up the sides, which I keep polished on my sideboard. On one side, it is inscribed with the words: *'To Mr and Mrs A.R. Small, A Token of Regard From Members of Lower Moawhango Farmers' Union, 1907'.* Moawhango, site of an earlier property, was a remote farming district from where, six years later, the first wave of Prime Minister Bill Massey's 'Cossacks' rode on horseback to Wellington, farmers armed with pitchforks and guns to break the waterfront strike that had locked up the ships taking produce abroad. They broke more than the strike, they broke heads and bones.

My grandparents had left the district by then. They may not have subscribed to the actions of the Moawhango farmers in 1913, but the New Zealand Farmers Union had been formed at the end of the nineteenth century to exert pressure on the government for free trade, free access to Maori land and security from the threat of trade unionists and socialists. And, the distance between my mother's family and my parents had something to do with the distance between town and country, farmers and 'workers', between Presbyterian and the Irish and Roman Catholics, or both, and between Maori and Pakeha. I look at the teapot some mornings when I am having breakfast and wonder about things I was not told.

It was to Ruakaka Station that my father came courting Flora, around 1931. Hugh Eakin, an itinerant English farm worker, was a tall thin young man with chiselled features and an olive complexion. He was good-looking, or so I thought, except for his large beakish nose, which I inherited, and a snarled tangle of teeth. He was born in Middlesborough, into what he described as the lower middle class, although it was clear that he longed to advance up the social scale. There was something of the dandy about him. I have a pile of photographs of him, mostly taken before he met my mother. In one he is a child wearing a frilled shirt and a huge Breton hat; in another he is a grown man wearing a one-piece bathing suit with straps over the shoulders, on a beach in Hawaii; in the next, he is a sailor with a pipe in his mouth, on board a ship; he wears plus fours in yet another, a serious business suit next, and here he is again, wearing tennis whites with a group of stylish young people; in several he has one foot up on the running board of a Model T Ford, in the Australian outback. In all of the Australian pictures, he wears a hat like Humphrey Bogart's tilted over one eye. He referred to his parents as the Mater and the Pater. His mother had died long before I was born. Her husband, my paternal grandfather, once a sergeant in the Royal Irish Constabulary, lived until not long before my birth on the other side of the world.

Here is another photograph: the only one of the Mater, my grandmother Eakin, born Ann O'Hara at Bandon in County Cork, Ireland. In the photograph, she wears a dark high-crowned hat with a severely cut brim. Above her stern mouth, the large eyes looking levelly out of the photograph are my own. There was talk, when I was a child, of a lost castle, of an educated Irish family, a vanished gentility. Unlike my mother's family, she already knew that the world was lost to her and her children. In letters to my father, which he kept, she tried to explain this to him, but he didn't believe her.

My father had emigrated to New Zealand in 1929 on a church-sponsored passage that required him to stay in New Zealand for five years. He was twenty-five and the Depression was biting hard. Despite several trips to sea, seven passages through the Panama Canal and living briefly in Vancouver, where he jumped ship and was rescued from imprisonment by his Irish uncles who were Mounties, he had already spent years out of work. He tried San Francisco for a while, where he sang in the chorus of light opera and became engaged to a girl called Sybella, but he left her and returned to England. Young people like him tried to hold onto their sanity through tennis parties and picnics. I don't know how my father came to meet the people he did, but by the time he emigrated he had a vision of himself as more English than the English. He landed in New Zealand with some of the colonising dream that had inspired the Wakefield colonists:

there would be cheap fertile land for farming, and local labour that was easy to come by. Soon he would be landed gentry. He had the accent for it. I doubt his family spoke as he did: this boy from Middlesbrough, with the Irish family background, spoke what we now call BBC Received English with an intermittent stammer. Something like Alistair Cooke, who had gorgeous British vowels despite his working-class origins in Blackpool.

Of course, it was too late. My mother's forebears, blunter, more pragmatic people, were the true inheritors of the Wakefield dream. My father was a johnny-come-lately, and by then New Zealand, too, was falling on hard times. I can see that if he had been born at some other time, he would have been an artist or a writer. He was to try his hand at both as he grew old. But he suffered disappointments that seemed to have little to do with my mother or me, although in time they would come to haunt us all.

Perhaps an accumulation of these sorrows had begun to burden his heart when he turned up on my grandparents' doorstep, and they detected them. Or perhaps they believed he was simply an adventurer, and an Anglo-Catholic one at that, not to mention the Irish influence. At any rate, while he captivated the heart of the youngest, seemingly most unlikely daughter to be attracted to this outsider, the Smalls were not impressed with his courtship. Just how they showed their displeasure was never spelt out, but he told me that he felt it. In later years I sensed an unease when he was present at family gatherings. At the time, matters were left to follow their own path. There were plenty of problems on the farm. My grandfather's woolshed was bursting with unsold wool as the bitter economic truth of the Depression bit even deeper. The unthinkable happened and the family walked off the land. Although my parents were engaged to be married, their future looked hopeless. My father's five years in New Zealand were up. He proposed to join Bill, his recently married brother, in Western Australia. He had a small inheritance from the Mater after her death in 1935. The letter the Pater wrote then breaks my heart. 'Lofty' is my father.

You will have a recollection of how mother used to complain of her stomach from time to time, and get a bottle of stuff from Pedlow for it, 'a tablespoonful 3 times a day'. During the autumn she got a few bottles from Dale the chemist, they seemed to suit her better, and that was all the difference that I ever noticed, a few days previous to Tuesday 15th January. She complained in the usual manner but nothing at all serious or to worry about. I had been for a walk after dinner as mother was keen that I should every day, and on my return just at dusk I noticed a light in the front bedroom. Mrs Fawcett was inside and informed me that 'Mrs Eakin had got a bad pain in her stomach and I've put her to bed and been for the doctor.' Well the doctor came and was on with the usual remedies which eased her a bit, but he began to fear obstruction of the bowel ... Pedlow decided that mother should go to the hospital for an operation. We arranged accordingly for a private ward in North Ormesby Hospital, you may recollect mother's horror of a public ward. Well the operation was on Saturday afternoon, at about 4.30 and at 11.30p.m. on Sunday dear mother breathed her last, quietly and without pain with myself and Fanny Thomson by the bedside. Cause of death cancer ... I have to send you some money, in accordance with the terms of your mother's will. There will be about half the amount we had in the Yorkshire Penny Bank, the whole of some saving's certificates (mother used always warn me that these were for Lofty, they are my own private savings she used to say, oh! All right I'd say, they are for Lofty) and the whole of the insurance amount, you remember the one-armed man—the agent—who used to come every other week for the money, mother used to call him 'Trouble the House'. It won't amount to a terrible lot but it will be a nice little start for Flora and yourself.

Later, the Pater describes how his cousin Fanny Thomson had arranged for a Mrs Murphy, a widow with nine children, to come and take care of him.

If my father seems to have been favoured by his mother's will, this was not quite as it appeared. Bill, the brother he was about to meet up with, had had fragile health as a child and was raised in Bandon by my grandmother's single sisters, Polly and Sarah (or Poll and Sal, as they were known). Most of the family wealth, and their house, had been set aside for Bill. Among my uncle's health problems was a cleft palate, which appears to have recurred in members of my grandfather's family. I am just one step removed from this condition. I have a distinctive voice that, in the years I worked as a producer in radio, prevented me from voicing programmes. There is a hollowness, an echo, I was told, because the very high roof of my mouth traps sound. I try not to think about this when I speak on radio now, and when I give talks. We would know that voice anywhere, people tell me. Yes, indeed.

My father felt that the money he had inherited might be put to better use in Western Australia and my mother agreed that she would shortly join him there. His newly acquired wealth lasted about three weeks in Australia. On the week-long railway trip across the Nullarbor Plain to Western Australia, he met a land agent who persuaded him to buy a worthless chicken farm, without first laying eyes on it. When he arrived all that remained were some broken-down cages on a piece of parched land, and not a chicken in sight.

Meanwhile, in New Zealand, my mother's family took up a piece of ragwort-infested land at Te Awamutu. My grandfather, the proud man used to riding though bush for days at a time, just for the pleasure of it, the strong and successful presence, grew out of touch with the world. My mother and her two brothers did most of the farm work. My mother also worked as a housemaid at various properties around the Waikato. Gradually she acquired a small nest egg.

Four years had passed since my parents' engagement. Possibly the Smalls thought my mother had forgotten about the itinerant Englishman, but she had not, although her heart had faltered more than once. She wrote to say that she would not go to Australia, then changed her mind again. One day she announced to the family that she had booked her passage to Sydney on the SS *Wanganella.* From there she too would take the train trip across the Nullarbor to Perth, where my father would meet her. By then he had a job as a herd tester, and he promised he could support her. Her journey became a family epic, part of the legend by which the three of us, my mother, my father and I, would live.

Once, years after my father died, I followed that train journey across the huge limestone plateau that spans the width of the Great Australian Bight. Like many people, I thought Nullarbor was an Aboriginal word. I should have known better because I learned Latin for a time at school: it is simply Latin for no trees. But while it took my parents a week to cross the plain, my journey took only three days. I remember the way dingoes slid away from the stations, the scarlet stain of the sun erupting over the horizons at dawn, the little huddles of houses that people on the train called towns—Watson, Loonana, Rawlinna (a big 'town' with twenty buildings)—the absence of people out there among the ghostly blue-brush and the grey green salt-brush. As I climbed off the train beneath the great dome of Perth Railway Station, I tried to imagine my mother stepping down to meet my father, as he waited there, dressed in his best Donegal suit, *sans* fortune but still set on marrying her. He was such a funny man then, she would say; he used to make me laugh. Then.

When I arrived, there was a cousin there, virtually all that remains of his family. She looked more like my father than I do, but she didn't, as I do, have my grandmother's eyes.

A few weeks after my mother's arrival in Perth, she sat down to breakfast in the boarding house where she was staying. It was the time of the wild flowers in Western Australia. Primrose orchids and mondurup bells scattered the plains and crowded the parks.

'And what are you doing today?' asked the woman sitting across the table from her.

'Getting married,' my mother said, to the surprise of her companion.

Later that day, she and my father were married at St Andrew's Church in front of two witnesses. My mother wore a spray containing kangaroo paw flowers on her pleated linen dress, and a big-brimmed hat.

They might have stayed there in Australia. My father spent weeks travelling the countryside in his Model T Ford with his terrier Mac. My mother was happy in Donnybrook where they lived. She ran the local library, played tennis and owned a bad-tempered pink and grey galah called Cocky, which screamed with maniacal laughter at people it disliked. Her lifestyle was relaxed and, despite her married state, she was able to exert some independence during my father's absences. With dismay, she learned that he was restless again.

They might have gone to Tasmania. Instead, with the thought of starting a family on her mind, my mother said that, if they must shift, she preferred to return to New Zealand to be near her people. In the end there was a compromise. He would return to New Zealand, provided there was a distance between him and her relatives.

I was born in Hawera on 26 March 1940, at a quarter to midnight in Mount View Private Hospital facing Mount Taranaki. I was delivered by Dr Andrew Young, standing in for my mother's regular doctor, while he was on holiday. I was a seemingly healthy nine-and-a-half-pound baby, with strawberry-red birthmarks scattered across my nose and forehead.

Two hours later, the Labour Prime Minister, Michael Joseph Savage, died. One great light replaces another, my family joked, but that's all it was, irony, grim humour. They were not socialists. My mother knew nothing of these events. She was unconscious for two days. Out there, the crowds were gathering to weep as Savage was borne through the country by train to his funeral. When she woke up, it was over.

Chapter 3

Shortly after my mother left the hospital with me, I became ill. Jean had come to stay and help, and to fall helplessly in love with me. She had married a year or so earlier, and was hoping for a baby of her own. There never was one. The visit did not last long, owing to coolness between her and my father. I was to be christened in the Church of England, not Presbyterian, and Jean did not stay for the ceremony. But she would become, in her own mind at least, and perhaps in some respects in mine, another mother; I was the link that would hold the family together whatever fallout and quarrels might follow.

My father was a door-to-door insurance salesman at that time. We lived at 49 Egmont Street and then at 10 Nelson Street. I have no idea what these houses looked like, yet sometimes I dream of a house I don't recognise. My dreams are often about houses I have lived in. This one has a long rectangular lawn with a path leading through it in a straight line and there's a single tree in front of the door. The house is narrow; inside the walls are painted light green, and it's full of shadows. A woman with dark hair sits at a bare table with her head bent. It's cold in this dream, cold and still outside. I don't know whether it was one of these houses in Hawera or not, although my mother tried to describe one of them to me once, and I think this is where the dream comes from. I do know that my mother couldn't feed me and I had an allergic reaction to milk. She paced the floor at nights while I screamed and projectile vomited.

'You'll never raise her,' the landlord said.

Her pacing increased. Someone, possibly my father, suggested that her nerves would be improved with cigarettes, so she took up smoking. Her regular GP, a Dr Cameron, had returned. Neither he nor the Plunket nurse could provide answers. I was dying. The medical director of Plunket, a specialist in child health called Dr Helen Deem, was due to visit Hawera and it was suggested I be taken to her.

As my mother told it, she was kept waiting for several hours while I continued to wail. It was a bitter Taranaki afternoon, with snow licking around the mountain, and my mother's appointment was the last of the day.

When she finally saw Dr Deem, she was greeted with chastisement and criticism for failing to care for me properly. There was nothing wrong with my lungs and perhaps my crying had rattled the specialist while she looked at the other babies. The only answer was for me to be placed in the Karitane Hospital in Wanganui (which specialised in looking after sick children), on condition that my mother didn't see me until contacted by the hospital authorities. It was clear, Dr Deem said, that she was unfit to raise me. Bewildered and distraught, my mother turned me over to the hospital. As she left me there, she had already said goodbye to me in her head.

Months afterwards, the hospital got in touch to say I could go home. I was well and merry, and at first my parents didn't recognise me. Whatever my temporary mothers in starch had done for me, I was healthy. Yet, well though I was, it is impossible now to imagine the thinking that led to a supposedly dying child being so arbitrarily disconnected from her mother. My mother and I might have withdrawn from each other, but the reverse happened. We became mutually protective in a way that is hard to explain, and that never stopped.

There was another ordeal in store. Dr Cameron had been giving some thought to my birthmarks. They would make life harder for me when I was older, he told my parents, and offered to try a new technique to remove them. The earlier it was done the more likely it was to succeed. The process involved burning the birthmarks off with dry ice. I screamed thinly and desperately through each session.

'I'd never let anyone experiment on my child,' the landlord's wife sniffed.

Eventually the marks were removed, and although I had pale pink scarring until I was ten or twelve, my only tangible reminder of the birthmarks is a nose that peels in both summer and winter.

Throughout these various trials, my father waited with my mother, but there were other matters on his mind. The pickings were lean in insurance: he was selling on commission. The Second World War had broken out and was well under way by the time I was considered strong enough for him to think about enlisting. Conservative as he was, my father endorsed Michael Savage's words, spoken in 1939: 'Where Britain goes, we go'. At thirty-eight, my father need not have gone to war at all. But he did. He joined the air force as an armourer, and we left Hawera.

It would be more than fifty years before I returned. It was not an intentional absence, the timing was just never right. People often ask me about Hawera because it is the place where my birth is recorded, but there has been nothing much to tell. Only this: Hawera is a town where I almost lost my life and my mother nearly lost her mind.

Although she did not know it then, my mother was also saying goodbye to another part of her life. At the end of my novel *Mandarin Summer,* a woman and her mother sit reminiscing after a funeral:

> I met a woman years after I left the north, a large sad woman who as if in some desperate acknowledgement of the past had borne many children to a man brain damaged in the war, and she said this to me, that some women's men never came home. But for her it had been different. The man she knew never came home. That was the difference she said.
>
> It was not like that with Luke, not exactly, but the war came between him and a wider vision, and my mother was caught in the wake of that fact.

That is a version of what happened in our family. When my father joined the air force, he expected to be sent abroad, but it didn't happen. The reason seemed ignominious to him: after his embarkation date was set it was discovered that he had flat feet. A succession of chest ailments, worsened by sleeping in tents, put his health under strain. There was no way out so he served for the entire war, being shifted from one air force station to another.

My mother, still in love with him, followed him from city to city, living in boarding houses to be near him. Sometimes we travelled on trains at night, and when he was on leave, he joined us wherever we were. Once we went south on the night express in a carriage full of American soldiers. My father was wearing his blue air force uniform and the Americans offered candy for me, which he took. They were hard round sweets like small white moons. When my parents thought I was asleep, I saw their hands steal towards each other in the dimmed glow of the carriage light. This is the first exact memory of my life, the first thing that wasn't told to me, about this period during the war.

Because it was often difficult to get rooms with a baby in tow, we ended up in a variety of unsavoury places. As always, funds were low, and there was growing pressure for women to work in factories and on farms as part of the war effort. But it was clear that I might well be an only child, and my mother didn't want to be parted from me after so nearly losing me. In one place, she barricaded herself in at nights with wardrobes pushed against the door to keep out American Marines visiting other women; her engagement ring was stolen in another rooming house, and in yet another she was called upon to retrieve the dead body of a pregnant woman from a bath in the flat below.

In the Waikato my grandparents and my mother's brother Robert had taken up a new piece of land at Morrinsville. My grandfather had developed Alzheimer's disease, just as his mother had, although in those days it didn't have a name. Robert was working the farm single-handed. He made an offer to my mother she couldn't refuse, especially as women with one child were now being compulsorily called up for war work. In return for a two-roomed cottage on the property and a wage, my mother would join the family and milk cows. It wasn't the first time she had done farm work, although she had no experience of dairying. Before long, we were installed on the farm.

This is the point at which my memory actively and continuously begins to record. An enchanted life had begun. I became absorbed into a household of grandparents, uncles and aunts. Jean's husband, Fred Dickinson, was a bluff kindly builder, who practised his Masonic pledges in the bathroom behind closed doors. He had built her a handsome house in town and took her to the races often. He called me 'the little tart', which made me very happy. Jean would come to the farm during the week to help with the wash in the steaming laundry along the kitchen path. If I close my eyes, I can still hear the clothes bubbling in the copper tub, feel the heat of the fire beneath, smell the table linen being blued and starched.

Roberta had retired from nursing. Her last position was matron of the YWCA in Wellington. Before that she had nursed for several years at Te Puea Hospital north of Gisborne. She never married, although it was hinted she had a lifelong attachment, a mysterious doctor with whom she kept in contact for many years. In middle life she was becoming a professional invalid, moving from house to house to stay with various relatives; she followed royal tours, kept a drawer full of expensive kid gloves and a wardrobe crammed with silk dresses. Margaret, now forty-four, was on the brink of a new life after years of being matron of a hospital in Samoa. One evening she arrived at the farm, sparkling eyed and accompanied by a sawmiller from Waiuku. He was a widower with two small children, and they were about to be married. The room glowed with laughter and excitement, and firelight reflected in the crystal sherry glasses. I was to have cousins at last although, as it turned out, I didn't meet them for several years. I am the flower-girl in the wedding photograph, a pudgy child with straight hair, wearing an organdie dress, a wreath of flowers slipping over my eye.

Without the company of other children, I lived in an adult world, which I proceeded to recreate on my own account. I had an imaginary husband called Eric McKay, who was serving in Egypt. As it happened, my uncle's middle name was McKay and my father's Eric. I've always been interested in where names for characters come from; I guess this invention was pretty simple but my aunts called me a clever little thing. I sat under the hedge beside the vegetable garden having endless conversations with this 'husband' of mine. I watched cats stalk mice and captured their prey from them so that I could study them; I misbehaved and ran away to hide in a wool press from which I was unable to escape and went missing for half a day; I hunted for eggs with Robert, who called them cackleberries. Robert belonged to the Highland pipe band and often in the evenings after milking he donned his McKay kilt and strode around the hilltops playing Scots laments. But, more importantly for the family, I had become a warning beacon for my forgetful but beloved and delightful grandfather, whom I followed on his ramblings on the farm. The day began with breakfast in the sunny farmhouse dining room, while Father, as I called him, spread his porridge with honey and butter and planned the day's 'work' with me, before we set off. Wherever he went, the sound of our voices located us, and spared the family from having to keep watch over him.

My father came and went from the farm during leaves, but by now bitterness was seeping through him. The family didn't appear to welcome his visits. Perhaps my father felt like an outsider, or perhaps the disappointment over the war had soured him. He was no longer the devilish, slightly foppish man who would have a go at things. During the war, he became a different kind of person from the one my mother married. I think the lost castles, the lost estates, took on a new meaning in my parents' lives.

When the war was finally over, my father returned to live with us. Life must have looked bleak: he had given five years of his life to the war effort, but because he had been unable to fight overseas, at that time he was ineligible for a rehabilitation loan. I get angry when I think about that, it was so absurdly unjust. The flat feet had certainly cost him. Although he had loaded bombs and made armaments, he wasn't a returned serviceman at all;

he was a sick man turned loose with little or nothing to show for it. It was not until 1954 that retrospective legislation was passed to correct this situation, but by then there had been some changes in his fortune that perhaps rendered him ineligible again. At any rate, after the war, we had very hard times.

I don't think I was particularly welcoming either. I had a glorious band of acolytes in the form of my grandparents, aunts and uncles. And until then I had shared my mother's bed; each night in the smoky little cabin she read to me before I settled down. I was resentful of the stranger who had turned me out to sleep on the kitchen couch. My father had been diagnosed with tuberculosis, although this later proved incorrect. Whatever it was, the damp Waikato air made him cough until he was nearly sick every night.

But plans were afoot. During the war he had become friendly with a man from Kerikeri in the Bay of Islands. He had heard such engaging reports of the climate and the lifestyle that he was determined we would up stakes as soon as possible and live there. My mother had accumulated some money from her wages while working on the farm, and through saving my father's air force pay, and this was used as a deposit for a piece of land in Kerikeri. Again, this land was bought unseen. Towards the end of 1945, he left ahead of us to prepare somewhere for us to live. Shortly before Christmas, my presents were placed in the suitcases my mother was packing.

Mandarin Summer is essentially a work of fiction, and so are most of the characters, but I have long ago given up the pretence that Constance and Luke Freeman are not based on my parents, nor Emily on myself.

> When we left the south my grandmother and my aunts and uncles all came to the railway station and wept over me, as if I was going to a far country. My grandmother wore black, presumably to suit the occasion. My mother wore her best clothes with a cherry-red pudding bowl hat over her short-cropped greying brown hair as if to say, well, it's going to

be all right, it's going to be fun up there amongst the orchards and the hibiscus, the pukka sahibs and tea on the lawn.

My mother's hair was jet black, and she didn't have a red pudding bowl hat. This is a fiction, an example of the writer's dilemma when drawing upon life, about what to put in, what to leave out and what to invent. There's no mention of a grandfather, but in real life he was there, weeping a perplexed old man's tears. I never saw him again. After I left, he wandered the farm calling for me. 'Oh, where is the little girl?' he would ask my aunts.

I did see my aunts and uncles again, many times. But as time passed, like a gypsy whose palm is crossed with silver, I often felt that I was different in some indefinable way from my mother's staunch Presbyterian pioneering stock. I loved them fiercely, and that love possibly divided me from my father in a way that makes me look back with sadness, although the difficulties were not all about them.

As I grew older I sometimes displeased these relations. I wasn't so much a 'clever little thing' as 'a funny little thing', said with an edge in their voices. In the last photograph in which all the brothers and sisters are together, indeed the last time that they were all to meet, I stand among them dressed in white bridal satin. They are a solid, respectable bunch, some more prosperous than others, hiding disappointments well. They do not show, on that day, the slight wariness some of them had developed towards me. I wasn't turning out to be quite what they expected, and no doubt they believed that I would have been better off had I stayed in the south with them.

I see their faces on the railway station at Frankton Junction, the steam from the engine billowing up through the railings of the overbridge, blurring my last view of them, waving to the child I had been. All my life I will be shaped by that separation, and the journey to the north, taken in a slow train, in the company of my mother.

Chapter 4

When my parents and I first went north, we lived at Shropshire House with a military family called Voelcker. Colonel Frank Voelcker was a decorated military hero, who commanded a retinue of servants that would include my parents, ordering life around him in much the same way that he had done in the East. His family was typical of people who lived in the area.

My first introduction to the colonel was at Auckland Railway Station at the end of the first leg of our journey to the north. He was wearing beautifully laundered tropical kit. It was an uneasy meeting. My mother wanted to be gracious in accepting this enforced hospitality, but there was something in his manner that suggested a misunderstanding. He can't have stayed long, not more than a few minutes, but I remember the feeling of disquiet he left in his wake. Although of course I didn't know this at the time, Voelcker had been appointed the resident Administrator of Western Samoa by

Prime Minister Peter Fraser in October of that year. Apparently, he was on his way home for Christmas.

I must have still been upset when we set off again the next morning, on another train. My mother said, 'Look at you, you're nearly six. You've never been to school. Now that we're going north, that's what you'll do, you'll go to school and play with other children and learn to read and write. This'll be an adventure.'

So the train lumbered on through the little stations—Warkworth, Wellsford, Kaiwaka, Maungaturoto; the names slip like music from my tongue. How many times I would pass through them again, backwards and forwards to the farm at Morrinsville, the other home that beckoned from the south.

My father was waiting for us at Otiria Junction. He showed us from the train to an elderly green Morris Eight. I recall it clearly, because it was the only car I ever saw him drive. Soon after, he stopped driving and refused to do so again. I never found out why. With him was Norah Voelcker, the wife of the man we had met the previous evening. Norah had fly-away grey hair, a thin face, lined and tanned. She wore a yellow blouse and green slacks, and I would learn that she was Irish. My mother and I climbed into the back of the car while my father and Norah talked in a voluble easy manner in the front. Later, Norah and my mother became close friends, but that all lay ahead, beyond a good deal of grief. In the meantime, it was clear that a friendship had sprung up between her and my father, from which my mother and I were excluded.

My father showed signs of being nervous about our arrival. There are unanswered questions from my adult perspective. It was never explained to me why we had had to leave for the north so suddenly, just before Christmas, and before the house at the end of Darwin Road was ready for us. Perhaps I am naïve, even now, but my father's nature was such that an improper friendship with a woman seems unlikely. But I'm sure he would have found a confidante in a lonely Irish woman. There were some things I did discover as time passed, and one of them was that Norah's husband was anxious to divorce her. The novelist in me wonders if my father, innocent or not, was about to be used as an excuse. With the colonel's return for the summer, did he urgently need to be a married man with a family? Voelcker had some kind of hold over my parents. But, who knows, it may have been the obvious tedious business of money, as it was so often in my family. My mother preferred never to speak about these events.

That afternoon, as we drove through the countryside, we saw how it was burnt with the sun's fierce heat. The grass was bleached and fallen tree trunks were like the bones of long dead cattle. We travelled for some distance through this landscape and then, suddenly and dramatically, it changed. We entered a world full of green and shifting liquid light. Avenues upon avenues of hedges lined the perimeters of orange orchards. The foliage was pale green and light red at the tips, and at every turn the skyline beyond was etched with the branches of blue gum trees, their trunks white beneath slender inky leaves. The car swept past a row of them, along a white gravel driveway, and we were at Shropshire House, an imposing building set in the grounds of a large garden.

Through a hedge, I heard the thunk, thunk of tennis balls being hit backwards and forwards, and scores called. I'm not certain now if there was a tennis court at Shropshire House, or whether people were just playing ball, but in my head there is one. The house doesn't exist now, hasn't done for nearly sixty years, but I do know it was raised high off the ground and surrounded by balconies and luxuriant gardens. Behind it stood a place known as The Bunkhouse, also slung about with long verandahs, used to accommodate people coming to settle in Kerikeri before their new houses were built. This was where my father had been living, although my parents and I were being elevated to Shropshire House itself.

Norah showed us to our bedrooms, reached by one of the verandahs at the side of the house. Whatever explanation lay behind our early arrival, and Norah's part in it, if any, she was clearly not the mistress of her own house. After that day, I wouldn't see her face to face for a long time, although I knew she still lived there, and from time to time I caught glimpses of her, in the shadows of a dimly lit bedroom.

Soon after we put our suitcases down, my mother was shown to the kitchen door, with me following close behind, then Norah disappeared. The kitchen was large, the matchwood timber walls painted cream, with wooden benches running right around them. A middle-aged woman, her face lined by the sun, stood in the middle of the room, her hands resting on her hips.

'Ah, you're here,' she said, and took off the apron she was wearing. 'I'd heard the new cook was on her way.'

My mother stepped back.

'You'll be needing this,' said the woman, handing over the apron. She introduced herself as Mrs Starr. (She was Mrs Starr, in the years that we knew her. I think her first name was Agnes.) 'They've got sixteen in for dinner tonight. I'm off.'

My mother shook her head in disbelief.

Mrs Starr paused long enough to say, 'You won't have to do it all tonight. The daughter's made choccy shape for dessert. She's good at choccy shape.'

And then she was gone. My mother stood there and took in what there was to cook—a roast of mutton, some potatoes and silver beet. She lifted the cover on a basin. 'How disgusting,' she said. It was the dessert.

She fed all sixteen of the family and their guests. They were served with golden syrup sponge for dessert. I don't know what happened to the choccy shape.

It took me a long time to go to sleep. At some time in the night I heard banging and a woman's scream. The sound was further away than the room next door where my parents slept. Rather, it was muffled and, over the months that followed, I came to recognise it as an insistent pleading cry. I never knew for sure where it was coming from.

One person who wouldn't have done any screaming was my mother. It's been suggested that I write as if my mother was a saint. She was nothing of the kind and could be as armed and dangerous as the next person. Her weapon was silence, a familiar trait among her and her siblings, as painful as loud words in others. I rarely felt the weight of this displeasure, which is not to say that it didn't cause grief in our household. My father folded in its presence. When my mother woke me, that first morning in Kerikeri, her face was paler than usual, set and still.

'You're invited to breakfast. The colonel says you must go,' she said.

I understood, without being told, that she and my father wouldn't be there.

I was startled to see Colonel Voelcker, the man in the cream suit at the railway station, seated at the head of a long table, where I must now take my place. Also seated at the table were his two daughters, both older than me by several years, and an elderly man, totally deaf and unable to speak, who, I learned, was a permanent resident. His name was Schroeder. I know nothing about him, or why he lived at

Shropshire House. He communicated by grunts and pointing.

The dining room had sliding doors that opened out onto another huge balcony so that the room could be used for dancing when the furniture was pushed back. This furniture, made mostly from dark wood, included chairs ornamented with carvings, desks scrolled with illustrations of dragons, silk screens mounted in elaborate frames, pictures of women in Chinese robes on the walls, statues made of silky green jade. I didn't know the word Oriental but I soon would.

'Those are Daddy's,' said the older of the girls, following my gaze. She was in her late teens.

Soon my mother came in bearing a tray set with boiled eggs, toast, butter and marmalade. She didn't look at me, and I knew I must be silent.

When she had withdrawn from the room, the older girl said, 'You have to do the victory sign.' She held up the first two fingers of her left hand in a 'V'.

I studied this for a moment.

'Daddy, she doesn't know how to do the victory sign.'

I raised my hand and imitated her.

'You do that every time you see Daddy, doesn't she?'

The colonel nodded in agreement, as he placed a linen napkin across his chest to guard the lovely cream clothes. I remember that he liked his eggs soft boiled.

Breakfast seemed to go on forever, punctuated by grunts from Schroeder, until at last I was allowed to leave the room. I wandered outside, not knowing which direction to take. Before long I found myself in the orchard. Orange and mandarin trees stretched on either side of me, late windfalls on the ground. I gathered a mandarin up and began to eat it, dropping the peel on the ground.

'Ah,' said a voice behind me, 'so you're going to eat all my fruit as well as eat me out of house and home.' It was the colonel. Perhaps it was meant as a joke; all the same, I pulled myself back into the shadow of the trees, with a feeling of helpless dread.

The colonel put his hand up in the victory salute. When I did nothing but stare back wordlessly, he sighed. 'So the servant's little girl has forgotten already, eh?'

I turned and ran. Happily, I wasn't asked to breakfast again.

The early months at Shropshire House, before I went to school, passed somehow or other. Odd things happened. Schroeder spent most of his time in a steamy conservatory that formed part of the house; I saw glimpses of Norah, her hair growing stragglier by the day, flitting through the house from time to time, followed by a piquant herbal scent. Tobacco was scarce in those days and when cigarettes were unobtainable the women of Kerikeri rolled fat purple lasiandra buds to smoke.

Some of them had hand bells on ropes to ring for toast from the cook. Some wore long silk scarves tied in bands around their hair with the ends trailing behind them. They tinkled when they laughed.

Some years ago, I launched *Women of Kerikeri,* a book recording accounts of those days by some of the old women who had lived there when they were young. Their lives don't make easy reading. One acknowledged that the biggest battle of her life was alcoholism, and she wanted other women who shared this problem to know that hers had been overcome. It seemed a brave and defiant statement.

You can't always see across these divides, not at the time.

Chapter 5

What was this place my father had brought us to? The Stone Store, established as a mission station in 1814, stands on the waterfront tucked into a tidal estuary, with Kemp House alongside it, the first European dwelling to be built in New Zealand. These are the tourist places that make Kerikeri famous. But the town has an odd other story.

George Edward Alderton was a Whangarei journalist with a commitment to developing the North. He was instrumental in obtaining road and rail services in the area, early in the twentieth century. His other great interest was horticulture, and he considered Kerikeri's unusual subtropical microclimate ideal for a large-scale horticultural experiment. Shelter belts of gorse already existed, planted by the missionaries for protection and as supplementary animal feed.

Alderton had developed his concept of a citrus settlement from the Riverside Scheme in California. Once the land was bought, he went to Australia and returned with 10,000 citrus trees. From Australia, he also brought the idea of planting gum trees as shelter in place of the gorse, which was fast turning into a pest. By this time he had a vision of a 'garden city' with each plantation being turned into a miniature park. His dream was to turn a part of Northland, an area of wasted potential, into a national showplace. One of the obstacles in the way of this plan was the length of time it would take for the citrus to bear fruit. He needed a fast-growing, quick-yielding crop to plant between the maturing citrus trees. His answer was passion fruit, which looks at first glance like a purple plum until its carapace is broken to reveal seeds floating in sacs of sweet amber juice.

Having got the plan this far off the ground, there was still something lacking—the right people to become the residents of the settlement. The North Auckland Land Development Corporation already had its eye on the increasing number of the country's unemployed for development projects in the North. A few of these people did find their way to Kerikeri, but clearly they didn't have the means to become part of the dream. And then there was the gum diggers' encampment at Waipapa but, at the time, they were seen more as labourers than as orchardists, although later many did become successful horticulturalists. Maori were not considered at all.

Instead of drawing on New Zealanders to fulfil his dream of a town based on orchard wealth, Alderton looked to expatriate British living in China, and wanting a place to settle as the Sino-Japanese wars, and Russian communism, advanced upon them in the late 1920s. The only account I've found that puts the Kerikeri story in context is a Massey master's thesis called 'Kerikeri Gold', written in 1971 by Christine Elson-White. It's a little known work that deserves a wider audience than the book stacks where it shelters at Kerikeri Library and at Massey University. As she points out, 'British stationed personnel found themselves in an unenviable situation. They were seeking to retire, preferably in one of the English speaking former colonies, free from political troubles—and one that provided an attractive pest free climate!' Alderton hurried to advise these potential settlers about Kerikeri's charms.

He wrote newspaper articles for the *North China Daily Mail* and the *North China Daily News,* published a book called *Income Homes That Grow in Trees* (1925), and, in 1927, issued the company's prospectus. Soon he received over 400 replies. That same year, he formed the Alderton Group Settlement Scheme under the direction of the North Auckland Land Development Corporation, purchasing a large block of land in partnership with five other directors, of whom Voelcker was one.

Intending settlers arrived to inspect the place. After the riots and open street battles, the snakes, insects and diseases such as malaria and the plague, Kerikeri presented an idyllic spectacle. There were no vermin or wild animals, and the surrounding water, including numerous splendid waterfalls, was unpolluted. Not only could they escape city life, but they could become involved in a 'back to the land' movement.

A man named Edward Little, a respected expert on fertilisers who knew how to evaluate soil and its potential fertility, became Alderton's agent in China. He had soil samples brought to China for testing by ICI (China) Limited, and the results encouraged him sufficiently to buy 160 hectares of Kerikeri land. Next, he established the Shanghai Club, a group of people from Shanghai and Tsientin who planned to settle in Kerikeri.

Before long the exodus from China began, along with a handful of the Indian Raj. In all, about 100 arrived, although more had been expected. These settlers brought to Kerikeri a way of life that they had enjoyed in their heyday in the East, including sentimental imitations of the style of housing they had left behind. Little himself established an estate known as Kingston, distinctive for the rows of palms planted along the driveway. Kingston was encircled by a broad brilliantly coloured belt of scarlet gums, golden wattles and wisterias. In addition he planted an imposing forest of redwoods and gums, and filled the gardens with Oriental flowers and shrubs brought from his home in Shanghai.

Another settler, Daniel Fergusson, formerly a civil engineer with the Hankow Railway in China, decided to create a 'little China' at the end of Pah Road. He landscaped an Oriental garden with hundreds of exotic plants such as Chinese lanterns and Japanese anemones, moss roses, a Chinese silk tree, mulberries, custard apples, bougainvillea, frangipani, avocado pears, crepe myrtles and fragrant ginger trees.

Some new arrivals built pagoda houses in which to store their treasures, before they had kitchens or running water. Massive stone pillars were erected and beasts of Chinese mythology were installed. In the township the Cathay Picture Theatre was built. Tobacco fields and a tung oil nursery were planted. Tung oil trees are indigenous to the Yangtze Kiang River Basin; oil extracted from the richly saturated seeds was used in the manufacture of paints and varnishes, and was an ingredient of 'India ink', used for lustrous finishes on wood. The Australian hakea plant, with its distinctive pale red tips, was introduced as a faster and bushier shelter belt than the gum trees.

Soon the newly made roads rattled with horses' hooves as galloping majors surveyed their new kingdom, issuing orders as if they expected coolies to come running. They and their wives drank gin and boogied and, if later accounts are to be believed, spent much of their time wondering how to escape back to civilisation. Pioneering orchard country was more rugged than they had anticipated. In their wake came believers in the unusual—Zen Buddhists, Scientologists, Anthroposophists and Theosophists—and dreamers like my father.

My father's habit of buying land unseen had again led him to make an unfortunate mistake. If he had done his homework more thoroughly, he might have noted letters from earlier settlers writing back to China which warned that 'bare land could not be cultivated without adequate capital to pay for extra labour'. One resident, writing to a prospective settler in 1930, said:

> Naturally the ideal condition would be to have a small income, of say two hundred pounds per annum to ensure any contingency that might arise ... It has been demonstrated that a woman interested in poultry or special gardening can earn sufficient to meet her housekeeping service expense and requisite pin money.

Most of the people from the East did come sufficiently well equipped to survive through bad times—and there were plenty of those. The passion fruit failed owing to mismanagement, and citrus canker had earlier forced the destruction of many of the first plantations. The pukka sahibs and their ilk carried on, seemingly regardless of fate, surrounded by their fabulous Oriental collections. They sang all the songs that would one day feature in *Pennies from Heaven.* Once, when we'd been in Kerikeri for some years, we were on a picnic arranged by Norah who, after an absence, had resurfaced in our lives. We came to a beach where the Kerikeri Cruising Club was holding a regatta and the crowd was singing, 'Cruisin' down the river, on a Sunday afternoon...' How very apt. Norah stood there, humming to herself, watching them all, without making a move to join them, for by that stage she no longer belonged. They drank their gin slings and jitterbugged at dusk, and ignored upstarts and servants. For us, on the outside looking in, theirs was the life.

Darwin Road was really a grass strip with a layer of gravel sprinkled roughly over the centre line. The small holding at the end that my father had purchased was a dry paddock lined by blue gum trees on the far boundary. We were undercapitalised for orcharding, and water supply was a constant problem; we depended on rainwater collected in tanks. The planting of a small orchard of passion fruit, tamarillos and kiwi fruit—the last two were called tree tomatoes and Chinese gooseberries then—was started. A few cows were bought, which my parents milked by hand. All three of us took turns at the Alfa Laval hand separator that divided the milk into cream and whey. A truck came past the other end of Darwin Road each morning to collect billies of cream to take to the dairy factory. But in 1946, our first year in Kerikeri, the North was experiencing the worst drought in its history, then or since. It was an inauspicious beginning and some things, such as the water supply, were never resolved, even though, when I was older, I developed the odd talent of being able to divine water. There was none to be found at our place, except in a shallow area of swampbed that yielded nothing but brackish surface water.

The house transported to the land was a medical army hut, to which lean-tos were added as funds allowed. It arrived in two halves on the back of trucks and was set down a short way from the gum trees. For the first two years we had no electricity, our illumination at night coming from candlelight and a Coleman lamp, our hot water from pots boiled on the stove, or in the copper for our laundry and baths. The front lean-to housed a bath and copper, partitioned off from a porch where a canvas camp stretcher stood. Two steps led from the lean-to up to the kitchen that I describe in my story 'All the Way to Summer', which is about that time, my father's secret lives and the Walter Mitty-ishness of his character.

The room in which we ate was narrow, not more than six feet (or perhaps eight) across by about fifteen long, a bench at one end and a coal range on one wall, our gate-legged dining table, oval when it was folded out, creating a barrier between the kitchen and the other end of the room, where a wooden-backed sofa stood. Seeing it like this, it is not a beautiful room, ugly in fact, its cream walls stained with smoke, red congoleum on the floor. But consider our table, laid with an Irish linen cloth, heavy silver cutlery, the knives bone-handled, the plates willow pattern. This was my mother's dowry, the remnants of some other life.

The kitchen was always dim and full of smoke. The coal range smoked. My parents smoked. They rolled their cigarettes from loose tobacco. Acrid little butts collected on saucers. Letters and bills and requests for payment of bills were stacked on the kitchen table. When the power was at last installed, Uncle Robert sent my mother a radio encased in green bakelite, which stood on a shelf above the sink. My mother and I listened to it constantly.

A window, covered by a curtain, linked the kitchen and the bathing area in the lean-to. I peeked through it once and saw my father naked. In 'All the Way to Summer', the narrator thinks of Oliver Reed in the movie version of D.H. Lawrence's *Women in Love:*

> I raised the curtain and he was rubbing himself dry in the dark room, lit only by a single bulb and the reflection of the flames from the copper fire ... that same pale English flesh, the colour of potato flesh. He was long and spindly, his chest slightly concave, and yet in the flickering light I found him mysterious and oddly beautiful.

By this time, the Voelcker household had been abandoned for some years. The colonel had returned to Western Samoa in his administrator role, while the United Nations thrashed out the future direction of self-government for the territory. Norah went away for some years for an undisclosed 'treatment'. Later she returned alone, to build herself a small house along Hone Heke Road, doing most of the labour herself. Shropshire House was sold as a boarding establishment to a couple called Jack and Cora.

Cora was a blonde merry woman, who acted in local drama productions, and got dressed up once to play the part of Fame in a play. I don't know what it was called, but I do know she wore a white sheet draped around her like a toga, and held a trumpet with a long handle—actually a broomstick with a petrol pourer stuck to the top of it, painted silver. Jack, who was an older man, once took me to a country fair where I was allowed to ride all morning on the Ferris wheel at sixpence a ride, which was fifteen times round. Fifteen times around on the Ferris wheel, and each time I could see the countryside as far as my eye could follow, every time a little closer to flying.

My mother returned to work at Shropshire House, in a happier environment, observing with amusement the foibles and affectations of some of the guests. The town had its reputation for the off-beat, so there was a steady flow of guests, all in their own way different, all vying for attention. The pianist Lili Kraus visited from time to time. Considered one of the world's leading interpreters of Mozart's work, she had escaped with her husband Otto Mandl from Nazi Germany and spent the war in the Dutch East Indies, before coming to settle for a few years in New Zealand. (Afterwards she moved to the United States where she became celebrated anew.) She toured the country for the CAS (Community Arts Service), giving scores of concerts on dilapidated pianos in little country halls. There was no doubting her charm and vitality. As soon as she arrived the household brimmed with her presence. As well as a base for performances, her visits to Kerikeri were for holidays and respites from touring. She often took me swimming to one of the nearby river holes beneath a waterfall. I remember her white shoulders in the sunlight, and the torrent of black hair released from its plaits, floating on the water. I would sit on a rock until she put out her arms and said, 'Come on, little girl, come here to me.' At that point I would entrust myself to the water and the certainty that she would catch me.

In the evenings, she put on dramatic dresses, velvet and richly coloured, to dine by the glow of specially lit candles. I think she behaved well enough towards my mother, although Flora didn't warm to her, because Kraus brought her own cook. I've only recently learned that these were the years when she became a vegetarian. That would have seemed outlandish to my mother.

All of this came to an end when Shropshire House burned down in a spectacular fire. In the middle of the night a young woman who worked as a cleaner at the boarding house, and slept over, banged violently on the door just a few feet from where I lay asleep, shouting, 'Mr Eakin, Mr Eakin, the big house is on fire!'

My parents sprang out of bed and raced to the scene, stopping on the way to leave me at a neighbour's house so that I would not see the fire. Not see the fire? The house contained gunpowder and throughout that night it exploded like cannon. The fire leapt 100 feet in the air, the smell of burning penetrating every recess of the house where I waited. As flames stung the citrus trees that ringed Shropshire House, the night smelled like boiling lemon juice.

Thus, in *Mandarin Summer,* Emily Freeman wakes to find the house where she lives on fire:

> The dry timber of the house was erupting, a fierce conflagration, brighter fireworks than I could ever have imagined. Already flames were leaping from the roof of the west wing of the house.'

Emily helps her father to rescue one of the characters, Lilian, from the flames:

> Half-carrying, half-dragging her we made our way clumsily through the glassroom, and the glass had begun to shake with the heat and then, just as it seemed that we would be engulfed, we found the door, and when we opened it, the

shaking glass started to explode behind us.

I wasn't inside that house. I smelled and heard the fire, but it didn't burn me. Or did it? I can't tell you that exactly.

In another of my stories, 'Paradise', a child listens to a group of adults sitting and talking by a river; the women have all, at one time or another, lived in the same house, later burned to the ground. The child in this story is more forthright:

> My mother did try to shield my view so that I wouldn't see the leaping flames above the gum trees, the blinding arc of light reflected in the clouds, the sparks which showered the night with dazzling, ferocious gaiety. This was the house I had briefly known as home. She wanted to save me from the terror of watching it perish. But of course I saw. I felt the heat of the flames. I heard the confused birds waking as if night were day. Of course I remembered.

I've never been able to get away from this image. The sight of a burning house at night causes me a trauma I find hard to describe. I run about crying 'Help' in a small terrified voice, even when I've rung the fire brigade. Fire is the hidden, mysterious image in my life, both terrible and beautiful.

People ask me if, because I've described in my novel a real fire that happened, I've also described the lives of the people who lived in the real house. Well no, not exactly. None of them were in the house at the time and if there were motives for burning it down, which some believed, they were certainly not ones that could be attributed to the characters in *Mandarin Summer.* I might not have entered the burning house but it doesn't take much to smell a fire; it takes little more to smell trouble.

But the women who sat and talked by the river in 'Paradise' were real enough. They are Laura, Nora and Cora. Or not. My mother Flora had morphed into Constance in the novel, then Laura in this new story; her friends, Nora and Cora, go shamelessly by their own names, although Norah loses her 'h': Flora, Nora and Cora. Their conversation happens some years after the fire. Norah had come back and built her house. Jack had gone for good. After the house was destroyed, the police had come up from Auckland because there were some unexplained circumstances about how the fire began. They stayed and asked questions for days. My mother was interviewed. Did she know where Jack and Cora were that night (for they were both out of town)? No, she did not. Then, when the police weren't satisfied with the outcome of their inquiries, they sent an insurance assessor to try to dig up the truth. His name was Edward. He stayed and that was when Jack left. Edward and Cora now lived in a bungalow by the river, surrounded by leafy green bush, and we were all very happy when we met, the three women, Edward, my father and me.

Chapter 6

Darwin Road. The place where we lived. There was a hill beyond our land, no more than ten miles away at most, shaped like a long thumbprint, the way the thumb lies when holding a page open. I find it hard to describe that hill's particular shade of blue, dark and distant.

The paddock beyond the house was planted with silk-tasselled maize and sweet corn, the swelling green ears stirring among the leaves. Food for the three cows we milked, food for us. The path along the house was flanked by banana passion fruit, the vines in summer were heavy with furry pale yellow erotic fruit. Snapdragons grew in clumps in our garden—electric pink, ruby red, shadowy lemon. The trees rustled and whispered to us.

While the exotic world of the Alderton settlers unfolded about us, and our piece of land was planted, I had of course begun school. Sooner or later it had had to happen. I was nearly six when I was put on a bus one day and packed off to Riverview School. Its motto, 'Be Worthy', loomed in large letters over the entrance. I started school on the same day as John Jurisich, Frank Zivkovich, Billie Smellie, Ngaire Bates, Lily Tango, Lovey Apiata, Bobbie Tucker and some of the Dixon girls, plus children with double-barrelled surnames. On the third day I wet my pants and cried. I got sent out by my teacher, Miss Templeton, a round-featured peach-complexioned woman with crisp grey curls, and pronounced facial pores. Her affair with a one-legged man was a source of interest in the town. When I had been dismissed, leaving the shameful puddle on the floor, I ran as far as I could, to the pine belt at the back of the school. There I concocted one of my fantasies. In the story, I was back in the Waikato with my aunts and uncles and grandparents, and they were sending a gunboat to rescue me.

'The cat sat on the mat' was not for me, and I couldn't make sense of the letters. I stumbled through my lessons, considered not very bright. My mother had read to me a lot before I began school, but the first books I remember owning were A.A. Milne's *Winnie-the-Pooh* and *The House at Pooh Corner,* both given to me by Jean for Christmas of 1945, and opened in those first weeks at Shropshire House. It was certainly the world of Tigger and honeypots. I felt like Piglet on the outside but in my head I was pure Christopher Robin, the introverted outsider who lived a make-believe life, with reality nudging perilously close to my elbow. Pooh, as he was for millions of other kids, was the alter ego, the person who listened and forgave.

Two children joined the class, new neighbours in Darwin Road, Madeleine and Michael Gross. Their grandfather, Tom Graveson, who had grown citrus trees from pips in tubs since he was a child in the north of England, owned the property across the road from ours. He was a remarkable orchardist who developed techniques of grafting fruit trees, his experiments aimed at discovering which trifoliata stocks withstood local conditions and were resistant to drought and disease. His gorse-covered land very quickly became a flourishing orchard, and in time he transformed the economics of the citrus trade in the North.

Madeleine and Michael were exactly a year apart in age; I was roughly in the middle. They had a smaller brother, Peter. The family was from Dunedin, where their mother had recently been separated from Frank Grosz, a French/Viennese designer and artist who had emigrated to New Zealand in the 1930s. Madeleine already had exquisite copperplate handwriting, and a few days after their arrival she was moved ahead two classes.

'She's much too bright to be in this class,' Miss Templeton told her mother. I felt envious and stupid.

The misery of life in Miss Templeton's class ended when I developed abscessed glands in my throat. I was dispatched to Kawakawa Hospital, some thirty miles away, for an operation, but it was a month or so before I was able to go home, as pneumonia and other complications set in. A few days after the operation I was visited by Miss Brown, the visiting hospital teacher.

'Where are you up to in your reading?' she asked.

Miserably I confessed that I couldn't read at all.

'Oh dear!' She regarded me with concern. 'I'd better show you how.'

We spent a busy afternoon. This is a word and it sounds like this. Yes? Yes, although sometimes there are tricks and some words sound the same but mean different things. Gosh, that's like a jigsaw: you've got to work the bits out? Mmm, that's right, and then you put all the words together and you get a sentence. But that's a bit out of a story? Right, the words start to tell you things. Really? Yes, so they do, oh, oh ... This is reading, isn't it?

'You should be all right now,' she said as she left. She was confident and so was I. The hospital had a small library of books, mostly for adults. When Miss Brown came back the following week there was a stack of them beside me. If she was surprised that I had read them, she didn't show it.

'This afternoon I want to learn to write,' I told her.

This took longer, but by the end of the afternoon I was ready to tackle the first project.

'Dere Mum,' I wrote. 'Come and get me, I hat the fode hair.' This was the first of a number of letters designed to cause misery and guilt at home. Eventually, they had the desired effect. I was pleased with myself. Writing worked.

Miss Brown may have accepted my learning curve without comment but Miss Templeton was incredulous. 'We'll have to start the child all over again,' she told my mother, when I arrived back at school.

'She can read,' said my mother.

'I doubt it,' said Miss Templeton, rolling her eyes and sitting me down for one of the detested lessons. Later in the morning I was promoted to standard one. I was still a class behind Madeleine, but I was blissfully happy at this elevation. As it happened, I couldn't do much else but read and write, and I continued to fail dismally in other subjects. But I had this trick—I had become literate, apparently on my own, and I wanted to show off my aptitude again and again. The following year saw a return to hospital and I was able to read even more. This apparent 'cleverness' didn't make me a huge number of friends, and I was also developing a strange hybrid accent. My father insisted that I copy his classy, if stammering, tones. The deal was simple: if I didn't speak as he thought I should, he didn't answer.

Things weren't all bad between us. He taught me how to fire a gun, although I missed whatever I was supposed to be firing at (often quail, which he shot for food although it was poaching), and how to float stamps off envelopes and mount them in an album, how to study birds and their nesting habits. He taught me how to hold my knife and fork at dinner, and how to address important people when I met them. Who knows, he said, one day you might meet the King and Queen, and you must know what to do. And, although winter was just a cooler time than summer, punctuated by days of fat flat grey rain, we sat by the wood stove with the door open and read to each other at night.

But he was decidedly Victorian in his view of how a child should be brought up. The first time I was strapped for disobedience was a dreadful shock. Lying down afterwards was a painful experience. When I was a small child, my life had generally revolved around rewards rather than punishment; this physical shift was frightening and humiliating.

I see now that my father was unhappy in ways I couldn't have imagined then, that he had left behind some friends in the air force with whom he could tell jokes that my mother and I didn't think funny. In particular, he had befriended a much younger man, who perhaps offered reminders of the youth he felt he had lost. All the same, I often felt I was meant to be born a ready-made grown-up, and a boy. Both my parents told me it had never occurred to them that I wouldn't be a boy, whom they would call James.

Among their more recent regrets was a baby who slipped from my mother's grasp before it took a breath, as she was hoeing rough ground. She worked on the land as a man would, not sparing her body at all. I was there when it happened, although I remember only her cries, and something I wasn't allowed to see. I don't know whether it was a boy or a girl, but the pregnancy must have been well advanced. I asked her once, when in a rare moment she spoke of the matter, trying to console me when yet another of my own babies eluded me. She merely looked vague. I think women were expected to turn their heads at times like this. I know this, actually—miscarriage has always been one of those things people prefer not to talk about. They will shrug and say things like, 'Well it probably wasn't meant to be', 'It might have been damaged', 'Nature's way of dealing with it'—all those platitudes that ignore the grief, the lost anticipation.

My mother began telling me stories that had as little to do with life as possible while I followed her around on the land they were breaking in. She was absorbed in *Portia Faces Life* and *Doctor Paul,* serials broadcast from the green radio in the kitchen. I listened too, in the school holidays, and during the polio epidemic, when we all stayed home for months and did lessons by correspondence. She and I began to live out some of the dramas in plays of our own. 'You can pretend I'm Delia,' she would say, and start vamping among the tree tomatoes. The fruit had drum-smooth red skin binding the rouge-coloured flesh and black seeds inside. She clipped and slid the fruit into a bulging apron with a big pocket. 'You can kiss me if you're quick, but nobody must know' could be an opening line.

'My wife no longer cares who I kiss,' I might say.

'Ah yes, but she does, that's half the pleasure,' my mother would breathe. 'We have our little secrets.'

'How about we sail away in a boat together?'

At which point she would snort, 'Is that the best you can do?' The question was meant for me, not the character. While we held these sultry improbable conversations, anyone glimpsing her at work in the orchards might have mistaken her for a man, with her overalls and close-cropped hair. I think my mother was in despair at this point in her life. I had reached an age when children know if things are not well in their house. These private fascinating role-play games made me endlessly inventive in my mother's company, but I have wondered since how much of it was for herself, whether this fantasy world was what kept her together. When she met people she was shy in her manner.

The collection of people along Darwin Road became increasingly colourful, a neighbourhood of extreme personalities. As well as the Graveson and Gross ménage, there was an old Scotsman with an accent as thick as broth and his maiden daughter, who moved into a rough cottage along the road. Miss Stewart painted watercolours and had an acid tongue reserved for children who interrupted. Then there was B, a man with a charming smile who invited me into his cottage one day and held me on his knee while he showed me photographs. I told my parents, with pride I suppose, that someone had taken a fancy to me. They were outraged. No doubt it was my good fortune to have boasted of the encounter, as I was never asked into his house again, nor, so far as I knew, did my parents speak to him after that. He turned his attention to adult females, although he remained a bachelor. Alongside the property adjoining ours was young Rod MacDiarmid's orchard, where my mother and Madeleine's picked lemons and oranges for a shilling a case. MacDiarmid had arrived earlier, a clever successful orchardist from the beginning. His brother Alan was later awarded the Nobel Prize for his work as a scientist.

My father was often irascible with other of our neighbours besides B. Mrs Starr and a man called Joe Johnson, who looked more Indian than Maori, tall and swarthy, with a scar on his face, given to wearing wide-brimmed dark hats, had moved in further along Darwin Road. When I read Robin Hyde's *Passport to Hell* many years later, Starkie's character reminded me of Joe. He began a campaign to castrate all the tomcats in the neighbourhood. When our black cat came home neutered, my father was beside himself with rage and an odd despair. I had begun to develop a temper of my own. If my father thought the world inherently unfair, I was beginning to agree.

The answer to life's uncertainties seemed to lie in books. I read and re-read Arthur Ransome, whom I loved because kids got to do things on their own. And Ethel Turner's *Seven Little Australians,* Rolf Boldrewod's *Robbery Under Arms,* R.D. Blackmore's *Lorna Doone,* which broke my heart, and Grey Owl's *Sajo and her Beaver People.* I was especially excited by *Pilgrims of the Wild,* in which he described the process of writing adventure narrative. This was the first time I had read anything about how a writer wrote. I liked the way Grey Owl described wanting to 'paint a picture in words', the sense of excitement he brought to writing things down and 'getting them off his chest'. I especially enjoyed his description of how, alone in the forest except for the company of a beaver called Jelly, he 'often awoke from sleep to make alterations, made constant notes, and to get the effect of difficult passages, read them aloud to Jelly, who, pleased with the attention and the sounds of rattling papers, would twist and turn in contortions of queer delight'. I revisited the book recently, and it all came back, the way I too began writing with this in mind. Even now, I suppose that unconsciously, when I write, I practise versions of this process.

I had also met a 'real writer', a man called Eric Kingsbury. He and his wife Mary had moved in next door, on the rise slightly above our end of Darwin Road. They had come for peace and quiet, and to live off the land, so that 'Mr Kingsbury' could write books. His typewriter sat on the end of their kitchen table amid a confusion of papers, while he sat pecking away at the keys. Mary, a pink-cheeked woman with a short brush of grey hair, planned to grow vegetables and raise hens. They kept a milking cow, but Mary couldn't master milking so her husband had to leave his work twice a day to perform this chore. Now and then I had to take messages to the Kingsburys because they didn't have a phone and an arrangement had been made with my parents to allow people to send urgent messages on ours. Most of them were to do with medical appointments for 'Mr Kingsbury'. When I entered the room where he worked, I was allowed to speak only in a very quiet voice, so as not to disturb him. It was clear, even to me, that he was sick: his face often had a glassy pallor that turned to a flush when he coughed. Nor did he seem to make money from his work. My mother sometimes sent gifts of food, even though we had little enough to spare. She produced astonishingly good meals from the wood stove's tiny oven.

The person who did earn a little money in the Kingsbury household was Mary, who sent 'pars' (paragraphs) about country life to the *Woman's Weekly,* for which she received five shillings or so. This would be reported with shy excitement to my mother. It was hard to tell who was the 'real' writer between them, but there was no doubt that her husband was the one to whom the deference was offered. I have sometimes wondered what Eric Kingsbury's novel in progress was about. My father tried to discuss books with him once or twice, but whereas his tastes ran to adventure stories, or H.E. Bates—*The Darling Buds of May* was his favourite—or Leo Walmsley's *Sally Lunn,* which my mother spent a precious shilling buying him for Christmas one year, the writer thought these unworthy of his attention. Although the Kingsbury novel never saw the light of day, I glimpsed a world where writing was considered important work, something for which sacrifices were made.

My mother, meanwhile, had taken over running the small local library that opened one afternoon a week. There she met a man called Lawrence Donald, who wrote plays for radio and had published a book. She spoke of him with some awe, although my father dismissed him as a conscientious objector, and refused to meet him. Donald's book was a strange prose poem called *Towards the Dawn,* with a foreword by educationalist Professor James Shelley. In his own preface, Donald wrote of the island where he lived, just off the coastline of the area known as The Inlet, reached by the road that passed Darwin Road. It was:

...an existence of utter simplicity: eight shore miles, by rugged road and track, from the nearest store or established post-office; the only conveyance along these miles—the legs which Nature provided for that purpose. Sans electricity; sans telephone; sans wireless; sans stove; sans carpet; sans newspaper; evening illuminated by the soft, amber beam of a kerosene lamp or candle...

It was not too far removed from the lives of many of us, although, after our first year or so in the army hut, our family had acquired all these seeming essentials except for the carpet. And we had bikes so we didn't have to walk everywhere. But along the road, although Madeleine's mother and her children lived in a Spartan three-roomed cottage, Tom Graveson had built a handsome brick house, luxurious by local standards, and very soon a swimming pool was added.

Madeleine's and my friendship had developed into one of the most important aspects of my life. Separated only by a hakea hedge and passion fruit vines, we had become children apart from our other lives. My father, increasingly hostile to outsiders, didn't welcome Madeleine's visits. She appeared not to notice. A small girl for her age, with a voice just above a whisper, and large navy blue eyes, she seemed insulated from anger and disapproval. When things went wrong at home—and they did, because her mother was a divorced woman, and that mattered then—she managed to glide over them as if they hadn't happened.

I wrote an essay called 'Caught by the Tide' (oh, the originality, but I think it was a set title), which was entered in the school essay section of the Bay of Islands Agriculture Show. It won, and was published in the Bay of Islands newspaper. In response to this, I received a 'fan' letter—or at least a letter of encouragement. 'One day,' wrote this unknown woman, 'you may grow up to be a journalist or a librarian or a famous writer.'

A famous writer. I wonder if that woman had any idea what a glimpse of heaven she offered. I still have her letter, written in green ink on paper that has worn so thin it has holes in it, one of the most crucial letters I have ever received. I was nine years old, and now I knew, covertly at first, what I was going to do. I would write books that people read, and I would perhaps live on an island. (I don't think the idea of living like the Kingsburys interested me a lot but there was definitely something romantic about life on an island of my own.)

I did tell Madeleine that I wanted to be a writer. In fact, we both wanted to write stories, and she wanted to be an artist as well. We became regular contributors to Anne Shirley's children's pages in the *New Zealand Herald.*

My Aunt Roberta, the delicate one, began to take an interest in my work. She sent me a battered copy of a favourite book from her girlhood, *Dorothy's Little Tribe,* by Joan White. It begins:

> It was Dick who decided that one of us must keep a diary of our summer holidays...

Billy (a girl) is one of a family of rather toffee-nosed children who for a summer acquire a down-to-earth governess called Irene. I warmed to Irene, who seemed to know what was what about life. But it was her idea of a magazine that really caught my fancy:

> The magazine proved to be a far greater success than we had dared to hope. Lawrence had been reading some of it aloud to us. He had contributed two nice little poems entitled 'Our Lady of the Bow' and 'The Wreckers Paradise'. The former was awfully sentimental; he didn't read that one aloud, I am thankful to say, but the latter was very realistic. Charlie had written criticisms of two imaginary novels, crying up the one and slating the other. He began by sketching the plot and then reviewing it. Helen's contribution consisted of a few riddles and acrostics ... and I did a short story about the Civil War in the time of Charles.

I showed this to Madeleine and we decided to spend the summer holidays writing our own magazine. For some time it became an annual event. I wrote several of the stories, and Madeleine copied them out in her beautiful handwriting, and drew the pictures. At best, they were punctuated with *Radio Times* and *Fun Times* humour, papers on which I spent my pocket money. But most of my efforts were daffy, silly stories that pandered to the prevailing atmosphere of Kerikeri, with white adventurers chasing bad brown guys. Yet, in Madeleine's hands, the magazines became small objects of art in themselves. She still has copies, written mostly from within our 'office', a hut woven from gum tree branches.

For a time I was in demand to act in school plays. My brash manner and odd exaggerated accent had their uses. I was also a sharp mimic. But at some stage, there was a change. Miss Templeton still hovered in the background, supported by the headmaster, a tiny scrunched up man called Frederic Strumpel, who had a will of iron and played blatantly to the Shanghai set and their children. Strumpel appeared to deliberately set me aside from these children, perhaps to ensure that I didn't get ideas above my station, the impression that I was equal. I didn't need his reminders: I suffered enough longing over exclusion from birthday parties run along class lines. Jillian Brady, a gentle, self-effacing girl, was the only real friend I ever had from the China crowd.

If Strumpel saw me as an exhibitionist, it's true I had begun to draw attention to myself in a different way, although it wasn't intentional. It was around this time that I began to divine water. The North Auckland Land Development Corporation had had a significant success when they installed the first power station north of Whangarei, harnessing electricity and pumping water from the rapid river with its many waterfalls. But reticulation was not widespread, and people depended on water tanks, which filled with rainwater during the winter, and were refilled with water trucked in during the summer, or the building of reservoirs, or sinking bores. My parents built a reservoir at the back of the house, but the water was brackish and unfit for drinking. I swam in it a bit, and floated like a log so that frogs could hop on me, which they often did. When my parents considered putting down a bore, they went along to see a man who did this work, and I went with them.

First, he said, you had to find the water. This was what a dowser did. He showed us how you took a forked live twig and trimmed it, and then, holding it on either side, bent it towards the earth. If there was water below, the twig would turn in your hands. He walked around showing us, and the twig quivered half-heartedly. 'I reckon,' he said, 'there's water on this property, but I'm buggered if I can find it.' My parents tried, and then when nothing happened, they looked bothered and said perhaps if he found water he could let them know. The whole thing seemed risky.

And then I tried, although nobody had offered me the twig, and soon I felt the wood move, like an electric shock in my hand. I thought *water, water* as if I was thirsty and the twig curled down towards the earth. It's almost impossible to tell how something as insistent as this feels in your hands: bucking, stronger than the kick of a gun. I think now that it was more like a sexual tension, not something children are supposed to have. By the time I was grown and married, this ability to locate underground springs had all but vanished.

There was water where I said, and a bore was laid on that farm, and later on another. But my mother put a stop to it, realising that this talent was adding to the view of me as different or in some way odd. And, no matter how hard I tried, I couldn't find deep water on our property.

Whether it was anything to do with the water divining or not, Strumpel and Miss Templeton decided they didn't want me to eat lunch with the children in my class. I was dismissed from the area and sent to eat with the 'big children' (intermediate level) on the bottom playground, 'seeing I thought I was like them'. The children of the Shanghai families were sent away to boarding school as soon as possible so the older school consisted mostly of Dalmatian and Maori children. Many of them would never go to high school at all. 'Janet Gray says she's going to marry a Maori,' I reported to my mother. 'Oh, does she just,' my mother said, grim-lipped. She had become more withdrawn on the subject of her own childhood companions.

At first, inhabiting an odd in-between world, I entertained these older children with mimicry and tall tales, peculiar stories that hinted of sexuality, based on my reading of adult books and my keyhole habits. Eventually they got bored with these stories that led nowhere—because the outcome of sex was unclear to me—and fed up with being imitated. Bitten, they bit back and imitated me. I quickly became ashamed and tearful and shouted at them. These outbursts were fuelled by the daughter of a rumoured remittance man, the third son of an earl, who hadn't yet managed to send her away to school. The truth was, I suppose, that she and I were both smart, both out of place, but she was older and held her own. Getting me in trouble, riling me up, gave her an authority that I had temporarily displaced.

Strumpel swooped and open warfare developed between us, his aim to silence me, mine to maintain a voice. I was constantly stormy. Strumpel called in his 'big boys' to deal with me. I spent many lunch hours locked in a toolshed in the school grounds, where I had been thrown bodily by these boys. 'Take her away and let her cool down,' Strumpel would cry, his tiny malevolent frame dancing up and down in the playground.

I still remember the cool earth floor where I subsided at the end of these screaming outbursts. People write to me now, others who felt like misfits. 'You were brave to stick at it, to be different,' they say. But no, I wasn't. I was foolhardy and desperate and I didn't know any better. I wanted to be a famous writer, and I was getting my first real taste of the critics. Anyone who could survive Strumpel's 'big boys' didn't have to learn bravery at some later date.

Days of heat and shame. On 1 January 1950 my father said, 'Well, I hope the next ten years are better than the last. They couldn't be any worse.'

Around this time I noticed that whenever anyone asked him how he was, in even the most casual manner, he would say he was feeling dreadful and begin a detailed medical bulletin about the state of his health. His hypochondria was of the purest form and would lift only when he was dying of cancer thirty years later; then it appeared almost as a relief, the burden of dreadful possibilities lifted. His health was the reason given for his frequent trips away to the south, where he met up with his 'cobbers' from the air force, and stayed in Auckland to see musicals.

He decided it was time I did a bit of work around the place, and offered some incentives. I bought *Pride and Prejudice* on the proceeds of learning to milk a cow. I have always been fond of the dreadful Lydia Bennet, who ran away and got married to the wrong kind of man. Elizabeth and Jane are very fine, suffering for Lydia's misdeeds, and winning happiness of their own the hard way, not to mention fortunes, but they are not, as Lydia is, on her return from her elopement, 'still untamed, unabashed, wild, noisy and fearless'. Now that seemed like living to me.

It was a short step from the Bennets to Becky Sharp, whose lack of scruples and effrontery captivated me, even if she did come to a sticky end. I reread *Vanity Fair* several times, and for a while it became my favourite book. The Victorians now took hold of me as I started on Dickens, and it was only much later I learned that the books I enjoyed had so troubled their prudish readers when they were published—they did not seem shocking to me. I wanted to know about good and bad, actions and consequences. And love, of course, there was always that, the great unknown, and I was considered far too young to know anything about it.

Chapter 7

A boy came to work with us. He must have been just doing odd jobs, because when I was ten or so he wasn't a lot older—perhaps in his early teens. He was Maori, with sleek brilliantined hair and a thin face. His name was David. One day he didn't do any work. He and I sat together on the camp stretcher in the lean-to and read comics. I don't know where my parents were. Perhaps they were around somewhere, or had biked into town; children were often left to their own devices. This boy and I may have leant on each other's shoulders as we read. I had forgotten about David until, on a trip north, when the gums first began to be cut down, I saw the stand on the property where he and his parents lived back then, dense and inky blue, the way I remembered them, and it came back to me. The next day, after we read the comics, he disappeared. He would never return, my parents said, because he had stolen something. They wouldn't say what it was. I recall nothing at all except sitting on the camp stretcher, reading comics, David's black hair and being hot.

This is not confessional stuff. There was nothing to confess. This was no older man sitting a child upon his knee in secret, it was two kids who laughed at the same jokes and liked comics. I'm sure of that.

But later I had a friend who I used to meet in the weekends and she was a secret. I think now that it was because of David that I kept this friendship to myself. Topsy Witihera was a girl with a wide concealing smile and a thick lustrous plait that hung below her waist. She was being brought up by her grandmother, and felt different, as I did, only more so. If my mother knew I met her she didn't say anything. But by now I was old enough to understand difference and I seemed to cause my parents problems enough. The poignancy of Topsy's name in a town like that was inescapable. She was called a lot of other names, too, that reflected her dark skin and lack of a father.

We sat on the doorstep at her grandmother's house and talked while the thick blue gums rippled and whispered in the background. In Topsy's presence it was possible to speak of unhappiness, to give sorrow a name. Our world was not make-believe and bullshit, it was about real things. And at school she saved me more than once from the physical attacks of older children. She would emerge as if from nowhere, her fists flying with a precision that left the opponents doubled over in agony. I got more peace after she took on the bullies. At some stage she disappeared, passed on to another family when her grandmother died. It took me thirty-six years to rediscover her.

This life with Topsy was far from the bookish fantasy world I inhabited with Madeleine. In fact, Madeleine doesn't figure much in this existence. She was still a class ahead of me and our school lives didn't cross much, although we walked to the bus each day, and if one of us was late we waited for the other, walking along Hone Heke Road where the yellow-green bamboos were packed so close together you couldn't see light between them, only above. The air stung with cicadas in summer; the scent of citrus flowers seeped through the hedges. Sometimes there was a sweet rottenness in the air.

Madeleine's own life seemed complicated in some respects—I was never sure whether her family was happy or not—but in this respect Madeleine remained loyal, close and inscrutable. Tom Graveson's fame as a horticulturalist was spreading and for many of the orchardists who had endured the 1946 drought, his new methods of raising trees were the salvation of their orchards. His swimming pool was a great luxury: in the summer I used to join the family and their many guests there almost every weekend.

Things continued to go from bad to worse for my parents. My father worked where he could but he found manual labour difficult and his job hopes were being constantly dashed. My mother had turned her hand to everything she could think of after Shropshire House burned down: the lemon picking, the library, growing vegetables for sale and raising chickens and ducks for the table—which I plucked for days on end over kerosene tins of hot water, round Christmas time. At times she glittered with a brave optimism, illuminated by small satisfactions in her garden. Her sunflowers were tall, strong and golden; her cut flowers won first prize at the flower show—a five-shilling prize was worth having. There were the picnics with Cora and Edward and dinners with Norah. One evening after dinner at her cottage there was singing round the table. My father loved this: his personality changed, he could hold a tune better than any of them. Then Norah sang 'I get along without you very well—of course I do', and when she cried we all looked the other way until conversation was restored.

At other times, my mother's health descended in sudden terrifying spirals: intolerable headaches, measles that turned to pneumonia and, worst, a carbuncle on her head that the local doctor, known for his drinking, lanced cold. It turned into a thirteen-headed creature that crawled across her head like a living thing. She was taken to hospital where they had just started using penicillin, and eventually recovered, despite heavy permanent scarring. While she was in hospital, I was sent south to live with Jean and for a time went to school in Morrinsville. I had spent many holidays at Jean and Fred's, travelling on my own to Auckland since I was seven, my name on a label pinned to my coat. Jean would pick me up there and we would take the next train down to Frankton Junction. Robert or Fred, usually both of them, waited for us as the steam engine snorted under the bridges while we climbed down from our carriage, and drove us over the dark Waikato roads. Home again, the other home.

    I loved my aunt's house. There was a huge kitchen with varnished wooden doors and a refrigerator—an early Frigidaire, of which Jean was very proud. Deep inside the house was a wide passage with a recess, which was Jean's special domain. A low seat made of plaited leather on a carved wooden frame sat beside a highly polished oak table. On this stood three objects: a brass box containing photographs of the family, several of her holding me as an infant; a swirling cloudy green Crown Devon jug, kept filled with flowers, either Michaelmas daisies or hydrangeas, according to the season; and the telephone. She would sit on the low seat for hours on end, talking to her best friend up the road, or to her older sister Margaret.

Although you had to go outside to it, they had a flush toilet, not the long drop across the paddock that I was used to. Jean and Fred had decorated it like a joke, with dozens of pictures of local football teams, and of racehorses, especially of the famous Phar Lap, whose heart, it was discovered when he died, weighed fourteen pounds. As well, there were cartoons cut out of the newspapers reflecting their enthusiasm for the right-wing politicians of the day, of whom they spoke in hushed tones of respect.

My grandmother now lived with Jean and Fred in the big and once too empty house. Jean was happy being busy, with several people to care for.

In earlier holidays, I had made some friends in Studholme Street, who now became classmates. My life seemed ordinary and regulated, nobody worried about money, and Jean did nothing except prepare dinner, bake, clean her already spotless house, and adore me. But I did rock the boat one Sunday afternoon. I had been reading *Palgrave's Golden Treasury* and decided to try my hand at some poems in the same portentous Victorian style. When the aunts were gathered for one of their frequent get-togethers I announced a poetry reading. The first poem began along the lines of an ode to 'love child of fair lady night'. Margaret was there. 'Love child,' she muttered into the silence. 'Love child.'

I got the message.

Still, going home to Kerikeri was like returning to another country. Starting all over again, and getting into trouble along the way, often without knowing why. I developed a fear of heights, got stuck on a swingbridge and had to be rescued by another teacher I didn't like, who turned out to be as frightened as

I was. The lecture, delivered back in the classroom, seemed unjust.

Things improved when Strumpel left. He was replaced by an apparently more liberal schoolmaster. His name was Hal Maingay, a man with kinetic brows and cool grey eyes. My writing was shortly to get me into another different sort of disgrace with him when I was almost expelled for writing my first love letter to a pimply curly-headed boy called Eric. (Why did Erics figure so often in my life?)

'I thought you were a decent girl,' said the headmaster.

I was terrified. What was a decent girl? I didn't know. I supposed that all the grown-up books and my secret conjectures, the tall and horrible tales I told other kids from time to time, were catching up with me. I felt particularly guilty because I had just read Warwick Deeping's *Sorrel and Son,* which my father had made clear I was not to touch. 'It's about nasty sordid people,' he said. Blissful. Just what I wanted, although when I read it, I couldn't make head or tail of what was going on.

And I didn't see myself reflected as a girl who wasn't decent. I knew that Mother Starr, as we called our neighbour down the road, used to wave brooms at girls who came up the road after her handsome son. Fighting them off, my parents muttered to each other. But nobody had had to fight me off Eric. I was eleven and the note handed in to Maingay had said only: 'I still like you. Do you like me?'

I ran away from school but was spotted by two maiden sisters, descended from missionaries (truly old Kerikeri), whom we called Flip and Flop as they trundled along on their bikes, with their skirts billowing around them. I took a short cut, running through their garden, shaking the wisteria and scattering Iceland poppies. I ran home into the waiting arms of my unhappy parents, who had already been phoned and told of my defection. After being delivered a lecture on not getting too friendly with boys, I returned to school the following day where Maingay told me he would be 'keeping an eye on me'.

He did this in a way that was not altogether unkind. Perhaps my disappearance had shaken him into taking a closer look at me. He may have understood that, as well as a precocious interest in boys, I had a frustrated longing to express myself. One way or another I was getting a pretty fair idea of the power of the written word. It was not just other people's words in books that made waves, but my own as well. I was awarded the *New Zealand Herald's* annual essay prize for a story called 'The Wrong Day', about a girl who gets Christmas Day mixed up, and thinks she has been deprived of company and presents. My prize was a copy of Robert Louis Stevenson's *Kidnapped.* People were starting to take notice of what I was up to, and despite the occasional setback, it seemed worthwhile. It's odd to look back and realise that, for almost all my life, the way out of anything has simply been to write, and when I don't I'm not satisfied with myself. If there has been a driving incentive to keep going and produce more books, an urge to communicate, to put things down, it began in those years at primary school.

I certainly had an early view of myself as a writer, but it was the *act* of writing that mattered so much, and has gone on for so long. I am glad I discovered books in the random way I did, without an internal censor saying what is suitable and what is not. By the time adults noticed that my reading was an eclectic ragbag, it was too late to change my ways. I was becoming possessed by a knowledge of light and dark, and I was already learning that the undercurrents I saw in people's lives were the kind of things people wrote books about, and not just an aberration of my own vision.

My school life entered a more tranquil phase as I became a senior at the school, and Hal Maingay began to offer me responsibility. As the school librarian, I kept order, in a dim little room at the end of the cloakroom, over the school's motley collection of books. I was the school mail girl, and at eleven every morning I set off to collect letters from the Stone Store. I was the bell-ringer who signalled the two minutes' silence we were required to observe on the day of King George VI's funeral. When he died, the school bus went to all the stops and the driver told everyone to go home. Pleased to have a holiday, I went out into the paddock to chat to my father. He was weeping. 'Don't you understand,' he said, 'the King is dead.'

I raised calves for the school's calf club, collected a number of red ribbons and began to travel round the Bay of Islands showing my charges and winning prizes for the school. At night I held their heads in my arms, as other children hold dogs and cats, and sat with them till they slept, often lying down beside them. In several of my stories, countrywomen lie with their faces near grass and earth—that is what I did.

Madeleine and I had grown closer at school, and began to assume independence. In the holidays, when we were not writing and drawing, we organised picnics at the river with her brothers, or went south to stay with relatives, both hers in Thames and mine in the Waikato. Madeleine suffered from travel sickness, so the trips were an ordeal for her. I liked fussing over her, walking her briskly up and down country railway stations for fresh air when the train stopped. Because of her motion sickness, the prospect of high school became a dilemma. Northland College in Kaikohe, the nearest high school, was over twenty miles away, reached by a bus that wound its way over gravelled roads and took several detours to pick up students from remote villages. It was decided that she would stay on for a second standard six year, which meant that at school we were finally equals.

It was around this time that I became possessed by a concern for my mother. The idea took hold of me that I must take responsibility, if not for her, at least for myself, so that I wouldn't be a financial burden. I lied about my age one summer holiday when I was twelve and got a job sweeping out one of the local grocery stores. When my age was discovered, I was given five minutes to get off the premises, but I did get paid for the two weeks' work I had done. Twenty-five shillings.

The following year, I set off for Northland College, while Madeleine went south to live with her aunt in Thames and start high school. She and I wrote to each other that year, but I think I wrote more letters in my head than in fact. The night Eric Kingsbury died was one that never got written. Towards dusk one spring evening, Mary Kingsbury had come running across the paddocks calling out, 'Mrs Eakin, Mrs Eakin'—always this odd formality in moments of crisis. Her distraught face appeared at the door. 'I can't get my husband to move. I think he's dead.'

Indeed he was. Earlier in the evening Mary had helped him across the paddock to milk the cow. He was very tired and seemed to have trouble walking. When he got back to the house he had lain down on the bed and closed his eyes.

My mother was gone a long time. My father made some phone calls to a doctor and others. When she came back my mother was pale and drawn. 'I've laid him out,' she said.

'Why didn't she get the doctor?'

My mother shrugged.

'No money perhaps, but she must have known he was sick,' my father persisted.

'No,' my mother said. 'It just never occurred to her that he'd die.' Her voice sounded flat, almost angry.

While she went back to the house to sit with Mary Kingsbury, I walked around in the moonlight, thinking about the dead body in the house on the hill, the not very romantic end to the life of a struggling writer. I had a vivid picture in my head of Eric Kingsbury stumbling across the paddock to milk the cow, a scene I had witnessed more than once. I remember being struck by the pity of it all—the surprised widow, the futile efforts to survive off the land. I wished Madeleine was there, but I couldn't think of anything to write to her about. I was in the habit of embellishing my letters to her with fanciful detail. But death was real, not an entertainment, and for once I was at a loss. Around this time my letters to Madeleine began to drop away.

When I set out for Northland College, I was the first on and the last off on the longest school bus run in the country. I was still only twelve, and the journey began at six thirty in the morning, when I cycled to the pick-up point. I was dropped off around six in the evening.

At this school, my life was transformed and a new world opened before me. Under the guidance of an English teacher full of infectious enthusiasm, T.J. Buxton, I flowered, could see direction in what I was reading and writing. He encouraged me to read Shakespeare, which I had timidly begun in my earlier reading experiments. It didn't turn me into a Shakespearean scholar—it was to be years before I turned back to what I learned then—but I began to understand the meaning of drama in a broader sense. Buxton had also been a friend and mentor of the Shakespearean actor, Ewen Solon, based in London, for whom I later wrote a television play.

I discovered at Northland College that I was good at mathematics after all, and also fell in love with Latin. 'Amo, amas, amat,' we chanted. I love, you love, he, she or it loves ... indeed. I did. I was giving more serious attention to the subject of boys, as real people rather than romantic images. As if in a magic reaction, my straight hair suddenly curled, and I stopped being plump.

I went to my first school dance during that year. A new frock was out of the question, but my mother had a collection of dresses in a tin sea trunk. She wondered if I might find something in there that we could remake. Opening the trunk was like discovering a whole new dimension to my mother. I was used to seeing her at best in drab floral cotton dresses, but mostly in trousers tucked into her gumboots. There was a pale apple-green silk dress with a rippling skirt, a straight cream linen frock with drawn threadwork on the bodice, a form-fitting sheath made of satin in wide horizontal navy and red stripes. These were the dresses she had worn on board ship on her travels to and from Australia. Perhaps this was where her alter ego in the Portia dramas had been born. I chose the satin dress.

I stayed with a new friend called Glenis that night, so that I could go to the dance. She and her mother tried to persuade me to wear one of Glenis's dresses, but I insisted on my choice. When I arrived at the dance, I could see it was a mistake.

'Where *did* you get that dress?' smirked several girls.

Seeing me sitting in a corner trying not to be noticed, T.J. came over to have a kindly word. But at the same moment a fair boy, with wide shoulders for his fifteen years, turned up. J was the son of the school caretaker, one of the Polish refugee children who had come via Russia and Persia to New Zealand, where his family was eventually reunited. My difference paid off that evening. J was foreign and exotic himself, from my point of view, and he thought I looked great, and much more grown up than the girls with wide petticoats and skirts. We danced every dance and for the rest of the year we wrote long letters to each other about our lives, although his was infinitely more dramatic than mine. Still, I had my first boyfriend, and one who caused some admiration and envy.

While this year was passing, changes were afoot at home. A year or so earlier both my Irish great-aunts, Poll and Sal O'Hara, had died in Bandon, County Cork, but it was some time before my father learned that he had come into money. In spite of the inheritance from my grandmother years earlier, my father had suffered the defeat of being the second son when it came to later estates. There had been some kind of falling out with his father's family. The cousin, Fanny Thomson, who was at his mother's deathbed, had distributed his father's money between my uncle in Australia, herself and the housekeeper, Mrs Murphy. 'The trouble is there being two sons,' she had written in a frosty letter to my father. Some lawyer's letters went backwards and forwards, but Fanny won.

In Bandon, Sal and Poll, who shared the family house where my grandmother grew up, had decided, after all, that both sons should receive an inheritance. When the sisters died within a few months of each other, there was money for a dairy farm, something my mother had long hoped for. My parents wanted, too, to move to a place where I could get to high school more easily.

At the end of the year I won the English prize, learning to curtsey for the prize-giving ceremony in my navy blue gym slip. My school report bore the exciting words, written by the principal, 'We expect that Fiona will bring a University Scholarship to Northland College.'

That never happened.

The day after prize-giving, we shifted south to Waipu. I had left Kerikeri behind me, even as we drove out of town.

Do I regret this childhood of mine? There are parts of it I wouldn't want to live again, but it has a certain curiosity value. All those remnants of the Raj, and the old China hands. Like a piece of cracked Ming at the back of the china cupboard. I wouldn't give it away, even if I could.

A day or two later, Madeleine returned from Thames. She had had a happy school year, full of academic success, but she missed her family, and me. She had decided to brave bus travel the following year. When she arrived home, I had gone without leaving a forwarding address. Perhaps I had got used to sudden departures and absences, and thought little of it. To Madeleine, it seemed that I had vanished off the face of the earth. It was years before I learned how this trauma affected her, although from time to time we exchanged letters and photographs. Madeleine became a dental nurse after she left school, before turning to law and later a career as a lecturer in law at Auckland University.

In the early 1960s, she and I met briefly, when we were both newly married. But it was not until 1973, just twenty years after my sudden disappearance, that I visited her. I was given the loft bedroom to sleep in, overlooking the estuary beyond her house. About ten thirty, after her children had gone to bed, Madeleine's head appeared through the loft door. She was carrying two mugs of tea. We talked until dawn about gaps in our lives, the great yawning stretches that only memory can comprehend and fill. Her eyes were still the same blazing navy blue they had been when she was a child.

I was beginning to make my way as a writer. Later, I would talk about my life in public, and the next time we talked she challenged accounts of my childhood in which she is missing. You and I shared a life, she has said, and we were happy.

Maybe, I said on that occasion, but I think now that I had two or three lives operating at that time; she was in one of them. She is not missing, she had just got into a different narrative. This is one of the writer's dilemmas, of course, to tease out strands of truth and make them whole. In fiction, it is not so difficult because truth is what the writer decides it will be. Real life is not like that—exact truth is an individual's personal nightmare and fantasy, which nobody else, however close, can really share.

I dedicated *Mandarin Summer* to Madeleine.

Everywhere you look in Menton there are flowers. A blaze of red poppies covers the bank beneath the fig tree outside the apartment window. Down the avenue de Verdun the beds are full of tall snapdragons that bring a lump to the back of my throat. They are just like the ones my mother won prizes for.

And yesterday the orange trees were being harvested for thousands of late fruit, the trees pruned by shearing off huge branches. Mountains of leaves, sparkling with the jewel-like fruit, lay on the sidewalks. The scent took me back, as it does here over and again, to that other place, the hot, dry place of my childhood, where the trees, heavy with fruit, or blossom, overpowered me with their perfume.

I am waiting for Madeleine. She will come any day. We are into the seventh decade of our friendship, but there is still much to be said. It seems to me now that Madeleine had another life too. We were talking in a Wellington restaurant one day, and she said, 'I don't feel like a New Zealander. I've always felt as if I was truly European.' I was surprised when she said that, wanted to repudiate it. But I thought of her father, Frank Grosz, that Austrian artist whose vivid paintings were to contribute to a significant corner of New

Zealand's artistic legacy of the 1940s and 1950s, and I could see why she might feel like that. All along, unbeknown to me, she had had this separate existence too. 'You were a fine one to talk,' I said, or words to that effect. Besides, I have always felt like a New Zealander, not tied to the countries our forebears left behind.

Now, quite late in my own story, I have a long-resisted British passport, thanks to my father's place of birth. It makes it easier to live in Europe, a territory without boundaries if you have this magic red booklet. 'Fiona,' a friend said gently to me, 'it's only a travel document, it's not who you are.'

But yes, in a sense, it is. I am the daughter of someone who never went 'home' after I was born, and yet in his head, in his heart, that is often where he was, and I missed him, more than I knew or understood at the time.

Anyway, that is the way it was. Other lives.

And, any day, any day now, Madeleine will be here in Menton.

Chapter 8

We arrived in Waipu just weeks before Christmas 1953, in the season of Advent. Seven Christmases had passed since our family had gone north. Now we were turning south again. I had seen Waipu, on earlier journeys. After the long climb up Brynderwyn Hill, I am still never prepared for what lies beneath its crest. For there, the blue floor of the world is stretched beneath the traveller, as it was for the Lotus Eaters coming upon a land of water 'along the cliff to fall and pause and fall'. The whole of Bream Bay stretches from Bream Tail to far-off Bream Head over beyond Whangarei. There are the Hen and Chicken Islands squatting on the sea and Sail Rock in the bright distance. When I arrive at that point it is a homecoming. It is only a short run down the northern slope of Brynderwyn to the flat plains of the Braigh, on the outskirts of Waipu.

But the day we arrived at the farm, we came in by a back road from the north. All our belongings, including three cows, two wire-haired fox terriers called Penny and Gay, and the cat, were loaded on three trucks hired for the journey. One showed signs of giving up by the time we wended our way in a trail of red dust down North River into the valley that would become home. Neither my mother nor I had seen the farm before we set off from Kerikeri. My mother had put her faith in my father's judgement again, and this time, it seemed, he had got it right.

The little house was square, with four exactly proportioned rooms and a lean-to bathroom and laundry. It seemed beautiful to me, after what we had left behind. It looked like a real house. Outside what would be my bedroom stood a plum tree. The long drop dunny, instead of being across the paddock, was in the back yard, separated from the living quarters only by another spreading plum tree. It became a favourite place for my father to read; he took his .22 out there as well as a book, so he could sit and shoot possums in the tree.

'It's not bad, Mum,' I said. 'It's not bad, is it?'

In fact, it remained wonderful to me, as was North River Valley and the people who lived there. Before we left Kerikeri, people said to us, 'You'll never get on with the Novies [Nova Scotians]. They're a clannish bunch, they don't like outsiders.' Which seems a bit rich when I think back on it. And it didn't turn out to be the case.

Perhaps an element of curiosity about our odd little procession brought the neighbours over that first day. Whatever it was, they came bearing gifts: scones, whipped cream, jam, a stew for our dinner, some homemade ginger beer. Their interest and concern for our well-being never failed. It might have helped that my mother was a Sutherland, descended from Sutherland County, the same as they were, even if she was off a different 'boat'. These new neighbours were, almost without exception, descendants of a migration that had occurred just over a century before our arrival, led by a charismatic Presbyterian minister called Norman McLeod. It was impossible to live in Waipu without being aware of the town's history; it was so central to living there in 1953, and it is even now.

In 1817 McLeod had led a breakaway group from the Church of Scotland to settle what became known as Nova Scotia on the eastern seaboard of Canada. He and his followers travelled from Ullapool, in the north-west Highlands, in a leaky ship called the *Frances Ann,* which would have turned back had McLeod's navigational knowledge not informed him that the vessel was closer to North America than it was to Scotland. He encouraged the passengers, in what would have been a mutiny had he been wrong, to persuade the captain to continue. His feats as a seaman, and in settling new lands, the manner in which he protected his followers from persecution by the lairds in Scotland, and the compelling rhetoric of his sermons are legendary. But he was also remembered as a harsh disciplinarian who had a repressive attitude towards women. He was said, too, to have cut off a boy's ear for stealing, although the child was later found innocent. Whether McLeod really did this or not is still disputed. In court records I later found in Halifax's Public Archives, it appears that although he didn't perform the deed in person, he did order someone else to do it. My fate, when I was a girl, seemed to be landing in places were history had happened.

After nearly forty years, a biblical amount of time you might think, famine struck Nova Scotia. McLeod decided to look further afield for a haven for his people. One of his sons had gone to Australia and he wrote to his father telling of prosperous farming land. At this point, one of the most extraordinary migrations in British Commonwealth history began. Virtually in their back yards, the Nova Scotians built six ships to carry them and their belongings to Australia. Many elected not to go and there were pitiful scenes as families divided for and against the migration. Some escaped on the day the first ship left, just as my own great-great-grandmother had tried to do at Brora, in Scotland. One of them was McLeod's favoured daughter, Margaret, for whom the ship was named.

McLeod was disappointed by what he found in Australia. By the time the ships arrived the goldrush had begun and many of the formerly law-abiding followers succumbed to easy money and the rousing life of the goldfields. While the settlers were camped under canvas, typhoid struck, and within six weeks three of McLeod's sons had died. Humbled, McLeod saw these events as a sign that he had offended God. He gathered together those still prepared to follow him and sailed for Auckland, where the settlers successfully petitioned Governor George Grey for land at Waipu. The green forests sweeping to the edge of the sea had attracted the voyagers as they travelled down the coastline: they saw the tall trees as potential masts in future shipbuilding ventures. Northland looked like a warmer version of Nova Scotia, a lotus land indeed.

Of course I didn't know all this when we arrived. What I did know was that everyone's names seemed to begin with Mac. There were eighty Macs in the two pages of the phone directory devoted to Waipu. To add to the confusion, people added the names of ancestors as nicknames to differentiate between generations. So a boy who was called Ian might have his father's name John added to it, and his grandfather's name as well. Jack's son might be Johnny Jack and Johnny Jack's son Ian Johnny Jack. Almost everyone had a nickname. A man might be known as 'Cave'; or as 'Bear', because his father had once shot a bear in Nova Scotia. A lot of them were just Mac.

They were solid, droll people in our valley. There was an unwritten but implicitly understood rule about being a good neighbour—you never locked your door, lest someone from along the road needed something they had run out of. A cup of flour perhaps, some sugar, or golden syrup, an item that couldn't be obtained without a journey into town, before the next weekly delivery of groceries came out from the Four Square.

Our dairy farm was just a pocket handkerchief in size compared with the ones around us, and we had no tractor, no plough, no cowshed, no haymaking equipment, not even a vehicle of our own, and we were five miles from the township, known always as The Centre. In a word, we were undercapitalised. I think the locals saw a kind of valour in it all, a bit like that of their own not so distant forebears.

Nobody had lived at the farm for some time, and when we arrived a thick crop of hay lay waiting to be cut. My father rang up Colin Russell, who cut hay, and asked if he could fit us in before Christmas. Colin had a vacancy the following week. When he came to cut the grass, my father asked how many men he would need to employ for bringing in the hay. That won't be necessary, Colin said curtly, it would be taken care of. This was puzzling, because there was a lot of hay. But on the appointed day, as if on signal, at least a dozen men appeared, wearing their trademark black singlets and gumboots. In the afternoons the women appeared with food baskets and scalding billies of tea, to picnic by the winding banks of North River. At the end of each day, I would lie beside the river and inhale the rich hot scent of newly mown grass. The river formed a natural boundary on our home paddock. On the banks grew massed willow trees, hawthorn and wild briar roses. Brown ducks nested there, a rare variety apparently, about which my father wrote to the naturalist Peter Scott. He replied, saying he might come and see us when he was in New Zealand, but in the end he didn't.

On Christmas morning, my mother appeared in the garden, her voice harsh with grief. There had been an accident, she said, at a place called Tangiwai. A train had been swept off a bridge and many people, perhaps hundreds, had died. It was difficult to absorb the dark cloud that had fallen on the country. The train had been derailed by a lahar from Mount Ruapehu, near Ohakune. The final death toll was 151. It wasn't long before news trickled back to us of people we knew, or who were touched in some close personal way by the tragedy. We felt overwhelmed by the scale of the disaster.

Like most, we 'did' Christmas, but the lustre was gone from that first celebration. As we did every year, we ate roast chicken and hot steamed pudding, and a special chocolate biscuit fudge my mother made called Oriental Chocolate Chew. The table was set under the plum tree and, as always, there was just the three of us, sitting in the wilderness, singing carols.

I was about to enter a period of family happiness I hadn't experienced before. My father's bookish ways and the years of herd testing in Western Australia now began to pay off. Although the farm was small, he had read a lot about managing pasture, and for a time he put this knowledge to good use. He would surprise everyone by prising a high butterfat yield from the small herd. In the beginning, a kind of idyll descended upon us. My mother was reunited with her Scots background, and my father became the true provider.

The neighbours helped to lay concrete for a cowshed, and a few days later, the building was erected. Then an uncle, Margaret's husband, came up and installed milking machines. My cousins by this late marriage of Margaret's came with them, and I finally got to know Louis and Elizabeth West. Lou played the accordion and knew all the hit tunes. Down south, my Uncle Stewart had also had a daughter, Catherine, when he was in his fifties. I felt less solitary, no longer the total focus of the older generation, and it came as something of a relief, although I doubt if I recognised it for that at the time.

My parents usually milked in the mornings, though sometimes I was rostered on at daybreak too. My father and I did the evening shift. We sang in the cowshed, his pleasant tenor voice, which had won him a place in musicals in Middlesbrough and San Francisco, in full flight. As well as the songs he remembered from those days we also sang 'Davy Crockett' and 'She'll be Coming Round the Mountain' ('when she comes, when she comes'), 'The Wild Colonial Boy' and our favourite, 'The Jones Boy' ('the whole town's talking about the Jones boy'). We could have been singing my father's own song. I relished this new and joyful family life. And, when life was quiet on the farm, I skilfully joined the local pastime of listener-in to the party line. The trick was to lift the phone without being heard, then cover the receiver to mask your breathing, and stand very still. Some did better than others. One elderly matriarch was often caught out by her clock chiming during her neighbours' conversations. I didn't make mistakes like that.

On pale turquoise summer evenings after milking, my father and I would sometimes go off with the McAulay brothers from across the road to gather scallops at Ruakaka Beach, where a mothballed oil refinery now stands. The scallops were so big and plentiful that the leftovers were fed to the farm dogs. The McAulays were our closest neighbours, their farmhouse over the paddock from ours. When night closed in, we could see the lights of their house, and one other, far back in the hills. The rest was a friendly darkness. Murdoch McAulay, weather-beaten, autocratic, yet still a very kind and funny man, would speak to his cows with a voice of thunder that I could hear from our place. 'You might as well speak to Jesus,' he grumbled, as he prodded them along. I was thinking of Murdoch when I wrote the character of a farmer in *Ricochet Baby,* a novel I wrote some forty years later:

> This land has been in [the] family for four generations. The farm lies among rolling country burned out of the bush a century or more ago ... He stands on the crest of the hill, holding his gun at his side. In the circle of light that surrounds the farm, all the trembling knee-high grass, the beautiful clover and rye, the cocksfoot and timothy lying before him is his. It is rich and luscious and soon it will be ready to cut for hay; it ripples and shimmers and billows; it surges with the day's early light, now purple and lavender in the shadow of a cloud, now flickering green like the feathers of a parrot. There will be a good crop of hay this year.

Murdoch. Or my grandfather. Or my father, if he could have just put his hand out and held fast to the dream. I knew these men, I knew what they loved, and it was not all beer and rugby, although they were rugged. With it, went a tenderness for the land, and what it stood for.

Nancy, the youngest McAulay daughter and the only one still at home, was sixteen and engaged to be married. She and I spent hours catching eels at the river, beneath the shed where the curds, left after the milk was separated, were thrown.

It was at North River that I began my habit, which lasted many years, of walking in the dark. On summer nights when the roof was still hot from the sun, and ripe plums reeked against the windowpane, I would get out of bed and steal out of the house to walk along the riverbank, often climbing a half-fallen poplar tree that stretched over the stream. I would lie in a comfortable crook in the trunk, watching moonlight play on the surface of the river and listening for moreporks. The scents of paddocks and animals and foliage are different in the dark—cooler, sharper, crisper. One night I could have sworn I heard God's voice, saying, 'Too late, *too* late'. Too late for what? To tell it all, I told myself years afterwards. There was something romantic about the idea of being spoken to by God, although I'm not a believer now. Towards dawn I would return to the house, feeling refreshed and whole, rather than tired. Something would have shifted in me. Being on my own didn't mean that I was lonely. The solitariness that had dogged me for so long was becoming a friend; I wasn't afraid of it any more.

Not everything was perfect. When the old and the new came into conflict some bad things happened. When people stepped outside the codes that operated within the Nova Scotian group they could be ostracised. A 'bad' marriage might mean a life on the outside looking in. And I was fascinated by a woman who lived in a tumbledown house at the edge of the village, in the first years I was in Waipu. She was referred to by some of the people in our valley as 'the witch'. I never knew much about the real life of Miss Kitty Slick, but it certainly appeared reclusive. She did not, it was said, receive visitors, nor had she left the house for many years, because of some transgression within the community.

When the school bus passed her house, we could see her, wearing long dark skirts, sweeping down her verandah. It wasn't difficult to see why the label 'witch' was applied to her.

But these things didn't affect me in my new life. The worst that happened was that once again school and I didn't agree with each other. There had been an inauspicious start during my second week at Waipu District High. I was assigned to a school house that was rostered on to do school duties for a week. The house captain had noted my unusual accent and I was asked to give the reading at school assembly. The reading I was assigned was the Twenty-third Psalm, 'The Lord is my shepherd'.

'Who does she sound like?' the headmaster asked the school at the end of the reading.

'The Queen,' roared back the school in unison. Queen Elizabeth had just made her first tour of New Zealand. I vowed inwardly that it was time to lengthen a few vowels.

What the house captain had omitted to tell me was that I was also supposed to clean handbasins each day of duty. At the end of the week I was summoned to the office of Miss Lucy Black, a gingery woman with an acid tongue.

'You gave the best reading this school has ever heard,' she said, 'so I suppose there must be some good in you. But I warn you, we have decent students at this school.'

Once again I was being chastised for not being 'decent'. I made a mental note not to put up with too much of this.

Waipu District High only went up to the fifth form, and there were just eighty high-school students. A district high school started from new entrants in the primary division, and went right through to the sixth form (today it would be the seventh, or year thirteen), where University Entrance classes were available, but ours fell short of that so pupils usually left at about fifteen. As in other country areas, those families who could afford to sent promising children away to board and attend city schools.

Nevertheless, we were blessed with a sprinkling of outstanding teachers. There was Roger Shaw, for geography, who showed me that the world was a bigger place than North Auckland; Alick, his small pre-schooler son, ran riot through the classroom as both his parents taught. History teacher Judith Bird, an elegant pale woman who reminded me of my Aunt Roberta, taught me to argue constructively; later she became a passionate street demonstrator in Wellington, an early anti-apartheid protester. And flame-haired Eileen O'Shea, my English teacher, introduced me to poetry. She was engaged to one of the primary teachers, Fred Larkin, and they walked the playground together in the lunch hour, she in wide full skirts, nipped in at her tiny waist. She told us that we would understand Francis Thompson's 'The Hound of Heaven' when we were older, and read us Gerard Manley Hopkins's 'Pied Beauty', with its wonderful opening line, 'Glory be to God for dappled things'. I wrote this in my English notebook, and some years ago, when asked to speak on a panel at

Wellington's Readers and Writers Week on 'First Loves' about the first poem that had made an impact on me, I chose the Hopkins poem, speaking of it and of Eileen. I hoped, I said, that somewhere out there Eileen O'Shea still walked with her own first love, forgetting that the panel was being recorded for broadcast on National Radio. The following year, I spoke at a lunch in Hawke's Bay; as if on *This Is Your Life,* Eileen appeared as a surprise for me, and yes, she had spent her life with Fred and they had been happy. Fred has died since then. Eileen gave me a beautiful green and white garden pot she had made, as if she had always known that these are the colours I love best. It sits in a corner of my garden beneath a miniature kowhai tree.

In spite of these teachers, whom I remember with affection and gratitude, the school didn't have much breadth in the education it offered. Latin was out of the question, I soon lost my hold on mathematics, and French was taught in a cloakroom, and later in the boys' woodwork room. There were five students in the French class; we had an elderly part-time teacher with some unfortunate personal mannerisms, such as losing her teeth when she was teaching us verbs, reducing us to endless hysterical laughter, the kind you can't stop once you've begun, which earned us daily dismissals from class.

In spite of this, I think poor Miss Hislop not only had a very good command of French, but a fierce love for France, and that she was a better teacher than we gave her credit for. I surprise myself here in Menton with the amount of French I know when I have no option but to speak the language, albeit in a shy and unpractised way. Somewhere between the faded board covers of our textbook, *En Route,* and our teacher's exhortations, I felt the first stir of longing that some day I would go to Provence and see fields of sunflowers for myself. And now I have.

But my thoughts of being a writer faded—that was something silly, a part of childhood. I was glad to be in Waipu but after Northland College the school felt like a let-down.

I had two close friends at school, Jennifer (Jen) Gates, now the children's writer Jennifer Beck, and Marina Markotich. I loved Jen's sense of humour and delight in practical jokes. She was the third of five children, and her family were generous in their hospitality. The Gates' farmhouse, up Finlayson's Brook, was a rambling many-roomed place where everybody read books and talked about them. Well, most of them—after some coercion, Jen's older brother lent me Mickey Spillane's *I, the Jury* which I read propped behind *Plain Sailing,* my English textbook. I don't recall any family discussions about that one. Jim Gates had a pitted face and a wide slow smile. The children were encouraged to say what they thought on a variety of issues, and to listen to each other with respect. In many ways, the Gates family came to represent the brothers and sisters I never had. The worst disgrace Jen and I brought upon ourselves came after seeing Edith Campion play Joan of Arc with the New Zealand Players, on a school trip to Whangarei. Afterwards, in a highly charged response, we went to the nearest hairdresser and had our heads virtually shorn in Eton crops. We earned rebukes at school assembly the following day and had to live with the consequences until our hair grew back.

I continued my night rambles. If there was a touch of religious fervour in them, it was possibly prompted by living in Waipu. Surprisingly, given the settlement's Presbyterian ardour, I was confirmed into the Church of England. The visiting minister at the tiny church on the northern boundary of the township was touting for young people to bring into the church.

Religion had remained a sore point in my family. Although my parents had been married in a Presbyterian church in Western Australia, the trade-off was my Anglican christening. Now my father wanted the job finished, and he was keen that I should go ahead with confirmation. My mother didn't seem to mind. Perhaps, here at home among Presbyterians, it didn't matter so much to her what I was, as long as she was free to be herself.

But it wasn't the anticipated Church of England, for the vicar was an Anglo-Catholic, known as Father F, all smells and bells, as my mother said when she found out. I think my father was a bit rattled too. Although he had grown up High Church, even he could see that in New Zealand it was viewed differently. But it seemed too late to change my mind. The girls up the road were being confirmed and I had thrown in my lot with them. All the confessing and kneeling and praying did bring out some rather phony exaltation, which kept us going to our instruction classes. My mother made me a white confirmation dress with intricate tucks in the bodice. She made me a brassiere as well, much to my shame. 'That will hold you in,' she said in no uncertain terms, and it certainly did, flattening me out like a pancake.

I didn't much like Father F. He elicited confessions from us girls, even when we had nothing to confess, and paraded through the dances in the church hall, looking for things to criticise about our appearance. When he saw me wearing gold hoop earrings, he warned me that I was headed for a life of sin, and threatened to tell my parents.

Not that my father needed any convincing. 'Don't come crying to me when you get yourself in trouble,' he said, the first time he saw me with lipstick. If only someone would tell me what trouble was. I convinced my mother to get me *Madame Bovary* from the Country Library Service van, in French, because the English version was banned in New Zealand at the time. She was doubtful, but when I insisted that I needed it to improve my French she relented. I think it did help the French along, but I didn't learn any more about the act of sex than I had from anything else I'd read.

I set aside this brief bout of religious mysticism as I grew older and became absorbed into Waipu's social life. This included square dancing, with a set of Scottish lancers thrown in, when we gathered at the local hall every month. We stamped and sang, circling to our left and to our right, 'and you choose your girl from the valley/oh you choose your Red River girl...' I used to go with H from a neighbouring farm, on whom I had a girlish crush. He was thirteen years my senior, and he started taking me only because I asked him, and because he was at a loose end after the collapse of a long relationship with a girl he had hoped to marry:

He was a dark nuggety man with a sinewy throat rising from his black bush singlet. His hair was crinkly beneath the battered grey felt hat he wore. Nests of hair covered his short strong forearms. When he lit a cigarette he balanced it for an instant with a delicate flick between the tip of his tongue and his top lip before drawing it down into his mouth.

He and I began to grow closer, but he was still unhappy about his life. He wouldn't be the last man I encountered who had failed to get a woman out of his system when he met me. He decided to join the Special Armed Services (SAS) and go away to fight in the Malayan jungle, to have an adventure that took him beyond Waipu. Before he left he said that perhaps, when he came back, we could think about the future. I knew even then what that would mean to my parents. A match made in heaven. He treated me as if I was grown up and yet he understood that he must take care of me. For a while I would have done anything for him, but he did nothing more than ask me to wait for him. I was too young for either. The last time I saw him, he was dressed in his olive green uniform with a brown-green shirt and tie. On his head he wore a maroon beret with a winged dagger, and the motto 'Who Dares Wins'.

Around this time, we stopped seeing Miss Slick out on her verandah. Nobody thought much of it. But then we learned that she had been found dead in her house, apparently, somebody said, three weeks after the event. You could feel a collective unease in the community. Nobody spoke of her as a 'witch' any more. But by this time, I had become drawn to the mythology of her life. When some months had passed, Jennifer and I were attracted to the swinging door, and the emptiness glimpsed through the windows. The house had been cleared of whatever furniture might have been there. One Saturday afternoon, we simply went in. The rooms were bare and plain. A ladder-like staircase led up to the second storey and we climbed it, clutching each other, suddenly afraid of the sound of our own breaths. At the top of the stairs were two bedrooms, facing out across the paddocks to an estuary. The branches of the big macrocarpa tree that stood beside the house were very close, almost touching the walls.

But what was remarkable to me was that these rooms were wallpapered with newspapers, brown and brittle with age, bearing the date 1898. Fifty-seven years had passed since this rough attempt to make the place homely, or perhaps just to paper over the cracks in the walls so the wind couldn't whistle through.

Over decades, I visited this house several times, watching its slow collapse, until its demolition ten years or so ago. I have a little piece of kauri timber stamped with the words 'Kitty Slick's House Timber, Waipu': these were sold as souvenirs when the place was finally pulled down. That house would later play a huge role in my own life. The kernel of a novel called *The Book of Secrets,* written thirty years later, appeared that afternoon. For a long time after its publication I would be 'expelled' from Waipu town myself. But then, all I knew was that a bleak sorrow had entered me, and that I could not get out of the house fast enough.

Soon came long summer holidays with the Gates girls, Lynette, Jennifer and Julie, and their younger brother Philip, without any parents present, at Waipu Cove, the long gleaming white beach that has been the haunt of surfies for decades. The Gates' parents rented a cottage for us that stood almost upon the sand. I swear they don't make summers the way they used to—the blue quilt of the mornings spread across each day, spilling over the edges of afternoon and folding into the saffron evening light. And beginning all over again the next day. We accidentally swam too close to sharks, looking back with a shudder at their fins slicing through early morning water. We resolved to be more careful. Apart from that, our holidays rolled past in a seamless pattern of scorching days.

The major event on the local calendar was New Year's Day, when the Caledonian Games took place. Some years, important visitors from Scotland arrived. Much of old Waipu still stands as it was: the Caledonian hall, the stone gates at the entrance to the park, a trickle of shops and a garage on one side of the road; on the other, a white rectangular church without ornamentation, a parish hall and a manse, the Waipu Heritage Centre, a stone building that houses an excellent museum, and, standing right beside the road, a tall monument topped by the heraldic Lion of Scotland. This road used to be State Highway One, but now a deviation passes behind the town. You have to go looking for Waipu. The monument is six-sided, each bearing the name of one of the ships: the *Margaret*, the *Highland Lass*, the *Gertrude*, the *Spray*, the *Breadalbane* and the *Ellen Lewis*. The pioneers' motto is written in Gaelic around the base: 'Cuimhinigh a nis do Cruithfear Ann an laithibh t'oice', the opening words of Ecclesiastes XII—'Remember now thy Creator in the days of thy youth'.

I left Waipu, and effectively the days of my own youth, when I was not quite sixteen. I sat School Certificate in the church hall, supervised by Mr McKay, a man known as 'Danny Ferry', an institution in the town, who had supervised the examination for as long as it had existed. For the occasion, he wore a suit and a gold watch chain across his waistcoat. He was known as a man with a big heart but it failed him that year. He went out of the hall, the day after I had sat my last paper in geography, while Marina was sitting home science, and died beneath the magnolia tree outside the church. 'I cannot go on today, children,' he is reported to have said, as he left.

At the end of school, my teachers urged me, and my parents, that I should go teaching. Although I was still only fifteen at the time, I was assured that with good School Certificate marks a way round the age requirements could be found. Nothing was further from my mind than teaching. For a start, I wanted to earn some money. I had had enough of making do and was fascinated by clothes. Miss Mary McKay, who ran the drapery shop, gave me a job the last summer I was there. I thought of her as quite old, although I don't think she was. She had a great deal of hair wound up in coils and loops. Like me, she was an only child, and I understood her to have worked all her life, since she was thirteen, in one or other of the Waipu shops. *Pride of the Lion,* an historical work produced by the people of Waipu to commemorate 150 years of settlement, recorded that the drapery:

> ...stocked a large range of items—men's women's and children's wear. Footwear was included—slippers, tennis shoes and sandshoes, which were then considered to be poor man's shoes, not like the high fashion sneakers of today. If a new suit was required, the measuring up was done at the shop, samples chosen, and the order sent away.

All of these were things I learned to do and Miss McKay said that I was 'a good girl at my work'. When things were quiet I would phone local farmers' wives and describe the latest dresses in stock with such verve that I was frequently invited to send a sample by rural delivery mail. None of the dresses were ever returned. Such aggressive selling seemed to appeal to the Scots. I also introduced some lines for young people. Miss McKay allowed me to order in some Whirl bras, which were constructed of spiralling wires that created a cone-shaped effect. I hadn't got over my confirmation bra. They sold as fast as we ordered them in.

I was asked to stay on as permanent staff. As in most of Northland's rural areas, where choices were limited, I would have been thought lucky to get a job. But I did go, fleeing, finally, in a kind of terror that I might stay forever in Lotus Land, without having sampled the world beyond. A message arrived from H, saying that he was sick and would be coming home soon. I knew then, as he had, that I wanted adventure beyond Waipu. I understood that if I stayed, I would almost certainly never leave.

As it happened, H was more ill than he knew and lived only a few years after his return, but long enough to marry. One day, I was sitting at my desk in a Wellington office, when the phone rang. When I picked it up, a woman introduced herself as H's daughter. She believed I had known him? And when I said yes, she asked me what I could tell her about him. As he had died when she was so young, she found it hard to get a clear picture of him.

Later, when I wrote 'Circling to Your Left', based on some of these events, the narrator recounts that when she is phoned, and the caller identifies herself, 'a shiver like violets shaken before a spring wind had passed through her. She thinks of Kathryn's father as tenderly as she thinks of any man.' I have since given this story to the daughter.

I didn't go very far when I left Waipu, just to Jean's place in Morrinsville, to work in an office. It was my first step into the world beyond. Fred and Jean came north to collect me. I have a photograph of my last morning. My mother, unusually, is wearing a dress, even though we must have just finished milking. Her face is strained and sad. More than that. There is something broken in her appearance.

I can see now that, when I left, all the struggling up north, the hardship and the breaking in of land, must have seemed for nothing. I was what they had, and I was going away and leaving them to it. Soon after I went, things fell apart on the farm. My father's health and newfound zest for life evaporated; he would sit for days at a time with his head in a book, just dreaming or staring into space. He wrote me loving and funny letters, my tangible evidence of the person he might have been.

Before long the farm was on the market. My mother hid in the hills when people came to look at the property, but the barking of the dogs gave her away, and it sold almost straight away. I could not bear to think of my parents leaving the farm I had so quickly and deeply learned to love, without my ever seeing it again. I asked for a week off work, and caught the bus home, appearing unexpectedly on the doorstep one afternoon in spring.

I walked all that haunted week. The hawthorn was already coming out around the riverbank and the wild briar roses and willow trees were in bud. I said goodbye to the animals: Toby, the dog who had worked the cows so well for me; the cows themselves, all of which I knew by name, including some that had come with us from Kerikeri; Deidre, the pig whose litters I had helped to raise.

When I return, I always go to the cemetery by the sea just before you reach the Cove. That is where McLeod lies. The place is full of old voices, which haunted me through the years, to the point where I was driven around the world in pursuit of the migration.

But the voices that follow me still are those of the first three names on the left-hand side going into the cemetery: the two brothers and their father from the farm next door, all the McAulay men. They remind me, all three of them, that despite a troubled early life, it was possible to have a perfectly ordinary rural childhood, in a quite exceptional and life-changing little town.

Chapter 9

In Morrinsville, I worked in the local Massey Ferguson tractor dealer's office, starting at £4 a week. My employer, Laurie Maber, was a debonair, good-natured man. He and Miss Betty Whitley, the tall big-boned office manager with a soft spot for young people who were 'triers', taught me office routine and how to calculate figures. Young farmers came to town on Fridays, and Maber Motors was their meeting place. Soon I learned to sympathise over broken crankshafts. In the evenings, I was to learn typing and shorthand at the local night school. My father was convinced that if I could acquire these skills my career prospects would be fine. In a sense he was right. Typing has stood me in good stead, though my skills remain basic: the first two knuckles of each hand are overdeveloped and misshapen from forty-five years of daily two-fingered typing. I never learned shorthand. Instead of attending class, I absconded to have a cigarette behind the bike sheds with new-found classmates.

It was a year in limbo. I learned a great deal about rugby football from my aunt and uncle, passionate followers of the game. Saturday afternoons were spent either watching polo with my aunts and uncles, or glued to the radio, cheering on the All Blacks. I heard Peter Jones, the Northland number eight forward, make broadcasting history when he said on radio, 'I'm buggered', at the end of a gruelling match. It shook the nation.

My Uncle Fred gave me sound instruction about the qualities to seek in a prospective husband. 'Don't look at him unless he can put a hundred pounds down for your engagement ring,' he told me. He showed me his bank balance and we talked about how a young man should aim for money like that. My Uncle Robert, on the other hand, offered me a set of dentures for my sixteenth birthday, because he felt it a great saving for the future if I didn't have teeth to worry about. I was less willing to listen to this, and kept my teeth.

I was happy enough in a day-to-day kind of way, but I was also missing my parents. It wasn't long before they moved to Rotorua to live. They planned to settle in Tauranga, after a brief holiday in Rotorua, but once they arrived in the Bay of Plenty they thought it would be easier to find work in the volcanic city, where mud pools bubbled and geysers erupted from the bowels of the earth. Most of the money they had when they bought the farm had gone in improvements that would have taken many more years to bring a return. They were back to being hard up. My mother took a job first in a factory sewing garments, and then in a bookstore, while my father became a clerk at the Forest Research Institute. They bought a small house at Hannah's Bay, on Lake Rotorua, five miles out of town with an infrequent bus service. This was a worry because my father still wouldn't drive a car, and transport was always a problem—it was beyond contemplation that my mother or I would drive. Nevertheless, I soon joined my parents at Hannah's Bay, and started work as a clerk in the Justice Department.

The tourist ethos hung heavily over Rotorua. The town was filled with hotels: the immense, pale grey old Grand, the shocking pink Palace and Prince's Gate, genteel and faded, at the entrance to the Government Gardens. On New Year's Eve barmaids ran a race through town from hotel to hotel carrying trays of beer. A non-stop carnival and float parade closed the town until the evening, followed by a lakeside party that went on until dawn. For its time, Rotorua was more cosmopolitan than most New Zealand towns, and I took to it. Later, I would meet some of the artists who lived there then: Theo Schoon, Jan Nigro, the Scholes family at Whakarewarewa.

But I lasted only two months in the new job. I might have heard Jones say that he was buggered, but I didn't have a clue what it meant in the literal sense. I learned suddenly one morning when the court registrar decided to take me to a private court sitting. Two pathetic, scruffy-looking men apprehended in a public toilet were brought before the magistrate. I took a crash course on homosexuality, without the benefit of modern sympathies or understanding. I was shocked and there was nobody I could talk to about what I had discovered. I still wasn't sure about the mechanics of heterosexual sex, let along any other sort.

I was almost as upset when a wedding took place in the office. In order to reach the registrar's room, couples had to pass between the desks of the other staff. The bride, on this occasion, was an older, highly made-up and heavily pregnant woman. The groom appeared little more than a child—I found out later he was sixteen. He sobbed noisily as he was chased through the office to the ceremony by angry relatives, cutting off his retreat.

I decided I didn't have the stomach for Justice Department work, and shut that door firmly behind me. My next port of call was the Rotorua Massey Ferguson tractor company where, in the light of my experience in Morrinsville, and a good reference from Laurie Maber, I was immediately taken on.

Percy, the owner, turned out to be a weasel words man, whose speciality was dipping into the petty cash without leaving IOUs, then blaming the office junior. I was becoming bored with office routine and it was difficult to see a way forward. I was moved into the spare parts department, where I worked alongside the men counting out nuts and bolts, and keeping stock sheets. I was seventeen, and at times I wondered if it would be possible to return to school. But young people didn't do that then, and I had no idea how I would support myself, even if the local school would have me. Besides, during that year I started an adult social life and it was difficult to contemplate a schoolgirl's life again. An only child comes to understand that brothers and sisters are impossible but a mate, a husband, is not. Unconsciously, I had begun to seek mine.

I had dispensed with my virginity, or rather someone had helped himself to it. The event was painful, unasked for and conducted in such ignorance that afterwards I went to the public library to see if I could find a book that would confirm that what I thought had happened really had. None of my reading, my search for descriptions of the act, had prepared me for this painful penetration. Finding no advice there, I turned a dress ring back to front on my ring finger and went to a bookstore for Catholics—only the hoarding had spelled it wrong so that it appeared as 'Cahtolic Supplies'. My aunts loved it, when they visited Rotorua. The Carrrtholics, they would purr, in imitation of what they believed to be an Irish accent. I found a book called *Ideal Marriage: Its Physiology and Technique* by Theodor Hendrik van der Velde, published in 1928. It was full of advice on positions in which to have sex, providing you were married. What I supposed had happened was true, only it was supposed to have taken place in such a state of exaltation, purity and lifelong commitment that I was still unsure that we were on about the same thing. All the same, I accepted this dismal deflowering for what it was, grieved for what was irretrievable and went out with some more young men. Girls in those days were divided into those who 'did it' and those who didn't, and most people knew which were which, if only because the boys they slept with told others they had scored. Because I had 'done it' in another town, I hoped that it was a secret. I wondered if people could tell just from looking at you.

I went out with a farmer who belonged to the Young Nationals and wanted to marry me. I turned him down, much to my relatives' disgust. There was a big fair Dutchman, who said if we made love I was not to worry: he would marry me if we 'made a baby'. That's what he told everyone he went out with and I didn't take the chance. There was an up and coming businessman who owned a pink and green-topped Chevvy and dated me when his girlfriend was out of town. Another told me he had bought a condom; I could choose between going to hear Billy Graham relayed into a Landliner bus or sex, and I'd probably get it either way. I managed to avoid it, and Billy Graham too.

Sex, sex and more offers of sex. If it was on their minds, it was on mine too, but these offers were not exactly tempting, and by now I knew that it was not necessarily all that was promised.

In 'At the Lake So Blue', a semi-fiction in which I unashamedly drew on myself as a central 'character', a young woman is invited to be a candidate for a beauty competition, in which she will be required to parade in a bathing suit and ride on a float in the New Year's Eve parade. I had been running with a crowd from the Blue Lake water ski club. All the girls in the club had had their turn as 'queen', so they insisted that now it was mine. I decided against it. For a start I couldn't stand up on water skis.

My life was beginning to seem out of control. Rotorua had two dance halls. On Saturday nights I ran from one to another:

> The Ritz had a vast glossy floor: the hall doubled for the A & P machinery show in winter. The band sat above the floor on a stage. The Master of Ceremonies (we called him the Emcee) announced the dances: Gentlemen, take your

partners for a foxtrot. A valeta. The supper waltz (keep the supper waltz for me; it meant you got to sit with a boy for the interval). Ballin' the Jack. A maxina. All the way through to the last waltz (keep the last dance for me).

The Ritz. It was also the place where nice girls told their mothers they were going, and left to go down to Tama.

Tama was Tamatekapua, a meeting house that stood opposite St Faith's Maori Anglican Church at the lakefront in Ohinemutu, surrounded by steaming vent holes and mud bubbling away in the night:

We took off our shoes to enter the meeting house. Outside, the air was thick with sulphur fumes, inside the smoke was so thick you could hardly see the other end from the door. The lights were always low in Tama. Sometimes they jerked and died altogether. Bodies flew beside the tukutuku panels, feet stamped out a rhythm, the blind saxophone player Tai Paul's music rippled up and down at the front of the small platform where the band played. To one side of Tai Paul, a young man with his hair slicked back was singing his heart out; his name was Howard Morrison.

Heavenly shades of night are falling...

Those dance halls. They appear not just in 'At the Lake So Blue', but in my novel, *Songs from the Violet Café*, where Hester Hagley and her fiancé haunt the Ritz, in formal evening dress. Bethany Dixon, in *The House Within*, has holidays in Rotorua, when she meets her future first husband at Tama. And, in fact, I didn't feel like being a 'bad girl' going to Tama; it felt more honest and free, more committed to dancing itself than the Ritz, which seemed dedicated to courting rituals. I danced and danced and my heart was ruled by Elvis.

One evening many years later I sat by Sir Peter Tapsell at a dinner party, when he was a Minister of the Crown, and before he became Speaker of the House. An ostensibly serious man, he had grown up in Rotorua. Testing the waters, when we had talked a little, I said, 'I used to go to Tama sometimes.' His face lit up. 'So did I,' he said, 'so did I,' and we talked on, about the huge feasts at suppertime, the way our lives felt electric when we danced.

The distance we lived from town meant I had to catch a bus and meet a friend before setting off to dances later in the evening. I struck up a friendship with a girl called Maureen Townley, older than me by three years. Maureen was a sturdy no-nonsense Irish Catholic, and her company steadied my life down. Her family provided a constant base in town. The deal between Maureen and me was that we would always make sure the other one got home safely. If the worst came to the worst I could stay at her house, although that created problems at home because my father now refused to get a telephone, hoping that he would keep boys at bay.

It was at Tamatekapua, when I was still working at the garage, that I met R. I remember him still as an important turning point, a person for whom I had to make real and adult decisions. I was exploring uncharted territories of love.

There aren't any maps of course, it's different for everyone, but I was finding out that it's possible to take charge of one's choices.

R's whanau was at Moerewa in the Bay of Islands, not far from where I grew up. He came from a large family and helped to support them from an early age. He was a butcher and I remember his hands among blood and flesh. When he finished work, flecks of fat and flying bone clung to his skin and hair like small white crystals. He hated what he did; when I met him, his dream was to teach.

Like most of the young men I knew in Rotorua, he played a great game of rugby. His club was Rotorua Pirates. With a group of team mates, he shared a house, or the 'flat', as Maureen and I knew it. Maureen was keeping occasional company with another Pirate. The flat was not unlike my aunt's house in Morrinsville: dark panelled and varnished, with beamed ceilings, and a rosy leadlight in the entrance way. You had to go there in daytime to appreciate its finer points—at night the lights were stark and the air filled with smoke. Cigarettes fizzled in puddles of beer. We sang such edifying songs as 'they put me on my wee wee pot/didn't care if I wee'd or not/so they put me back in my wee wee cot...'

Most of the men had big forearms and necks, and nipples standing up under their cotton Aertex shirts. R was different. I can see him, dark and lithe, almost delicate, among the rugged bodies on the rugby field. And in the evenings I could see the eyes of the other young men looking at us together, considering. Was it possible? Does she do that with him?

From the outset, my parents were uneasy about my relationship with R. We were 'different', they thought, too, but for other reasons. He was Maori and I was not.

He fell ill, and developed pneumonia. Worried, I went to see him one day in my lunch hour. His lips were dark and plummy with the heat of his illness. I lay down in my clothes on the bed beside him.

'We're playing with fire,' he said.

When he was better, R decided to go away to Australia with a journalist,

Dick Rutledge, who lived in the flat. There was a mournful farewell at the bus station, and R gave me a gold music box with blue velvet lining that played 'The Blue Danube Waltz' to remember him by. I think the strain of it all was beginning to tell, because when he left I remember feeling relieved. Years later, I saw Dick Rutledge on an American television programme about the shooting of JFK where he had been an eyewitness. He had become an anchorman on a regular news programme.

But R didn't get far. He returned to Rotorua, and me, the following week. I was not as pleased to see him as he hoped. I didn't care less about him, but I suspect my parents were right about us not being suited, although I didn't agree with their reasons. There was some feminine, febrile quality about him that I didn't understand. I just knew that this wasn't really love. Although I did continue to see him for some time, we seemed to have less and less in common. Some days we mooched down to a coffee bar near the lakefront in the lunch hours and he would put the jukebox on, playing Bing Crosby singing Cole Porter's 'True Love' over and over again. I can never hear that song without seeing his longing eyes. He was a constant, caring person and I felt I was heartless, that he deserved better than my on again, off again behaviour.

He dropped out of sight for nearly a year, then reappeared to tell me that he had bought a section and was in the process of building a house for me during the weekends. He had given up rugby to make the time. Sadly, I said goodbye once and for all. By then, several major changes had taken place in my life.

My employment with Percy had ended after a particularly nasty scene over the petty cash box, although I hadn't been in the office for months. My parents were devastated by having an out-of-work daughter on their hands, which was unheard of in those 1950s days of full employment.

Ashamed of the situation I found myself in, I determined to look for something that would provide a challenge. I turned first to the local radio station. Radio meant so much in those days and I had often thought about working in broadcasting. But it seemed a daring idea, almost as presumptuous as being a writer. Now there seemed nothing to lose by making an inquiry. I was granted an interview but it turned out badly.

'What do you think you can offer broadcasting?' asked the station manager.

I hadn't thought about that. I took a voice test and failed, as I would many times in the future. I didn't know then about the high roof to my mouth. Not that that was what the station manager seemed to notice. 'Very thick accent, I'm afraid.'

This was a blow, given that my father had been so conscientious about trying to iron out my New Zealand vowels.

'Maybe I could write the bits in between?' I hazarded.

'Scripting?' He shook his head and sighed. 'I don't think there's a future in broadcasting for you. I do suggest you look for a nice office job somewhere.'

So much for broadcasting.

Desperately, I began to make myself over, taking up fencing lessons and heading for the local Little Theatre, which was housed in a building known as the Shambles. I auditioned for a role as Colombine, as does a character called Marianne in *Songs from the Violet Café,* and was passed over in favour of an ample blonde called Faith. I was still unemployed and beginning to think I could get nothing right when a job in the local library was advertised. After some persuasion from my father, I applied. On a whim, while I was at Tractor Services, I had bought a plain grey tailored suit, perhaps to offset the racier side of my life. The suit did the trick. My neat appearance and School Certificate English marks impressed the librarian. The job was mine, and suddenly a door opened.

Kit Spencer, my new employer, was a woman I think of as a feminist before her time, though she might have been horrified to hear me say this. But it was true. In mid-life, she had an exquisite prettiness and a core of steel. Her eyes were the colour of violets, her prematurely white hair, worn in a

French roll from which small tendrils were always escaping, was palely rinsed with blue, giving it a freshly laundered look. Kit had been divorced and raised a daughter alone. Fifty years later, I met a son of hers whose existence I had never guessed, as circumstances had forced her to part with him as an infant. He is the only person I have met with eyes as blue as hers. Her love life was scandalous in the town; she appeared not to care what people thought. Although she had worked her way up through the library system without formal qualifications, her reputation as a public librarian in professional circles was of the highest order. She was the only woman fellow of the Library Association at that time. Her beliefs were straightforward. Readers, she declared, should have the best possible access to the books they wanted to read. Libraries should be welcoming places where people could have good conversations about books and receive well-informed advice about what was available. She expected her staff to be courteous, friendly, punctual and totally at her command. In many ways she was a hard woman, but I learned much from her, including self-discipline and a sense of responsibility.

And she introduced me to books and writers I would not have thought of reading—Simone de Beauvoir, some of the nineteenth-century French and Russian novelists, a smattering of New Zealand books, a broad spectrum of good modern fiction. I became more adventurous, trying some of the more contemporary French writers; the youthful hedonism of life in the South of France in Françoise Sagan's *Bonjour Tristesse* was seductive, and I was dazzled by Colette and her accounts of tough but vulnerable women who could have lived anywhere, but happened to live in Paris. It must have been about then that I encountered Duras, although my first clear memory of her work is in the screenplay of *Hiroshima Mon Amour,* which came later. Before long I was discussing the works of all these writers with borrowers, and recommending them.

I had found my place. I was in love with library work, books, new ideas, the very building itself, with its long, low, lemony-coloured interior and huge French doors opening out on to a flower-filled balcony. And although my grey suit had been a selling point, Kit didn't expect her staff to look like frumps. Most of us had our clothes made to order and these were the subject of interest to borrowers, especially when two of us introduced 'sack' dresses to the Rotorua fashion scene. It was just as well I had fallen so instantly in love with the job, otherwise it might all have finished abruptly. Before I left the garage, it had been arranged that Maureen and I would travel around the South Island with my parents for ten days, followed by Maureen and me going to stay with her aunt in Auckland for a long weekend. This plan had emerged after Maureen suggested she and I travel to Fiji for a holiday together. My parents were appalled, saying that I was far too young and, besides, they wanted us to go south as a family. Eventually, Maureen was included in this trip and the bookings made. Kit agreed to my taking this holiday when she employed me.

In the late spring of 1957, the four of us toured by bus and train, stopping at Milford Sound, Te Anau, Lake Ohau and Queenstown, all remote and relatively unpopulated places then. I knew my father was dubious about Maureen coming, but things appeared to go smoothly. I thought it a lovely holiday and I was happy that everyone had got along so well. My father had other ideas.

The morning after we came home, as I was repacking to go off to Auckland, he told me in no uncertain terms how unkind I had been to him while we were away, that I had hardly spoken to him, and had gone off with my friend on trips that didn't include him. He had had a miserable time. I was devastated. Suddenly I erupted and told him I was leaving, that he needn't expect me to come back from Auckland. I was sick of his criticism, sick of not having a telephone, sick of not being allowed to listen to the hit parade once a week, sick of being stuck in places without adequate transport. My mother stood by, tearfully begging and pleading with me not to do this.

I was still fairly resolute when I left. I spent the first morning in Auckland looking at advertisements for places to rent, quickly realising that all my savings had gone on the holiday and that without a job it was going to be difficult. So I looked, too, at the jobs vacant columns without seeing anything I felt qualified to do. On Saturday night, Maureen and I went to a dance in the city, then on Sunday, wandered about without much direction. I was terrible company. The only bright spot came when we were about to step off a bus in Onehunga, as a group of black American sailors were waiting to get on. When we appeared in the doorway, they fell to their knees in the street and began singing 'Hey there, you with the stars in your eyes', exactly as people do in corny musicals. It was a funny moment, and I could see how American sailors got around girls so easily. There was an element of this experience in my novel *Paddy's Puzzle*, when a young girl falls in love with a black Marine in wartime Auckland. Our sailors climbed onto the bus and leaned out of the windows, waving to us.

I had wondered if Maureen's aunt might put me up until I found somewhere to stay, but she wasn't keen. Maureen had to go back to work the next day. She didn't really understand what all the fuss was about because I hadn't told her the reason for the quarrel, not wanting to hurt her feelings. It wasn't hard to work out that my father had wanted me all to himself and resented her coming on the holiday. As far as she was concerned, too, it had been a great trip, and she thought she and my father had got along fine. Eventually she pointed out that as I had such a good new job in Rotorua, it would be a pity to lose it. She suggested that I go back and, perhaps, stay with her family for a while, until I found some accommodation in the town.

I finished up going back with her, deciding to return to the Hannah's Bay house to tell my mother what I planned to do. I found the atmosphere very subdued, but some changes had occurred. My father was clearly desperately sorry, and I think that, had

I left, my mother might well have done too. We agreed to put our differences behind us and try again. Things were never happy again in the way they had been in Waipu, but the changes were permanent, and although we often disagreed, my father and I never quarrelled openly again. There were times when he was a surprising ally. From that time on, we began to exist as three adults in the house, and I think I was better disposed towards living my life in a more sensible way.

Back at work, I began a correspondence course in library training, and went on a number of extra courses in Hamilton. Just a year later, I was elevated to assistant librarian, when Barbara Legge left to marry her fiancé of several years, Ron O'Connell. I was bridesmaid at her wedding. She gave both her bridesmaids a gift of orange perfume, very strong, in a small oblong bottle. I have kept this little vial, and when I prise the now perishing rubber stopper from it there is still a whiff of fragrance. Barbara has died, but there is this, the scent of orange lingering down the years.

With Kit, I was now in charge of the library and the seven women who worked there. I was eighteen. This was a remarkable position for a woman so young, particularly as my training was incomplete. My photograph appeared in the local newspaper, and I began to earn as much as my parents in their respective jobs.

Problems arose only when Kit was ill, and she often was. Although she demanded that her staff not take leave unless they were dropping in their tracks, and was ruthless at refusing even bereavement leave, Kit herself was frequently absent. In my first few months in the new job, she vanished for six weeks and left me to it. Some of the women I worked with were older, and at times they found it hard to take directions from me.

The real conflicts arose from socialising. It was still a small town and on Saturday nights I went out like everyone else, but on Monday morning I donned recently prescribed spectacles, and again became the person in charge. Not surprisingly, some of the staff could not reconcile my two selves.

I embarked on a new relationship with M, a banker. He was another rugby player, an All Black triallist, which was important stuff: his exploits were often written up in the paper. He was short, snub-nosed, neat and wore a suit during the week. He was also carrying old baggage from an engagement down south that had broken up the previous year. For a season we went to balls, a step up from the Saturday night dances, but he often took out other girls. I could hardly berate him, for there were no promises, although there was an expectation that I would be there when it suited him. I went out of my way to please him. Towards the end of the season we went to the Road Services Ball (yes, really) at the Ritz, me in a lime green chiffon dress, silver strapped shoes and elbow-length white gloves. We drank beer that had been sneaked in under the women's ball dresses, Howard Morrison, who had moved on from Tama, sang 'Twilight Time'. It felt like the happiest night of my life, and towards the end of it, M seemed to have come to some decision about me. Or so I thought.

Afterwards we sat on the lakefront at Hannah's Bay and watched the moon. Suddenly M began to shriek with pain. He could hardly drive me home. A week or two later he was in hospital after having surgery for what turned out to be a rugby injury. I visited him on a Saturday afternoon. Beside the bed sat a young woman, slim, dark and wearing a rather virtuous expression. She worked on the lolly counter at Woolworth's, next door to the bank. I couldn't think why she was there, and sat her visit out. I felt embarrassed for this woman I mentally called 'Lollies', and her unseemly presence. When she had gone, M gave me a sorrowful, forgive-me smile.

'I've had time to think things over while I've been here in hospital,' he said.

My heart melted at his fragility. 'Of course you have,' I said. I guess I was waiting for his proposal.

'I think it might be better if we didn't see each other for a while. I haven't recovered from the engagement really. It's just not fair on you,' he said.

I agreed. Of course. What else could I have done? 'I can wait,' I said.

I was working in the library stack room a few weeks later when Kit came through with the evening paper in her hand. 'Isn't this the boy you used to go out with?' she asked me, naming M, and looking at me hard.

'What's he done?' I asked, expecting a new report on his sporting exploits.

'He's engaged.' The new fiancée was Lollies.

'Oh, I expected him to marry her,' I said as airily as I could and walked out of the room. Kit didn't mention the subject again, but I remember that she was unusually considerate to me for a while. M and Lollies began their family of six soon after their marriage the following year.

I was deeply embarrassed by this episode, and appalled that I could have been so naïve. I was fairly certain that my innocence about this relationship had been joked about around town. I threw myself into my work, withdrew from the rugby crowd and went to fewer dances. The Pirate team members were already strangers when I saw them at Maureen's wedding to her Pirate, where I was a bridesmaid. We bridesmaids wore wide picture hats and frilly dresses, their huge skirts supported with Elizabethan farthingales. The newspaper dubbed it Rotorua's 'wedding of the year'.

It was the second wedding at which I had been a bridesmaid and, at nineteen, I was beginning to feel distinctly like an old maid. I began making tentative plans to go abroad. The big overseas experience beckoned, a rite of passage for young New Zealanders, particularly for women, before they 'settled down' and got married. My friend from Waipu days, Jen Gates, now a teacher, asked if I would sail to England with her, and I began to save in earnest for the trip, planned for 1960.

Around the same time, another change of house was in the offing. Night work at the library meant long days for me, and for my mother too. The bus we caught left soon after seven in the morning, so we waited at the bus station for more than an hour before there was anyone to let us into our workplaces. My mother had by now swapped books for work in an exclusive china shop. She had an instinct for fine china and before long her advice was sought by wealthy buyers. Later, she would manage the shop and have her own key, but this was a little way off. Our busy lives, and particularly my evening work, were getting harder to manage from Hannah's Bay. An advertisement for a large house to rent in town attracted my parents' interest. It was decided that the Hannah's Bay house would be rented out, and we would move to this house in Kuirau Street, owned by an out-of-town dentist, who had purchased it from the film magnate Robert Kerridge.

This, of all the houses I have lived in, is the one I still dream about most. Surrounded by beautiful trees, it was a long white stucco building at Ohinemutu, on the edge of Utuhina Stream, just around the corner from St Faith's Church and Tamatekapua. It had a raffish charm, filled as it was with elegant cane furniture, French doors and small sunny alcoves. A huge stone fireplace occupied the end of the long sitting room, and the ceiling was match-lined and varnished in a gable shape. In a way, it was a more upmarket version of some of the planters' homes in Kerikeri, and I felt as if we had arrived at last. Behind the house was a private bathhouse that contained a deep Roman-style steam bath with aquamarine tiles.

The house was ours for the time being, albeit with some financial juggling. As well as running the china shop, my mother now took in boarders. Two men, a lawyer and a broadcasting technician, joined our household. I studied hard for my library exams in the new house, and read more than ever. Kit's lustre had rubbed off on me, and my knowledge of books and management skills were becoming respected in the same way as hers. I kept my travel plans to myself, knowing that she would be upset to learn that I was planning to leave.

Chapter 10

One winter's day in 1959, I was standing at the issuing desk in the library when a local school group walked through the door with their teacher. When I looked up from the issues desk and saw the blackness of his hair and the whiteness of his grin, I stood stock still, my heart poised above the rubber stamp in my hand.

'Oh,' I said aloud. Inside me, I said, 'That's for me.'

'What's the matter?' asked the assistant at my side. She was counting change for the rental fiction.

'Did you see that guy who just came in?'

She flicked her eyes in his direction. 'Looks like Mario Lanza, doesn't he?' she said, and kept on counting.

I pushed my glasses down firmly on my nose and straightened my shoulders as I strode down the library, searching in my head for a great opening line.

'Will you keep these children quiet?' I asked the teacher, in a frosty voice.

These were the first words I spoke to my husband-to-be, Ian Kidman. From that moment, I had no doubts or hesitations about wanting to marry him, and nor did I expect him to have them about me. He was eight years older, and one of his teaching colleagues I knew laughed when I told her I was going out with him. 'You'll have to be quick to keep up with that one,' she said.

Our courtship was brief. Ian was new to the town. A teacher at Rotorua Primary, he was living at the Maori Apprentice Hostel where he had gone looking for accommodation close to the school. Instead, he was offered the job of housemaster in return for his board. The hostel was on the other side of Kuirau Park, a few minutes' walk from where we were living. My mother's cooking appealed more than hostel fare, and soon he was a regular visitor.

Ian was different from the young men I had known up until then. He listened to classical music, told endless tall tales that made me laugh, didn't play rugby (although he had done in the past) and didn't drink alcohol or smoke. He smelled healthy. And he dressed differently as well. One Friday evening, he picked me up after work at the library wearing a red cashmere wool cardigan and a rakish hat. This was at a time when young men had just about given up wearing hats. At the end of the street stood a group of the old rugby crowd. A couple of them called out, asking me who my well-dressed boyfriend was. I dawdled for a moment, hanging back as though looking in a shop window. But it was make or break time. I ran after Ian and clutched his arm, turning my face away from my old friends. There was no going back.

We fell quickly into routines that included the occasional Saturday night dance at Tamatekapua, some sailing on Lake Rotorua in Ian's Q class yacht (I was a very inept sailor) and regular attendance at St Faith's in Ohinemutu, where he was required to shepherd his hostel charges on Sunday nights.

My parents, however, were still concerned that I was too young to make a lifetime commitment. And there was more to it, which my mother was close-lipped about, although I knew more or less what had taken place. Ian had grown up apart from his mother. His parents had separated during a time when they lived in railway settlements along the North Island's Main Trunk Line. Like mine, his father was an English immigrant, who had come out to New Zealand as a First World War veteran, having spent years in the trenches, and gone to work on the railways. In the King Country he met and married Ian's mother, Ruby, a woman of Te Aupouri descent, with family connections in Piopio, but the marriage lasted only a few years. When the couple separated, their children were divided between the parents, the intention being that Ian would live with his father. This didn't happen for a long time, as Ian's father fell ill shortly afterwards with tuberculosis and spent nearly ten years in a sanitorium. During those years, Ian had been handed from pillar to post by at least a dozen relatives, and attended around twenty schools. He and his mother hadn't seen each other for many years. A woman my mother had met at the clothing factory now appeared in the china shop. She knew Ian's family back in the railway days and had decided it was her 'duty' to impart gossip about his parents' past lives. My mother sent her away with what she told me was 'a flea in her ear' but I knew she was discomforted. And, as I had expected from the outset, the issue of race reared its head again. Only this time it wasn't going to stand in my way.

In April 1960 my parents and I went north to the fishing village of Leigh, where we stayed for a week in a strange rundown boarding house called the Jolly Fisherman's Lodge, at the edge of the sea, approached on foot over wooden bridges and gangplanks. My twentieth birthday was spent there. For most of that week, all I did was read, stopping only to watch the spinifex turning over in the sand. Ian's letters arrived almost every day. 'Surprise, surprise,' he wrote, 'two letters from me and none from you. Send me a telegram when you decide.'

In a sequence of poems I wrote some years ago, called *Wakeful Nights,* there is a passage about that week of decision:

> ...Only
> when the distant lights of boats shone
> through the shadow of the navy sea burning beyond the granite cliffs, the haunted clay,
> was it cool enough to consider your proposal;
> in the end
> I said yes, a strange
> place to choose a life.

And here's one of those odd inconsequential things: the book I was reading that week was Elizabeth Jane Howard's novel, *The Beautiful Visit,* and the first book I picked off the crowded bookshelves here in this French apartment in Menton was a first edition of that same book; I read it again just recently. In a strange way, it's connected to the events of my life as they flowed on from that week in Leigh.

For really there had been no contest.

The wedding was brought forward on account of a pregnancy scare that didn't eventuate, but badly rattled my mother. My father remained remarkably calm. 'What will I tell my brothers and sisters?' my mother wailed. This was an indication to me of something I hadn't really understood before: that in spite of all that had gone on between them, my mother needed to keep face with her family. And I was the prize.

'Let them find out for themselves,' my father said, apparently without flinching. As it turned out, there was no need to tell them anything, but it was a close call.

In August, instead of going to England with Jennifer, I married Ian at St Faith's Church, the service taken by our friend Manu Bennett, later Bishop of Aotearoa. The date had been decided in consultation with Jean, whose husband Fred had died suddenly one Saturday afternoon the previous year. Although Jean and Fred's lives had sometimes seemed stormy during the last year I lived with them, she was bereft without him. To complicate matters, Roberta had turned up on the day of the funeral with all her suitcases, and hadn't left. We knew that Jean was considering abandoning the Studholme Street house in favour of something smaller, so that Roberta would be encouraged to move on. Jean didn't want a wedding on the anniversary of Fred's death, but it worked out in the end that we could get married on the first Saturday of the August school holidays.

On the morning of the wedding, I was due for a hair appointment. The main salon in town opened for 'brides only' on Saturdays, and that day I was the only bride. One of the uncles dropped me into town. The salon hadn't opened and he offered to wait, but I said I would like some time to myself. It was a dull day with rain in the air. A lazy newspaper wrapped itself around a lamp post in the deserted street. In the distance, a friend appeared. Bob Harvey worked as the projectionist in the picture theatre next door to the library, a gangly nineteen-year-old with large eyes and an air of constant startled wonder.

When we had exchanged greetings, he said, 'So what are you doing today?'

'Getting married,' I said, much as my mother must have said in the boarding house in Perth, nearly a quarter of a century earlier. Certainly, Bob looked surprised.

After a moment or two of reflection, he said, 'But Fiona, you can't get married in the hairdresser's.'

Quite. I couldn't really explain to him that I couldn't get married with*out* going to the hairdresser's. This seemed like a significant difference in the way men and women thought. After all, my intended bridegroom had gone out on a Scout bottle drive that morning.

Jennifer helped me to dress, later in the afternoon. I wore a cream satin dress with piping down the front and ruched roses at the back—because, the dressmaker insisted, this was what Princess Margaret had worn at her wedding to Anthony Armstrong-Jones three months earlier. I am not sure why I agreed to this, but the dress was pretty and showed off my twenty-two-inch waist, about which I harboured a not so secret vanity.

All my mother's family came, even Stewart, whom my mother hadn't seen for years. Robert had recently married an English nurse called Agatha, whom we've always known as Mary. She had been a ballet dancer and studied with a career in mind, but the war intervened and although her direction changed, she brought a difference to the family with her love of dance and the arts. They all had their photograph taken at the small reception at the Kuirau Street house, the last time they were all together. If they were puzzled by the wedding in the Maori church, they said nothing. Upon meeting Ian, they had decided he was Spanish, a view from which they never deviated. Ian's father and stepmother, Doll, came up from Wellington. Tom Kidman had met Doll during his sojourn in the sanatorium at Waipukurau. The old rift between Ian and his mother, brought about by many separations and Ian having spent his high school years with his father and Doll, had not healed, so there was nobody else from his side of the family.

The back of the church was crowded with library borrowers. Several older people had come in before the wedding to give me gifts of crocheted doilies and placemats, tea towels, tablecloths and kitchen appliances. I was overwhelmed by this unexpected affection for doing what was, after all, just my job. But, if I had not known it before, this was an affirmation of the importance of books and their accessibility in people's lives, and I was part of it.

As we were married, an immense hail and thunder storm struck the church, drowning out our vows.

Unbeknown to us at the time, Ian's mother stood outside to watch the wedding procession. Standing in the rain.

Our first address was 8 Lake Road, in a semi-detached less than a hundred metres from the edge of Lake Rotorua, facing Mokoia Island, where the legendary Hinemoa, strung with gourds, swam to her lover Tutanekai. I had arrived at that most desirable estate, the condition of marriage, not on 10,000 a year like the best of the Miss Bennets, but something like a combined income of £728. Never mind, marriage represented freedom and the right to sleep every night with the man of my choice. On blue days I watched the shining surface of the lake, a mirror of the sky, broken by fleets of black swans; in winter, the mists creeping over the lake, chill cruel waves slapping at its edge. Sometimes the rain was beautiful, as Elizabeth Hardwick wrote somewhere. For me, it was almost always beautiful. I liked winter better than summer in Rotorua. The purple light of rain over the lake appealed to me more than the sulphurous yellow landscape that intensified in the sun. You got used to it, as they say, but somehow the seeping yellow smell stained the senses.

Of course, most of us learn that, as freedom goes, marriage is a double-edged sword. Love on a permanent basis was an altogether sparkier, more demanding and labour-intensive undertaking than my friends and I had imagined. There had been an international nuclear scare some weeks before our marriage. Please God, I prayed, don't let the world blow up before I become married. Sometimes I think that it happened afterwards. Learning to share a bed was enough, let alone a life and the ironing. That time is so intensely personal, so much about learning to live with each other's differences, the hazards as well as the pleasures, that I find it hard to write about now. The story of the two of us. But we were deeply and irrevocably in love, and that saved us from disaster.

About ten years earlier, when Ian was just out of school himself, he had taught as an untrained sole charge teacher at the still operational whaling station on Arapawa Island in Cook Strait. At the time, it had been a young man's great adventure. He had to leave the island in order to go to training college, but he had vowed to return. When a job there was advertised in the *Education Gazette,* shortly after our marriage, Ian asked me if I would consider going. I didn't think much of the idea, and he understood, without much discussion, that it might not be the best place for us to begin a family, something we were both keen to do when we had some more savings. I don't believe he regretted this decision in the long run, but it was an early test of wills. Yet his tales about that period in his life have followed me through the years. The story of the Guard family, whose forebears had founded the whaling station on Arapawa, and that of Betty Guard, who had gone there as a child bride and been captured by Maori on the Taranaki coastline, eventually found their way into my novel, *The Captive Wife*.

Man first entered space a few weeks after my twenty-first birthday. For all it meant then, they might as well have shot an arrow in the air. But it was a transforming signal: the new Camelot burned brightly in America; I grew my hair in a bob and wore a pineapple straw pillbox hat that looked like an albino hedgehog to my cousin Louis's wedding. 'You can't put that thing on your head,' exclaimed one of my aunts; 'you look like that dreadful Kennedy woman.' That felt like success. At the weekend, I taught Sunday school at St Faith's, and in the evenings Ian and I walked over to evensong, the service in Maori. When Christmas came round the children in my Sunday school dressed as angels, wearing their fathers' white shirts turned back to front, with silver tinsel garlands in their hair. I made up stories as I went along which were about good and evil, although their biblical sources were pretty tenuous. That was just about my last serious brush with religion.

Soon it became clear that the demanding hours of my job didn't fit easily with the three o'clock end to Ian's day, even if preparation took up much of his so-called spare time. When a vacancy as a librarian at Rotorua Boys' High School came up, I gave it serious thought. Jen was about to leave for England, and I asked for two days' leave to travel to Auckland and say goodbye; it was the school holidays and I had little time to spend with Ian so the trip would serve two ends. Kit was furious, but I stood my ground, still smarting from her refusal of bereavement leave when Fred had died the year before.

At the wharves, Ian and I waved as the fluttering streamers linking shore with ship stretched and snapped. If I felt a twinge of regret, it was only because Europe was still a distant dream, and not at all because I had decided to get married. To farewell Jen on the wharf was her friend Peter Beck. Two years later, shortly after the birth of Ian's and my first child, I was matron-of-honour at the Becks' wedding.

On our way back to Rotorua, Ian and I talked over the situation at the library. It was clear that there would be more conflicts unless the library always came first. This was a huge decision for me. I would have to forgo the six-week course to complete my library certificate. All the same, on my first day back I handed in my resignation. In time, Kit and I would resume our friendship on a more equal footing, and I would work for her again. Later, Ian took up an invitation to join the high school staff, leaving primary teaching behind.

The high school was a curious experience. At the time it was a very wealthy establishment, but the library had been allowed to run down, or had never really existed. The new headmaster, a former All Black called Neville Thornton, gave me a free hand and as much money as I wanted to set up a proper library. He carried a suitcase of money in the boot of his car. Once he handed me £1000 from it to spend on books on a trip to Wellington.

During the holidays, Ian and I travelled south, staying with his father and Doll in the Evans Bay house where Ian had lived during his high school years at Wellington Technical College. It was the only permanent home he had known since his parents' separation. His father had sent for Ian after he had married Doll and gone to live with her in a tumbledown house on the Wellington waterfront. Her mother lived there too, a sharp spidery woman who rejoiced in never having a good word for anyone; if she did it would have certainly been a mistake. Ian hadn't relished his time there, often falling foul of the old lady. True to form, she didn't take to me when I put in an appearance. It didn't really matter; Ian and I spent a few happy days buying books and, with what we bought, I was able to establish the nucleus of an excellent library back at the school.

As we drove out of the city we stopped to buy petrol in Hataitai. It was a bleak windswept morning, with not a soul in sight. Four butcher shops, a post office, a Four Square, a hardware shop, some beauty salons—it looked like a country town on a wet day. 'I'd hate to live here,' I remember remarking to Ian, as rain lashed our windscreen.

In many ways, I had a great time at Rotorua Boys' High. I was not much older than some of the students, and as one of only three women on a staff of forty, I was fussed over, quickly gaining a sense of my own power. Several writers on the staff took an interest in me. Frank Gee, head of English and author of *Rotorua Trout,* was one of them. Frank—with his powdery pale skin, hair like a blackbird's wing, cigarette in a holder—was a man with a vast classical knowledge, and he loved to talk. He found fertile territory in me, talking through his spare periods at the back of the library about fly fishing and poetry, especially the Romantics.

Poetry!

I was like a greedy sponge. All this, from a man who wrote books about coloured feathers and fish. Phil Andrews, also in the English department, was toiling over his novel, *Terese,* published later by Blackwood and Janet Paul. And there was Nancy Ellison, the Latin teacher, a tragic figure in many respects, married to a disabled serviceman and working to provide a good education for her seven children. She wrote her life story in *Whirinaki Valley.*

But there was also a level of violence at the school that upset me, a relic of Dickensian attitudes of the past, and something Thornton had more trouble eradicating than an out-of-date library. The women's toilets were adjacent to the 'caning room', and through the thin walls I often heard strapping big teachers beating boys who were only children, some of them quite small, until they screamed and pleaded for mercy. This brutality was endemic in the school and only a handful of teachers, like the legendary Tom Tague, had the courage not to participate. Tom became a friend to Ian, who was also sickened by this violence. In later years, after he left Rotorua, Ian was among the leading teachers in a successful campaign to eradicate caning in New Zealand schools, making it an illegal act.

One of the results of this mayhem in the caning room was that, as the new library developed, many of the more vulnerable boys, or those who simply wished to avoid violent playground behaviour, took refuge in my department, acting as assistant librarians. I like to think that many of them also discovered a love of books and reading. Some years ago I was invited to the school, now apparently very civilised, for a Writers in Schools visit. It was odd, all those years later, walking onto that stage again, looking down at a sea of faces from that familiar angle. I thought of some of the brightest and best students from those earlier assemblies, whom I had known well beyond their school days, and who had already died: Warwick Flaus, lawyer and fearless anti-apartheid campaigner; Glen Garlick, leading athlete and national health administrator; Jim Booth, the sparky young film producer who had given Peter Jackson his first break when they made *Brain Dead* and *Meet the*

Feebles together. All of them gone, as if burned up by their brilliance.

I thought, too, of another young man for whom I had truly provided a haven. Jack was already a cross-dresser by the time he was in the fifth form. For a long time after I went to live in Wellington, Jack, known then as Lorena, would ring and tell me about life as a transsexual on Vivian Street's red light strip. After a while, Lorena stopped calling. I find it hard to imagine that she would have survived long; that she survived Rotorua Boys' High School at all was something of a miracle in itself.

Our social life blossomed in our two years at Lake Road. For a time we ran with a racy wealthier crowd, some of them seasonal summer workers, others locals, including Matt Le Gall, a good-looking man with smooth swarthy skin, who later disappeared in mysterious circumstances in one of the forests near town. They were too wild for us and we soon tired of each other, but that first summer there was a sense of adventure in streaking in fast motorboats over the dark lake at night, and dipping in the hot pool on Mokoia Island.

Bob Harvey, who was a frequent visitor among our stream of callers, was entrepreneurial in his manner of collecting friends. The theatre was owned by a Mr and Mrs Lightfoot, who used to dispense theatre tickets to worthy recipients, such as young librarians who saved them special books (while I was still at the public library). Bob took this a step further, and when the Lightfoots went home, opened the theatre to his friends for previews of upcoming films, starting around midnight. With about a dozen other young people, Ian and I saw *Butterfield Eight,* with Elizabeth Taylor, Laurence Harvey and Eddie Fisher; *Whistle Down the Wind,* with Hayley Mills; Jean-Luc Godard's *A Woman is a Woman,* with Jean Paul Belmondo and a crazy scene of a bicycle ride like a praying mantis mating dance inside an apartment; and a film about the Russian ballet. We would emerge bleary-eyed around two or three in the morning, stomping to keep warm in the deserted frosty streets. Of the Russian ballet escapade, my father muttered darkly that only communists would get caught at a film like that. Bob's rise and rise to mayoral and national eminence has never surprised me. He has a walkon part as a character in 'At the Lake So Blue'.

Needing to cater for so many visitors, I was earnestly learning to cook. I made some of my mother's recipes but I managed to mess up even the basics, with a bit of help from her. She had written out instructions about how to roast beef and lamb, and cook corned beef. 'Put the corned beef in the pot, add a sliced onion and some carrots, barley [sic] cover with water.' Dutifully I added a good portion of barley. Interesting. The simple route never appealed. I pored over fancy new recipes. Pasta that turned to glue. Iced coffee? An acquired taste, I murmured to surprised guests. Bombe Alaska? Nothing to it. So what if the flames were frantically lit in the kitchen with the aid of meths when brandy failed? This dessert features in one of my early stories called 'The Torch', as does a version of our friend Karel Pihera, a

Czech refugee, in the guise of a restaurateur called Vlado.

Karel had opened a restaurant near the waterfront. The red gingham tablecloths, spluttering candles in bottles and basket-encased Chianti bottles hanging around the wall gave what we perceived as a Continental flavour. The bottles didn't reflect the true picture. The sale of alcohol was illegal in restaurants, although sometimes, after closing, friends shared a bottle of wine with Karel. One day, *one day,* he would promise, we will drink like civilised people. His menus of filet mignon with asparagus and mushrooms, and beef stroganoff and coq au vin seemed sophisticated. We often ate on the house, and, in return, we actually did do the dishes when the doors had closed. We listened to his stories of persecution and escapes through icy European forests, drank rough red, watched the bright tropical silhouettes of aquarium fish on the wall. I felt bound to ask Karel and his English wife, Lynne, to come and eat with us. It felt like an ordeal, as I anticipated all the culinary disasters that might happen, but they were thrilled, going on and on about how nobody ever asked chefs to dinner, and praising the food lavishly. I stopped trying so hard after that, and just enjoyed sharing meals with friends.

Over school holidays, Ian and I worked at extra jobs to raise money for a car and a deposit on a house. Each day, I walked down Fenton Street's burgeoning boulevard of motels and neon strip lighting to my job as a waitress-cum-sandwich hand at the tearooms outside Whakarewarewa's tourist thermal area. I crushed bowls of boiled eggs that smelled like the sulphur pools for sandwich fillings, bore the brunt of tour bus drivers' shouted insults if I didn't move my backside fast enough, and 'picked up the spits' for local penny divers. Maori kids diving into the river for tourists' coins pocketed the money in bulging cheeks to exchange for a single coin of a larger denomination. My job was to offer a bowl of clean water for the divers to spit out the pennies, and count the money.

'Watch out for the rough tough Duffs,' I was told. Probably just popular alliteration—the bunch of freckle-faced brothers, Stephen and Alan Duff among them, didn't cause me trouble, although they liked to get to the head of the queue. Their father, a quietly spoken scientist, was a friend of my father's at the nearby Forest Research Institute.

The world was changing. Kennedy was shot. Camelot turned to crap.

My friends were becoming anxious that 'I might not be able to have a baby', and I wanted one anyway. It seemed like time to be 'real people', with our own Fiat 600 and a suburban bungalow. My career at Rotorua Boys' High School ended when, as one boy put it to Ian, 'You've knocked her up, sir.'

Knocked up I was. With a baby on the way, we opted for a shift to the polite new suburb of Lynmore, renting a house vacated by Tom and Barbara Tague, which we would eventually buy. Nev Thornton was a likeable easy-going man in many ways, but I was nonplussed by his view that it was time for me to put my feet up and knit some booties. The evidence of pregnancy did not sit well in a boys' school in the 1960s.

Finding myself at home and alone, I was not at all pleased. I didn't have the slightest idea how to knit a bootie, although I did try a mossstitch matinée jacket, made from peppermint green wool. That was it. In the afternoons the old lure of radio serials called again. I immersed myself daily in adaptations of the New Zealand writer Nelle Scanlan's *Pencarrow* novels. Some of the stories reminded me of those I had heard about my mother's family; the women in them sounded like my aunts.

As it happened, a group in Rotorua, connected with the Shambles Theatre, was running a playwriting competition so I decided to try my hand at writing a play, drawing on familiar themes. My play, about a young woman who gets caught up in the intrigues of a small town football club, bore the dubious title 'The Orange-Scented Tide'. All the old hunger to express myself on the page had returned.

I wrote in a state of elation and excitement, the pages mounting day by day. I looked forward to every morning so that I could begin again. It was as if the new creation within me had been transformed into another creation beyond. Motherhood, now it was almost upon me, was scary, but writing was not. I was certain that, whatever the outcome of the competition, I would continue to write, if possible, every day of my life. I didn't have a typewriter, so I paid a public typist to type up the play. I should have been warned by her response. She was shocked and told me so, but she typed it anyway.

I have often told people about the outcome of the competition, and they are astonished, as I was then. The judge, an older man, was not at all impressed with my work, and wrote a disapproving letter. Further, on being told by the organisers of my age and sex, he told them I must be one of the dirtiest minded young women in New Zealand.

When I think back now, I wonder why I was so surprised. Few New Zealand women had found a voice in 1963. I was a young mother and I had told men's secrets. I had told on men. I had broken the code. Of course it wouldn't do. The problem was, nobody had told me the code. Except for the library, I had mixed with men in a number of jobs, and they had been very free with their conversation; they had told me many things about themselves and their lives, and I hadn't found what they told me strange so much as interesting. Perhaps, even worse, I had adopted men's voices. Over the years, debate has raged about whether I write men who are 'weak' or whether I can't write men at all. It took me years, and a lot of heartache, to work out that the men I write about are not so different from women when it comes to experiencing pain or love or joy. But, for the most part, they have simply been conditioned not to show it, particularly New Zealand men. My men got hurt, as all people do.

Despite the outcome of the play, my determination to write did not falter. I might be young, but I clearly knew things about the world that made people sit up and take notice. I wasn't about to be silenced. At intervals over the years, I reworked the themes I had used in this play. Eventually a version of the early part of it emerged in the context of my first published novel, *A Breed of Women.*

Meanwhile, the birth of our baby had not gone smoothly. I had become ill towards the end of my pregnancy. Late in March, I was going to bed one evening when my waters broke, and a torrent of blood cascaded to the floor. Ian rang the hospital, but they said not to worry, it would only be a show. I was certainly not to come in until the pains were regular. Throughout the night he filled the bath with blood-soaked towels and sheets and continued to ring the hospital, meeting the same response.

By five in the morning, Ian could bear it no longer. He bundled me into the car and drove to the hospital. A long avenue of oak trees led up to Rotorua Hospital. As we walked beneath them in the breaking light, I said to Ian that I wanted to go home. I would have given anything for some way to get through what I had to do, without it actually happening.

I was bleeding so heavily that a ward cleaner followed me along the corridor with a pail and mop to clean up the trail of blood. But the same night staff who had treated Ian so casually on the phone remained unconcerned. A nurse told Ian they would let him know when it was all over and he could pop back to see me then. Dismissed.

In the ward where I was put, I tried hard to keep what my father would have described as a 'stiff British upper lip'. At nine, a woman in the next bed called for a nurse, alarmed by my paleness and noting that I was drifting in and out of consciousness.

Mercifully, there was a changeover of staff. Within minutes, my doctor and grave-faced specialists were hurrying to my bedside. My doctor was a short, genial man with a huge bristling moustache, who wore peaked tweed hats when he careered around in his little red sports car. He was furious when he discovered my condition. I had had a placenta previa the night before. Now it was too late to perform a Caesarean. During the afternoon it seemed certain that my baby, at least, would not survive, and I might not either.

My daughter decided otherwise. Galvanised into action, she made a sudden appearance later that evening. I could hardly believe she looked so well.

'She's a little beauty,' said my doctor, seeing Ian still outside, as he left the theatre.

The theatre staff left us to look at our baby in her bassinet, while they hurried away to another crisis. In the next theatre a young woman was having her baby under anaesthetic. Her doctors were not so kindly. As I discovered later, Barbara was an unmarried mother. The conversation carried clearly through the walls.

'Look out, Doctor,' said one of the nurses, 'there's some blood coming away there.'

'Black blood, I'll be bound. Who knows where this one came from,' was the reply.

In fact, Barbara's daughter was blonde. Over the next two weeks I often came across Barbara weeping. All our babies were kept in a dormitory ward down a long corridor. I asked her why she didn't go down to see her baby who, I learned, was to be adopted out.

'I'm not allowed,' she said, turning her face away from me. 'They won't let me.'

'There's nothing to stop you,' I said hotly. I suggested that she simply accompany me down the corridor and walk into the nursery.

'They'd stop me,' she repeated, over and again, and nothing would convince her otherwise. Her baby lay like a creamy star, alone in her bassinet. One morning I placed my hand on hers and her fingers curled around mine. I have often wondered if her mother ever learned what a beautiful little girl she had. Still, it didn't really occur to me then that there might be other options. When girls 'got in trouble', as we said, they either got married or gave their babies away to others.

Hers was not the only study in separation and grief. In a bed near mine was a Maori woman called Martha, whom welfare authorities were trying to persuade to give up her newborn child, because she already had three children, an absent husband, and a house with an earth floor and no running water. I understood their concerns, but not the need to remove her child. Another woman who looked more like a grandmother was off to the races the day after she got out of hospital. I asked her who would look after her baby. She looked at me as if I was touched in the head. She had nine children already and she certainly wasn't keeping this one. She would be giving the boy to her sister.

But on the evening of the twenty-fifth of March, Ian and I could only marvel that, after all the fuss, our daughter Joanna was so smooth, olive-skinned and lovely. She lay chortling in her bassinet, seeming to laugh at us.

The following morning I woke in the hospital ward. I had been placed alongside the bedpan sluice room and it was noisy, hot and steaming where I lay, hurting from many stitches. But there I was, a mother and a writer. It was my twenty-third birthday.

A few days later, the babies were wheeled out from the nursery on a long trolley, a dozen or so at a time, to be distributed to their mothers for feeding. When all the babies except one had been given out, a nurse wandered over with a puzzled look on her face. 'I've got one Maori baby left over,' she said.

The baby was mine. I couldn't have been more proud of her.

Chapter 11

We would take our daughter and our Siamese cat called Oscar riding through the countryside in the Fiat 600 we had bought not long before Joanna was born. As my parents had never owned a car, or not during my lifetime, it is hard to describe how complete I felt when we went Sunday driving, as if my truly grown-up married life had begun, filled with the freedom that roads and distance offer. There were routes leading out of Rotorua in several directions. The Fiat's tiny engine was at the rear of the car, purring along behind us. In the back seat, the cat purred too, and our daughter hummed. On sunny days we rolled the windows down, so that the warm air could trickle across our faces.

Once, we came to a place in the Bay of Plenty, where the sky was immense and blue, and a railway line ran through the golden-brown summer grass. It was like a Grahame Sydney painting. There was not another human being or house or car in sight, but in the distance we heard a train whistling. We stopped the car and stood on the side of the road as it came into view, surely the longest train in the world. Joanna clapped her hands. She had a dark sealskin cap of hair, and that day she wore a pink and blue cotton dress that belled around her as she stood on tiptoes, and we counted the wheels. Ian lifted her on his shoulders. We stood and counted the wagons, all one hundred and nine, rolling over the parched landscape beside an electric-blue sea. We weren't sure exactly where we were, though we thought it near Opotiki. Blue-eyed Oscar never stopped licking his fur while the train disappeared over the horizon.

Days like that have a dream-like quality. For a time I was very happy although often exhausted: our daughter was a restless sleeper. Sometimes at four in the morning, Ian would pour her and me into the car and we would drive around the deserted streets for half an hour or so until peace reigned. When she was christened at St Faith's, the ceremony was disrupted by television cameras being set up for the wedding of Maureen Kingi, Miss New Zealand, scheduled for later in the day. With Joanna's godfather, Quintin Burslem, a young Englishman we had met in the Lake Road days, we dodged the cameraman while Manu Bennett dashed distractedly backwards and forwards to check that sound systems were working. Jennifer was her godmother, but couldn't come to Rotorua as she and Peter were about to get married. I was going up to be her matron-of-honour in Waipu the following week. I leaked breast milk through my satin dress while I handed out the cake.

Ian was working hard at Rotorua Boys' High, endeavouring to carve out a niche for himself in secondary education. He was teaching boys with learning difficulties and troubled lives. His own life gave him a natural empathy for kids like this, and he was popular with most of them. In the weekends he put in long hours in extra-curricular programmes, so we didn't see as much of each other as I would have liked. He took over running the night school and this burgeoned into such a big enterprise that he was out most evenings. Before Joanna's arrival I had taken some courses myself in floral art, still practising to be the perfect wife.

That was turning out to be more difficult than I expected. Although neither Ian nor I knew much about conventional family lives, Lynmore seemed full of people who did. The wives took days to prepare for dinner parties; there were coffee mornings at least once a week when the hostess prepared elaborate food and the invited guests dressed up in twinsets and pearls. These descriptions sound like battered clichés of the times, but that is what it was like. And if you wanted to be anyone, you belonged to Plunket, the society spawned by Sir Frederic Truby King to protect mothers and babies. A group was to be found in almost every suburb the length of the country, run mainly by young mothers.

I desperately wanted to be someone. I wanted to be a proper mother, a good wife, a respectable person. I was accommodating to every request. Yes, I would wear my bridal dress again in a parade of former brides to raise funds for Plunket; yes, I would mind this or that person's children—nothing was too much trouble. I made jam and preserved fruit and made my own clothes, not that I was very good at any of these skills. Preserving fruit was a mark of how successful you were as a housewife. Anything less than 100 bottles was considered a failure. Although I make a wonderful tomato soup nearly every year, from a recipe given to me by Barbara O'Connell, it was years before I began to bottle fruit just for the pleasure of it.

The house at Lynmore was on a flat quarter-acre section, facing the road and a long dense row of macrocarpa trees. New Zealand Gothic. In winter it got bitterly cold in the shade of the trees, with hard black frosts that often didn't lift until three in the afternoon. Just behind us, houses lay in lovely sunlight almost all day. On the other side of the trees there was a poultry farm; Iles Road was a kind of demarcation line between Lynmore's more upmarket profile and the next suburb.

Anyone passing by could see me sitting at the kitchen table. A moment or two later, there would be a knock on the door, someone on the doorstep looking for a cup of coffee. If I had a book in front of me, I would guiltily put it away. If I was writing in my notebook, I immediately declared that I was writing out a recipe, or a letter to my aunts. It seemed easier than the truth. I was scribbling again but now I was getting to know my neighbours, I wasn't sure it was something I should be doing. We would chat for an hour or two, about the children and their health, or our finances. A frequent topic of conversation was whether we should wear our most glamorous outfits and short skirts when we called on the bank manager to discuss our overdrafts, or whether to go looking miserable, with the children in tow. We usually opted for the first. We gossiped about our husbands, and, more significantly, about other people's husbands. The grapevine worked like magic. People told long intimate stories about their lives. I listened, and told less about my own.

I made some good friends in Lynmore. A few of those friendships have survived all the years that have passed since I left, and the not always flattering accounts of life in the suburb that have turned up in my fiction. But it was becoming clear to me that I didn't really conform.

And some clouds were gathering over my life. When we first married, Ian and I had planned to have several children. As an only child, I had hoped for at least three, perhaps more, but I began to miscarry frequently. We were never sure of the cause of this problem, although later we had a theory. One summer, Ian's long holiday job was working on Lake Rotorua spraying lake weed. At the end of each day of spreading chemical poison, he would load the drums on the back of a Marine Department truck and bring them home to wash out on our back lawn. It was about then that the miscarriages began and I can't help but think that the poison affected one or both of us. At the time, it was just grief and more grief, without any explanation.

There was nobody much I could talk to about it; it didn't seem to be one of the things people discussed over coffee, although my mother did sympathise. My doctor, the one who had delivered Joanna, had driven his red sports car into the side of a bridge and died instantly. My new doctor wasn't sympathetic when I went to him about the miscarriages. 'I don't suppose you kept the pieces,' he said. When I admitted that that was the last thing I had thought of doing, he snapped that women never did.

Nev Thornton was due to move on from Rotorua Boys' High, but before he left, he had a surprising guest to speak to the boys and their parents, and invited guests such as myself, at the school prize-giving. I was in the audience when Phoebe Meikle first delivered a speech that became famous and was published afterwards in various places. When she appeared on stage she was mild-mannered in her appearance (although, as I later learned, she could be very firm), with grey hair, large glasses and an understated elegance. She spoke directly to the assembled boys without patronising them. She said, among other things, that it was possible to be happy when you were alone, and she expressed her abhorrence of violence, her opposition to war. Then she said:

> The masculine orthodox Kiwi is likely to be pleasant and friendly in speech and manner, but to have few graces, and to suspect that elegance and effeminacy go together. He may spend his week-end painting a boat but not painting a picture; fishing but not bird-watching. He may show uproarious excitement over a rugby match or a Peter Snell, but not over the Beatles or a ballet. He may read a novel, provided it has plenty of action and not much 'psychology' (and provided it's not written by a woman), but he mustn't read poetry or plays. He may get drunk, preferably on beer, but he mustn't be a teetotaller.

I found myself wryly thinking, so this is why I chose a man who listened, and introduced me, to Chopin. Ian had 'difference' written all over him in more ways than one. I understood, in a moment of sharp recall, the way I had had to 'choose' between him and the rugby crowd. As she spoke, the level of discomfort in the theatre was palpable among the adults, although many of the boys were listening intently. They were hearing something that nobody had talked about in school. She continued:

> ...the standard male Kiwi has been trained from an early age to repress some of his deepest emotions, such as tenderness, remorse, pity and sympathy freely expressed, generous pride in the success of others, and joy in their well-being. And these are the very emotions we must develop, must educate instead of repressing, if we are to achieve good relationships with people...

I sat there quietly, hardly believing that a woman was standing there saying these things in public. It occurred to me that it was not just young men she was talking about, but men in positions of power, like the doctor I had recently encountered, and some of the teachers

I had known as a child. The people who should have known better, but were conditioned to a 'blokeish-ness' that destroyed their empathy. I thought about my father and how unhappiness had blinded him, for a time, to the sensitive artistic side of his nature, how he had become so confused with notions of what a Kiwi bloke should be like that he had felt one way, and behaved in another. It would take me a long time to figure out that these divisions also occur among writers and artists. To be 'artistic' doesn't necessarily guarantee empathy, particularly when it comes to women's work.

At the end of Meikle's speech, some women in the audience, and a few of the boys, stood up and clapped, while others sat in stony silence. After a moment of hesitation, I stood up and clapped too, aware of sidelong looks.

Despite some reading on the subject, this was the first speech I had heard about the role of men and women in a more equal society. The fact that Phoebe Meikle said these things aloud somehow made a difference. Between the covers of books, the ideas seemed vaguely fanciful in the society we lived in then. I learned afterwards that Meikle had made an earlier speech to the Goethe Institute (in Auckland, I think), in which she had talked about New Zealand not being a very friendly environment for women, and that thinking was considered:

> ...essentially an unfeminine practice; therefore women who indulge in it must be unfeminine. Thus all except the most fortunately placed intellectual women were accustomed to being patronized and considered unwomanly by many men (by some women also).

All of this made a great deal of sense to me, and explained some of my own uneasy feelings about the work I was trying to do, while living the life of a wife and mother in the suburbs.

Meikle definitely put some iron in my soul. When Joanna was a little over a year old, I read a newspaper advertisement inviting women writers to a week-long seminar at Auckland University, run under the auspices of the University Extension Department. The residential venue was O'Rorke Hall.

I decided that nothing would stop me from going. I cajoled friends into minding my daughter during the day, and my mother into taking a day or so away from the china shop. Ian would come home early for that week. Nobody thought it was a good idea, but it was agreed that I needed a change.

I remember that week as one of intense excitement. About sixty women had gathered from all over New Zealand. Only two were published writers: the novelist Frances Keinzley and a children's author called Joan Harland. The course director was John Reid, Professor of English at Auckland University. He was urbane, charming and erudite. I could have listened to him all day. Reid was followed by a succession of speakers, all well known in their fields. I was taken aback when the poet Kendrick Smithyman glared around the room and greeted us with the words, 'Lady writers. Lady writers, eh? Well, I guess you all need a little hobby.' Some years later I met Kendrick and he told me about the years with his sick wife, the poet Mary Stanley, author of *The Starveling Year*. On that later occasion, Mary had been particularly ill all the previous week, and he was almost weeping with exhaustion, his hands grimly clutching the sides of his chair as he recounted nights of sleeplessness and unhappiness. I understood something of the frustration of his life then, but on the day when he made his comments to the seminar, I felt charged with righteous indignation.

But what mattered, from the moment the course began, was my sense of not being alone in my desire to be a writer. All these women shared my longing. I was by far the youngest person there and I was hungry for the 'word', the voices of wisdom and advice. I had my hand up often in question time and earned a sharp rebuke from Sarah Campion for asking if there was any *limit* to what one could write about. Illicit love, homosexuality, whatever ... I was thinking about the reproach over the frankness of my play. Why would anyone want to write about things like that? she responded witheringly. So our tutors were a mixed bunch and some of them very self-opinionated, although I heard much that interested me and helped me make sense of what I wanted to do. Pat Booth offered practical advice about writing fiction, and journalist Cherry Raymond made useful suggestions about writing for the media, as an end in itself, or as a way to become known as a writer across genres.

And for a whole week I was totally independent. I could come and go as I pleased and walk around Auckland in the middle of the night if it suited me, talking, talking all the time to my new friends. I had never experienced this level of freedom before, this not accounting to anyone else.

I returned to Rotorua in a state of exaltation and with new determination. By this time, I had bought my first typewriter, a battered Remington that I practised on at night. My children have told me that some of their earliest memories are of going to sleep to the clatter of the keys. At the seminar, Raymond had suggested that if we had a special interest in a topic, our local newspapers might be interested in articles. It was, she sensibly pointed out, a way to get into print and put our names in front of editors. The following week, I bowled into the editor's office at the Rotorua *Daily Post,* without an appointment, and offered myself as a book reviewer. The reviews in the paper were so few and far between as to be hardly noticed. Ian Thompson was a grey-haired old lion of a newsman with a reputation for gruffness. He asked me what credentials I had to be a reviewer. I reminded him I had been deputy at the library, and that I had been one of the book buyers there and at the high school. He looked at me for a long considering moment. 'The job's yours,' he said.

'You mean I can review some books?'

'I mean I want you to run the book page. Once a fortnight.'

'How much will you pay me?'

'Twelve and six a page.'

'Who else should I get to review books?'

He looked impatient for the first time. 'You review all the books,' he said.

Over the next six years I must have reviewed at least 500 books. I was in a happy state of innocence and ignorance. Apart from Keinzley, who had proved a remote and somewhat haughty figure, and Harland, whom I liked immensely, but who drowned soon after the writers' seminar, I didn't know any writers at all. As far as personalities were concerned I was truly impartial. At one stage, Maurice Gee was living in the town, but I didn't know that and we didn't meet for at least another twenty years. I commented, on his novel *The Big Season,* that his was a 'dazzling' new voice, and that he had 'an authentic ear for dialogue'. The quote was picked up on the dust jacket of his next book. I felt a touch of envy about *The Big Season*—it was about the world of rugby. I had begun to turn 'The Orange-Scented Tide' into a novel called 'Club Litany'. Although it was never published, a later novel drew on similar aspects of my early life.

The more I reviewed, the more New Zealand books began piling through my letter box. I had come across Marilyn Duckworth's work by then, and was impressed. When Jean Watson's 'roadie' novel, *Stand inthe Rain,* appeared in

1965, I was bowled over. Jean's spare style packed a punch, and I thought her waif-like face in the dust jacket photo quite beautiful and wild. I could identify with the work of these women. When I learned that they were both mothers, I felt more certain that if they could write a novel, it was an attainable goal for me. I had formed a private ambition to have all my children, and to publish my first novel, by the time I was twenty-eight. I don't know why this seemed such a magic age, but it did.

It was increasingly clear, however, that this might be unattainable because of my unexplained and frequent miscarrying. In 1965, Ian and I made one of the most momentous decisions of our lives. We sought approval as adoptive parents, and were quickly accepted, perceived by welfare authorities as an 'ideal couple'. We thought we would like another daughter, and barely a few weeks had passed before a call came to say that a little girl who fitted our family profile was waiting for us in one of the St Mary's Homes (for unmarried mothers) in

Auckland. We travelled north by train, taking Joanna with us, clutching a carry-cot and some clothes for the new baby. The matron of the home greeted us with a long appraising look. She would bring the little girl out to meet us soon, she said, but she gave the appearance of being busy and bustled in a few minutes later carrying a baby boy, already more than three months old. 'Would you mind holding him for a few minutes?' she said.

She knew what she was doing. We looked into the face of a child who returned our gaze as if he had always known us. He had a mass of dark curly hair and his brown eyes and olive skin matched Ian and Joanna's colouring so closely that he looked part of our family. As we were to learn shortly, his colouring was not due to Maori ancestry but was that of his Greek birth father. When the matron returned, the question forming on her lips as she walked in was already answered. This was our son, whom we decided to call Giles.

We stayed for a night or two with Jennifer and Peter while the paperwork was done. Already we didn't want to be parted from our new baby. How does one explain such an instant and lifelong attachment? I can't really; it just felt right from the beginning. On the morning we were to pick Giles up, Jen drove us to the home in her small elderly Renault and came with us while we signed some papers, before delivering us all to the railway station. On the way home, Giles seemed to smile all the way. The train had a brief stop at Morrinsville station, where my Aunt Jean sat waiting, the news of our new baby having preceded us.

By that stage, Jean had sold her house in Studholme Street, but Roberta moved to the new place with her. It appeared that they rarely spoke. Jean had got a job as the Morrinsville librarian and left the house first thing each morning. This was her lunch hour and she cut a lonely figure, sitting on a bench with her handbag upright in her lap. But when she jumped on the train and saw Giles in his bassinet, her face lit up with a damp-eyed smile. 'Oh Fiona,' she breathed, 'he's just beautiful.'

In Rotorua we climbed aboard the local bus and made our way home, Ian carrying Giles up Iles Road, Joanna and me trailing along with the carry-cot. From the outside, we must have seemed an ordinary enough family of four returning from a brief holiday. But even if we did not fully realise it then, we were a family that had just made an enormous cultural transition.

Clyde Olsen, a friend from Ian's school days in Wellington, came up to act as Giles's godfather, and this time the occasion went off smoothly. Clyde was a scientist, a warm-hearted delightful man who loved kids but hadn't married because of severe hearing loss. It makes me sad remembering this, because when he was older, too late, he felt, to think about a family of his own, his condition was diagnosed as a minor defect, corrected by a simple procedure. He was passionate about life, raucous and opinionated with strong left-wing sympathies, smoked like a power plant, and died while his hair was still black.

I continued to work hard at my writing, but with two children my routines had to change. There was less time available in the day to write, however much I tried to create the space. I began to get up at three in the morning, while the house was totally quiet. I would sit in the still kitchen with the night pressing against the windows and pick away at my typewriter until dawn broke and the first of the children woke. That usually happened when the roosters crowed at the poultry farm beyond the macrocarpa trees.

 I knew Ian was often dubious about these preoccupations of mine, but he tried hard not to show it. He sensed the gradual withdrawal that had begun among some of our neighbours. I wasn't turning out like a conventional wife and although, if he'd had one, I doubt he would have been happy, I can see it must have been hard to have one who so increasingly turned her back on what was expected. I turned down an invitation to chair the local Plunket committee, and people started asking, 'Who does she think she is?' This came back to me via a well-meaning friend, and it hurt. But it was not just the time the position would have absorbed, I was uneasy about what I sensed as a ripple of racism running under the surface of the Plunket committee. I disliked the jumble sales that were held at a nearby pa on benefit day: it felt like the white Raj all over again. Later, our daughter learned the meaning of being 'brown' while we lived there.

I began sending short stories to literary periodicals, as well as a number of articles. The stories came back, but several of the articles were accepted. I was now drawing in a modest income. When I sold an article to the *Woman's Weekly* for £20, Ian was impressed; in those days it meant a lot. If I could keep this up, along with all the extra work that Ian had taken on, we could stop renting and buy the Lynmore house. I figured that if I really wanted to earn money, I would have to give up some of my household chores. I began to pay for my jam, and buy the children's clothes ready-made. From time to time, I put Joanna and Giles in a nursery for an afternoon while I went off to do interviews. I could afford to dress more snappily. The *Daily Post* gave me more and more assignments and I had also a regular radio slot on books, although my voice was still considered unsuitable, and the monthly contributions were voiced by a local radio personality, Helen McConnochie.

In another year the house was ours. We quickly began to transform it from a grey square box into a place that was light and airy, in summer at least, with a cheerful pretty kitchen and a deck. Together, we laid down paths, and Ian built a 'pit' in the concrete floor of the garage, which every home mechanic aspired to—a hole where you could stand upright beneath your car when it needed repairs. All the necessary things of life.

Then I began having miscarriages again. Friends, those I was still seeing, thought I should get the message and settle down to a less ambitious life. After a while I stopped talking about what was happening. I had another new doctor but nothing much altered. I went into hospital a time or two for dilation and curettage, or D and C, as it was known. Cleaning out the nursery was another way it was put to me. A specialist I consulted said, 'You're a sparky young woman round town, you've got two children. Why don't you just treat that womb of yours like an old handbag and throw it away?' But that wasn't what I wanted either.

Then one morning, out of the blue, we received a phone call from Ian's father. A close relative had died, and the husband was left with four children under the age of six. I had never met this relative, but Tom asked if we could step in and take one of the children. Without really pausing to think, we said yes. It seemed like the right thing to do. Suddenly, we were about to become the 'parents' of another little girl called Christine. She was eighteen months old, just eight months younger than Giles.

Later that morning the matron at St Mary's rang us to say that a little girl had been born who she thought would be ideal to complete our family. With very mixed feelings, we said it would not be possible for us to take her, as we already had another little girl.

We drove over to Napier, and I met Christine. She was a ragged little scrap of a girl, with wispy fair hair. Her mother had died of a brain tumour. Nobody had suspected that she was ill, although she probably had been for some time. Christine appeared to have spent most of her short life in her cot, for she was malnourished and could barely walk. But she had a sweet crooked little smile and she put up her arms to be held. When I picked her up, she buried her face in my shoulder and I was lost. Her father said, 'She's yours. What can I do with four children?'

Unfortunately, I believed him.

My life now entered a frantic stage. I had three pre-schoolers and no clear idea of what lay in the future. I wasn't sure whether the arrangements for Christine were really permanent, or whether her father might recover enough to want his family back. Joanna was often sick, and the winter damp seemed to intensify as the trees across the road grew ever higher, blotting out still more sunlight. When we first rented the house, and again when we bought it, we had had an assurance that the trees on the Crown-owned land would be trimmed and kept under control, but that hadn't happened. I was beginning to regret the purchase of the house.

There were so many napkins to deal with and I could never get enough dry. I stayed up at nights burning the wood-fired booster stove in the kitchen with the door open, holding up the napkins. Another test of good motherhood was having sparkling white napkins on the line but mine always looked a sullen shade of grey. The woman next door always had luminously white ones, but then she was in the habit of turning her two children loose at eight o'clock in the morning while she did her housework. They invariably ended up on our doorstep, and I didn't have the heart to turn them away. The house teemed with toddlers. Of course the writing work fell away.

On a more positive note, we had another assurance that Christine was ours to keep, and we began adoption proceedings. As the months and nearly a year passed, she had grown into a plump healthy little girl whom we regarded as a daughter, and the children thought of as their sister. Friends rallied with support when they saw that I was finding it hard to cope. They understood that acquiring a less than robust addition to the family at such short notice wasn't easy; the age difference between our youngest two was close but not close enough to think of them as twins. Time out was offered more generously than when I needed time to write. This was a side to living in the suburbs that I could appreciate.

It all crashed to an end when an old family animosity, which I hadn't really understood, reared its head, but then I barely knew Ian's family. Christine's father had been reproached for not gathering his children back together. He appeared unannounced one morning and said he had come to collect his daughter. Twenty minutes later she was gone.

Nearly ten years passed before we saw Christine again. What angers me still is that although I didn't discover it then, she didn't return to her father's home for several more years, but was sent to another family, unrelated to her. When she was thirteen she was taken out of school to care for a half-brother by her father's second marriage; this nonconsensual truancy was never followed up. In time, we would resume a relationship with her, which we still maintain. Her father died long ago. Although she is a person whose courage I admire, her life has been unnecessarily harsh, and it's hard not to think how much easier it might have been.

When she left my world collapsed. Thinking back to the little girl who had been chosen for us at St Mary's, I felt that I had lost not one daughter, but two, even though I had never met the second. There was a night when I cried hysterically for hours. Ian became afraid for me, and I tried to pull myself together. But in the days that followed everything around me seemed dull and disconnected. I sought to establish a routine that I could follow day by day. In the mornings I moved like an automaton through the house, picking things up and putting them away. I counted the rooms that still had to be tidied—three more to go, two more, one—and then it would be time to start putting things away again in room number one. In the afternoons, while

Joanna and Giles took naps, I sat and looked into space or at my hands lying in my lap. I didn't always understand my hands; they didn't seem part of me. As they lay there I could see that later in the evening they would appear somewhere else, round a child or a teapot, or sitting outside me on the covers of the bed. Just anywhere.

I need hardly say that this was a very bad time in my life. Joanna was old enough for me to talk to her about Christine's disappearance, but Giles was agitated. He told the mother of a kindergarten friend that I had a baby I kept in a cupboard and only took her out to feed at nights. It was something of a neighbourhood joke, but not to me. When Christine left, the supportive friends melted into the distance again. After all, Christine was alive; it wasn't as if she had died. But I had reached a point where I didn't really want to see people anyway.

My mother was concerned, but there was little she could do. Her life at the china shop was busy. People flocked from all over the Bay of Plenty to buy from her. She had been offered the opportunity to buy the shop, but my father was totally opposed to this idea. He wanted his wife at home with him. He had retired the day he turned sixty because, he said, most of his relatives had died young, and he was likely to do so too. This might have been true but as I knew very little about his family either, there was no way of knowing. The older I got, the less I felt I knew him. Sometimes he said odd things that left me confused. I was nearly thirty when he mentioned some uncles I had never heard of before, called Abraham and Isaac, and I discovered that my great-grandfather's name was Nathaniel. As he often expressed strong anti-Jewish sentiments, I began to wonder if he had some closet connections of his own. Later, when I was older and began exploring my family's history, I realised this wasn't so. What I think now is that he wasn't so much anti-Jewish as pro-Palestinian. He became increasingly passionate about his conviction that the Palestinians had been wronged by the establishment of Israel.

What I did learn was that he had nurtured a desire to paint. In retirement he began producing watercolours, painstakingly executed over long periods of time, delicate studies of flowers and landscape. There were never people in them. He started to exhibit and sell some of the work. Some are in private collections, but I have a few. When I look at them, I see how misplaced had been his ambitions to farm when he was a young man.

In a 1985 collection called *Going to the Chathams,* I published a poem for my father, which included these lines:

> *At mother's house your pictures*
> *of this place hang on the walls colours*
> *soft as tissue the wash of the water*
> *in the paint reflecting these*
>
> *mists and oh the sky over the water*
> *is darkening the waves on the lake*
> *sharpen like tousled lace the hem*
> *of my shift*

*...it's impossible not to think of you
(here) old
man now that you're dead and your
late drawings oh yes the light*

*on the wind shifting
the tops of the waves and the night
leaning in on me it's been
a bright day beneath the mountains.*

Now his ambition was to move around the countryside looking for subjects to paint. My mother was to be part of these expeditions and he was adamant that she give up the shop. My father would visit me on Tuesday afternoons, and talk enthusiastically about his plans, then become irritated with what he saw as my lack of interest. I don't think either of my parents realised how close to the edge I was at that time. Neither of them had thought it a good idea for me to look after Christine, and they were pleased she was gone. They had been certain from the beginning that it would all come to tears.

On a trip to town, I went into one of the bookshops I used to haunt in better times. The bookseller was someone I liked very much, a plain man with blunt black hair and a pitted face. He loved a man with sculptured features and a theatrical manner, who was about to betray him. I understood more about gay men's lives then than I had in the courthouse some years earlier, though not much. I did know that these sorrows had to be secrets and that they were shared only with people who could be trusted, and that day he confided in me. Perhaps he thought I needed someone else's trouble to take me out of myself. After we had talked for a time, he offered me a book that had been around for a while but he wondered if I had read it. The book was Janet Frame's *Faces in the Water*. I think he had worked out what was becoming apparent to only a few, that I might be moving towards some irretrievable point, that I was staring a total breakdown in the face.

Reading had become almost too great an effort. I still reviewed a few books, but the book page was in decline. After a few days, on one of my listless afternoons, I picked up *Faces in the Water* and began to read. I read it straight through and then started again, this time taking the book apart in my head and examining it piece by piece. I thought about the character of Istina Mavet, and her long banishment from the world into that place of chaos and madness, where the sun never shone. A paragraph that struck me with great force was one where Istina runs away. 'I rely so much on the sun; I think it is the sunflowers with their ebony hearts and their ragged searing corona and their heads turned to the sun. I think it is the removal of the sun's influence that made us mad...'

I don't remember how many times I read the book altogether. I'm not suggesting that, in some smug way, I had responded to a warning to 'pull myself together'—people do what they can. But I do know that I saw my own face in the deep water, the infinite dark lake, and that it became possible to think through what, before, had been unthinkable. One day I got up and left the rooms untidy. I took the children by the hand and marched up the road, a piece of paper and a pen in my bag. I knocked on the door of each of the twelve houses beneath the line of trees.

'This is a petition,' I said. 'I want you to sign it, so that we can do something about getting the trees taken down.'

'You're mad,' some said, or words to that effect.

I smiled to myself. I wasn't, that was the point. 'Well,' I said, 'perhaps it seems like that, but our kids are getting sick, and the paint isn't lasting on the houses. We were promised that the trees would be kept under control, but they aren't and it's not good enough.'

In the end, they all agreed to sign, except for a policeman who thought he might jeopardise his job if he put his name to a public petition. The trees were cut down, and our houses were flooded with sunlight. Without trying very hard, I had become a successful activist.

Chapter 12

I may not have been mad, but I had certainly been ill. A nervous breakdown of some kind, I have supposed since, triggered by my body's erratic disposal of babies, and the loss of Christine. I'm not sure why the illness passed. Perhaps it didn't pass as quickly as I thought. Afterwards I embarked on a period of perpetual restless activity that lasted well into the 1970s, punctuated by bursts of depression, regret and, later, too much to drink during bad patches.

In the meantime, we resumed some semblance of normality. The books page recovered. Joanna started school along the road. We upgraded from the Fiat to a Mini, although the cat had become irritable and didn't want to be driven any more. We would head for the seaside, or one of the lake beaches, and we came home plastered in sand, sticky with ice creams, and sometimes quarrelsome, but this was family life. One sultry Sunday afternoon, an odd thing happened. We had driven through an area of forest towards one of the sawmilling towns. The area felt remote, trees pressing close against the roadside, no houses or shops for miles. Eventually we came to a ramshackle store where we could buy cold drinks. Inside, a woman emerged through a fly-speckled strip screen. As she took our order at the long counter, a man wearing a filthy singlet, rough and unshaved with an unlit cigarette drooping from his mouth, appeared behind her. She turned and shoved him roughly back the same way. 'Get yourself out of here,' she snarled. By then I had started reading Katherine Mansfield; 'The Woman at the Store' immediately came to mind. I found myself shivering as we returned to the car.

On other Sunday nights we would head for the hot spa pools at the Government Gardens, and take a private pool, all four of us together, soaking up the spirited stenchy water, drying off and heading home dressed in our pyjamas. The house was stacked with children's books—lots by Dr Seuss—and Joanna and Giles were raised according to Dr Spock. We had television, and watched David Frost, the Seekers and Julie Felix. As well as 'Beautiful Brown Eyes' and 'Goodnight Irene' and 'Frankie and Johnny', I added 'Going to the Zoo' to my repertoire of songs to sing to the kids at night, then Peter, Paul and Mary brought us 'Puff the Magic Dragon'. The last thing the children would ask me every night was 'Mummy, sing Puff.' The song made me cry: it reminded me of Christopher Robin and the end of childhood, and how our own family innocence had come unstuck.

I began to write again and was rewarded with the acceptance of a short story. Noel Hoggard, who operated a small hand press to produce his literary journal *Arena,* had taken 'Murphy's Cow', about the slow and painful death of a cow as mirrored through the eyes of a young farmer up north. *Arena* was smaller than *Landfall,* but it was a prestigious publication nonetheless, and I knew the story would be noticed.

I wanted to go away to more University Extension classes but for the time being I was needed at home. I contacted the department in Auckland

and asked if they would fund some courses in Rotorua if I organised them. To my delight they agreed to send Pat Booth, whom I had first heard in Auckland. I liked his novel, *Long Night Among the Stars,* and because he was first a journalist, he was a very good communicator. (Years later, his work in overturning Arthur Allan Thomas's convictions for the murder of Harvey and Jeanette Crewe made him a national figure.) The seminar was held over a weekend in the Boys' High library, and more than sixty people turned up, including my father, who, it turned out, also had a secret yearning to write. One person who enrolled but later had to withdraw was a sixteen-year-old high school student called Ngahuia, with an open friendly face and long plaits. Her teachers said I would be a bad influence on a young girl and had forbidden her to attend. Ngahuia Te Awekotuku and I have been regularly in touch over many years since that early encounter. She is a more radical activist than I have ever been, but she managed that without any help from me.

The tutor at the next course was playwright Isabel Andrews, an older woman who wrote for stage and radio. Again, the University Extension department was willing to help, but thought the audience would be more specialised. It was decided to hire the Shambles Theatre. A group of about twenty spent a weekend improvising plays and writing dialogue. Isabel and I found an instant rapport. She encouraged me to start writing plays again and urged me to try for a place on a workshop for emerging playwrights that Bruce Mason was running in Wellington the following month. The organiser was Playmarket, an agency for stage writers that encouraged new work. Out of town writers were being offered billets with Wellington writers. I hadn't figured how I would get away, but I sent a play off anyway, which was a pre-selection requirement.

Not only was the play accepted but Bruce chose it for the rehearsed reading on the last night of the workshop in Stagecraft Theatre. This was beyond my expectations. In my mind Bruce, already famous for *The End of the Golden*

Weather, was truly distinguished. Of course I had to get there. Again there were complicated child minding arrangements to be made, but nothing was going to stand in my way.

I have never forgotten that weekend. Not only was I in the thick of greasepaint and make-up, but all the dreams and longing to be acknowledged as a writer, to be recognised, seemed on the brink of being realised. Bruce's trademark was his wonderful fluting voice, a voice that could soar with anguish, evoke loneliness, make you laugh, paint landscapes with words and people them with characters both Maori and Pakeha—in other words, transport you to wherever he wanted to take you. He was a consummate actor and writer, and he turned his full attention on me. At times I felt mildly uncomfortable, because there were other, more experienced people, who had also travelled long distances to the workshop, but I was clearly a new young protégée. There were a few mutterings, and one man said, in forthright terms, that it was because I was young and pretty. I've thought of that when I hear young writers being dismissed because they are attractive, and I know it's almost always unfair. I didn't think of myself as pretty but I had bought new clothes and they made me feel confident. The Beatles and Mary Quant had hit New Zealand by then. I was into short short skirts and dramatic make-up. Besides, Bruce wasn't like that; he was interested only in talent. True, he was surprised to learn that I had two young children at home. He felt I should be working in Wellington.

I was billeted with a woman called Marjorie Brooke-White who, along with her ex-army colonel husband John, became a friend for life. Marjorie had grown up in the select Day's Bay area across the water from Wellington, Katherine Mansfield territory through and through. The Brooke-Whites also had a connection with Kerikeri. John's mother had owned a bookshop there, and although she had a slightly prickly exterior, she knew books and allowed children who liked them to come into her shop and browse. But the Brooke-White family seemed different from the colonial crowd I had known up north. Their apartment on The Terrace was stylishly furnished and crammed with artworks, a salon for people from the theatre and the arts. They welcomed me as a young artist in my own right, and that weekend I met a number of their circle, including Constance and Max Kirkcaldie. In my memory, some of the meetings I had with their friends run into each other, but at various times I met George Webby, Peter Bland, Nola Millar, who later came up and took a workshop at the Shambles in Rotorua, David Tinkham and others. Marjorie and John's apartment would become my base for several trips south over the next two years.

I was falling in love with Wellington. Some nights we would watch old movies on television, with the lights turned off, and the city lights glowing beneath us, Marjorie sipping a brandy in milk, John and I drinking gin and tonic. One night we watched *The Red Shoes,* with Moira Shearer and Marius Goring playing the romantic leads. Shearer (Victoria Page in the movie) is a dancer who owns a pair of red shoes that want to dance even when her body says it's time to stop, even though her husband begs her not to go on. But she is in the grip of a compulsion. 'Why do you want to dance?' asks her autocratic ballet impresario, whose spell she is under. 'Why do you want to live?' the dancer responds. And one night, faced with a choice between love and art, the shoes dance her to her death. I found myself crying. I knew that I wanted to write as much as I wanted to live, but I wanted equally to be a wife and mother. I both craved and rejected an ordinary domestic life. 'No more gins,' John scolded, seeing my tears.

But it was more than that. I suspected that I was wearing my own brand of red shoes. Not for the first time, I was frightened of the course I had chosen.

After these interludes, I travelled back on the bus, over the long Desert Road and watched the mountains unfolding before me. On these journeys, everything looked different. Jessie Sandle makes that same trip when she arrives in a mid-island town in *Songs from the Violet Café:*

Jessie sat in an olive and mustard-coloured Road Services bus as it trundled through rolling plains, then the wasteland of desert space in the centre of the land, the starry tussock glinting under an erratic sun, the mountains leaning towards her from the west ... As the bus pushed north she saw a line of army tanks ploughing through the grass, firing practice rounds of shells that made puffs of dark smoke, and then the bus descended towards the lake country, the dark iris of Lake Taupo trembling on the horizon, and on past it, until they reached their destination.

It was through the Shambles, back in Rotorua, that I met a Turkish woman, Nina (actually Niyaz) Martin, now Niyaz Martin Wilson, who lived on the far side of Lynmore. We hadn't known of each other's existence up until then. Niyaz was the most strikingly beautiful woman I had ever met, tall, with tawny skin, huge kohl-rimmed eyes, and an irrepressible laugh that could easily turn to tears. When she was seventeen, she had married an older Englishman and the following year left Turkey against her family's wishes. She and her husband had moved restlessly to live in various parts of the world until he finally decided they would settle in New Zealand. Their son was close to Giles in age, and the two little boys got on well. Niyaz was not a Plunket mother; instead she was involved in setting up Playcentre in the district and became director of training for the Rotorua Playcentre Association.

There was an absolute electricity in the air when she walked into a room. We quickly became confidantes; I usually went over to her house, filled with colourful rugs and large gleaming copper kettles and pans, while she made Turkish coffee, then told my fortune in the cups. Both of us were chafing against life in the suburbs. Francis Batten came to take a mime workshop at the Shambles. He spent the entire day showing us how a man (but it could as easily have been a woman) tries to get out of a box in which he is trapped. I was entranced as I watched Batten's hands move backwards and forwards across the walls and ceilings of the invisible box, while we tried to tell him where he would find the exit. With him, we all believed in the box. And then, I don't remember how, the box vanished. It simply wasn't there any more. What fascinated me was that, even with the walls gone, his character still searched for them. At some point, he realised that they were not there, and began a little hip-hopping dance, reaching out for the freedom of space.

I stayed with the Brooke-Whites again in Wellington, this time on assignment for the *Daily Post,* which had asked me to cover the conference of the South East Asia Treaty Organisation (SEATO). Set up in the 1950s, it was an international organisation, in which the United States played a key role, ostensibly for the collective defence of the area, but primarily intended to subdue communist activity. The US was seeking, but ultimately failed, to make the Vietnam War into a SEATO problem. All the same, New Zealand had sent more than 3000 troops to Vietnam, and in the cities there were protest movements.

That much I did know, but apart from this, I barely understood what SEATO represented, let alone the dynamics of the war. I thought I was against it, but that was not very helpful. I wouldn't have dreamed of saying that to my neighbours or family beyond Ian. War was war, and you were staunch in support of our troops.

In Wellington, I was armed with a press badge, but woefully unfitted for my journalistic task. I didn't know where to begin. On the opening night, I went to a party bristling with gold braid and military stars, held at the White Heron Lodge, drank my first martini and persuaded one of the press officers to arrange an interview with the wife of Admiral Ulysses S. Grant. As far as the real business went, that was a men's world, not a job for a 'press girl' in an orange mini-dress with Indian braid on the sleeves. The next day I made my way along Lambton Quay towards Parliament, hoping that, with my magic press badge, I could fight my way into a meeting or, at the very least, a press conference. What I didn't know was that the Peace, Power and

Politics in Asia movement was holding its conference at the same time, with a line-up of leading international speakers. (A paper by Jean Paul Sartre was presented, although Sartre didn't attend in person.) All of a sudden I was in the middle of a crowd of placard bearers and a sea of slogans saying, 'Stop Your Bloody War', 'No Aid for the US' and the like. People wore headbands and scruffy jeans; I had on a twinset that day. This tide of people swept me along, and I found myself shouting, 'We don't want your bloody war.' Somewhere near the cenotaph, I pulled myself together. What on earth was I thinking about? Shaken, I made my way to Parliament, pretending I hadn't seen the protesters. I got into Parliament, but nowhere near the action. It was becoming clear that I might have to content myself with the admiral's wife.

I headed back out to the White Heron near the airport, where the generals and their entourages were staying. It was the morning of 1 April 1968. I was ushered into the presence of a small woman with iron grey hair.

Nancy Grant seemed pleased to have someone pay her attention. I asked all the usual patsy questions about how she spent her days while her husband was off at war and closed my notebook.

On my way out, I stopped to thank the press officer who had arranged the interview. Admiral Grant and a number of military personnel were clustered at the front of the room. A briefing was taking place and, from the corner where I stood, I heard that President Lyndon Johnson had announced he would not be seeking re-election to the American presidency, and also that he had ordered a halt to bombing over a major part of North Vietnam. Johnson, of course, was keeping the wheels of the war machine oiled. I can't remember the exact words, but they indicated that public pressure had played a role in his decision. Loud exclamations of anger erupted around the room, and quickly turned to turmoil and shouting. Grant's face was very red, several of the men appeared to collapse inwards on themselves and one began to weep. You could see their dismay as the news that the war might be about to disintegrate began to penetrate. A man looked over and saw me. 'Get that woman out of here,' he shouted.

Later that afternoon, standing in the central city, I found myself overwhelmed by a desperate need to get home. I had no idea what I was doing there. I felt foolish and ignorant. I saw that I had no real idea of how the world worked, that difference was not merely personal, but part of some wider global movement. Most of all, I wanted to be with my family. The whole trip had been a professional fiasco and, as I made my way home on the first bus I could get out of town, I resolved not to accept work that took me away like this again. I was guilty that I left the children so often. Joanna had had pneumonia in the spring and Giles had broken his leg at kindergarten a few months earlier. I carried him around on my hip for weeks with his leg trailing in a thigh to foot cast. Today, my life would seem staid, but back then troubles like this could be seen as neglect. I loved the children beyond words; my family was a major reason for my own existence. And yet I was in the midst of a turmoil that was more than I could handle.

Back home, I went through another brief bout of depression. I took long walks at night, as I had when I was a girl, tramping the Lynmore streets after Ian returned from night school classes. Sometimes, I would pick the children up in their pyjamas and walk along the road in the dark with one on each hip, waiting for him.

And I was not the only person finding life difficult. Somehow, in the midst of my own crises, I had not properly noticed the toll Ian's job was taking on him. He had now spent some years working for Ted Hamill, the principal who had replaced Neville Thornton. Hamill was, quite simply, a sadist. If there had been a violent culture in the school when I worked there, it was nothing compared with what followed. Those staff who didn't obey Hamill's edicts became the targets of his merciless tongue. The teachers were free of him for a year when he was contracted to an outside job in education, and for a while Ian saw the possibilities of life under a less brutal regime. On his return, Hamill was worse than ever, and Ian, who taught without caning unless ordered to, fell foul of him. He had had enough, and told me he was ready to leave Rotorua.

Nearly a year passed before a job came up that was worth the move, and it turned out to be a very full year. My spirits were sustained by Niyaz's exuberant companionship. When I was down she persuaded me that the answer wasn't to act more 'normally', it was to be myself. We decided that we really didn't want to conform and set out to show the world. We bought gorgeous hats and wore them to town in the mornings to have coffee. I had one, made of swirling peacock-coloured fabric, with a high crown and a brim that turned up at the front, which made heads turn. Gone were the staid morning coffee sessions in the suburbs. I had also met the radio playwright Julian Dickon, an English writer, living in Atiamuri. We met through another seminar at the Shambles, after a recommendation from University Extension to use someone close at hand. He was the most prolific radio playwright of the time, and his plays had a smart polish to them that much local broadcast drama lacked. I liked the universality of his themes; he had served in the Korean War, spent several years as a seaman and came from a strong literary background in England. He knew a lot about the world.

Julian turned out to be a generous friend, and put me in touch with Bill Austin, the head of radio drama in the New Zealand Broadcasting Corporation. As it turned out, Bill had already heard about me from Bruce Mason, and was very receptive to the idea of a meeting. I sent him a radio play called *Martha,* inspired by the Maori woman in the maternity hospital who was being pressured by welfare to give up her new baby. I got a contract for it the next week.

Shortly after I signed, a letter arrived from Bill containing an invitation to see him in Wellington, so that I could learn more about the art of radio drama; the invitation was accompanied by an open return air ticket. I had been burnt by my last expedition to Wellington, but this seemed more promising. Radio drama would be more lucrative work than the odd bits of journalism I was doing. *Martha* hadn't taken me long to write, and had earned me more than six months' income from these jobs. I was ready for something new. My twenty-eighth birthday had passed: the deadline I had set myself to become a published novelist had been and gone. I had finished a draft of *Club Litany* and sent it away to Whitcombe & Tombs, where it had been assessed and returned with a long list of suggestions, although not a downright refusal. The suggestions forced me to look at the material more closely. I decided that this was not really the book I wanted to publish after all. Radio drama seemed a promising alternative for the time being.

Besides, although man had landed on the moon, I hadn't yet been on a plane and I thought it was time I did. Rotorua dropped away beneath me, and the next challenge beckoned. The following day, I met Bill and his script editor, Arthur Jones. Bill had a big leonine head, a shock of blond wavy hair and piercing blue eyes. He was gorgeous to look at but appeared almost paralysed by shyness. I soon learned that he was an alcoholic, who binge drank till he was legless, then stayed sober until the next bout. In between times, he produced and acted with brilliance. But when I met him, he had so little to say I wondered why he had sent for me.

Very soon I found myself in the office of his offsider, Arthur Jones, and it was here that the trip began to take on meaning. Behind a perpetual pall of smoke, Arthur's face was the colour of grey suede. He had been a script editor for the BBC, and when he wasn't working in radio he wrote detective novels under a pseudonym. We talked for hours and then he took me along The Terrace to the broadcasting studios so I could see a drama in production. He was, he said, very impressed with my ear for dialogue and hoped we would work together in the future. I think dialogue was one of the strengths I brought to radio dramas. It was not until I wrote radio plays that I began to realise that I had a quick instinctive ear for the way people spoke. I was a good listener, thanks to years of childhood eavesdropping—on telephone lines, and in the way only children often do in the company of adults. I have always been interested, too, in what people are not saying—the sub-text, as they say in television.

Arthur and I became great friends almost straight away. When I got home, I wrote another play, and that was accepted too. Life rolled on at a steady pace, some of it, like Woodstock, via the television screen, but mostly, in real life. Tom and Doll came to stay, but then they often did. I liked my father-in-law, despite his odd insistence that his meat always had to be on the right side of the vegetables on his plate, but there was usually friction when Doll was around. Never an easy woman, she had had no children besides Ian, and her tongue was sharp when it came to telling me how to raise mine. When she and Tom came to stay, Doll always made a secret of how long they would be with us. It was like a game to her, having us ask questions designed to elicit a date from her. 'When you throw us out,' was her standard, challenging reply.

Then Clyde contacted us and asked us if we could provide a bed for a friend of his called Carole and her son, while the little boy underwent tests for autism in Rotorua. Carole hijacked her way into our lives. A latter-day blonde bombshell, she was born the night Carole Lombard was killed in an air crash over the Atlantic, so her mother named her after the silvery-haired film star. Lombard had been one of Hollywood's most popular blondes, rather like Jean Harlow, only more freewheeling, playing roles from sensitive drama to screwball comedy. Our Carole liked to live her role as a zany blonde to the full, with a stack of energy to burn. She did "Ello Sailor' routines in our living room and made us laugh. In spite of that, I suspected she wasn't very happy, and that it went beyond the difficulties her third and youngest son was experiencing. There was the hint of a marriage that wasn't standing up well to the strain of the situation.

Then Kit Spencer, by then Kit Wright, got in touch with me, and asked me to run Rotorua Book Week, as part of a national library promotion, and I did that too. Since I had last worked for her, Kit had married the town clerk, Len Wright, with whom she had had a long and tempestuous affair. When marriage was finally possible for them, they enjoyed a brief time together before Len was killed in a car crash. She was alone again, and devastated. The Book Week was supposed to have been her job, but she couldn't face it.

The national organisers were touring some overseas writers and the one designated for Rotorua was the Australian Max Harris, a key player in the infamous Ern Malley affair, considered one of the greatest literary hoaxes of all time and fictionalised in Peter Carey's novel, *My Life as a Fake*. Max, considered a young poetic genius at nineteen, was a founder of the *Angry Penguins* literary periodical in the 1940s. He thought of himself as an anarchist and published collections that ran contrary to the established poetry traditions of the time. Using the pseudonym 'Ern Malley', two conservative poets penned some work that was intended to send up the modernist principles espoused by Harris and his various friends, including the artist Sidney Nolan, to see if Harris would recognise them as a spoof. Max Harris took the bait and the poems were published to acclaim before the hoax was unveiled. Harris was not only reviled, but landed in court and was convicted for publishing obscenity. Yet the Ern Malley poems stood the test of time, Harris defending them as inadvertent works of art, a view that has been widely upheld since then.

Although Max's own poetry had declined in output after the affair, he had become a respected columnist and editor by the time of our meeting in Rotorua, nearly a quarter of a century later. Again, I made an unexpected friend. Max was an advocate of women's rights, declaring himself a feminist, and also believed in people being 'self-made', the way he was. We spent several days in each other's company, his wild mood swings and gaiety perhaps fuelled by the freedom to be himself in New Zealand, without the eye of the Australian establishment upon him. We finished up a spectacularly successful week with a party at our house. All manner of people turned up, including some television folk from down south. Max finished the night sitting in the branches of our nectarine tree throwing green fruit at us and shouting poetry at the top of his voice.

The following week, Ian got a call from Derek Wood, principal of Naenae College in the Hutt Valley, to offer him a job as head of the school's newly established Special Services Department. We were on our way, out of Rotorua.

Almost. In what were to have been our last weeks in the town, I threw caution to the winds and wrote a long piece called 'I, the Suburban Housewife' for *Eve* magazine, billed as a periodical for 'thinking women', which had carried work of mine for a year or so. My essay was intended as an exposé of women's existence in the suburbs, and drew heavily on the lives of those around me. When I submitted it, I reasoned I would be gone by the time it was published.

But I wasn't. Ian was invited by the Taiwanese government to set up a special education programme based at the East-West Center, University of Hawaii. So we decided to put off the move until his return. I was left to face the music of publishing a piece that caused a small scandal of its own.

Over the summer, I went to work for Kit at the library again. My parents, now both retired, helped with the children. It was a strange time, living on my own with the children, and now considered something of a scarlet woman, in thought if not in fact. I was perceived as frank to the point of raciness, and caused considerable interest at work. Kit joked that she had never had so many people in the library at one time. It was a good place to take refuge from a none too happy neighbourhood, as well as a chance to say goodbye to some of the library borrowers I had known for so long. There were some I would miss very much. One man who liked talking about books and art with me said wistfully that he would never get past the 'green apples and a jug' stage, but I had the chance to do something more. But on the whole, I was glad to be leaving Rotorua, and Lynmore. I think the suburb was pleased to be seeing the back of me too.

Ian arrived back from Hawaii, bearing leis made from fresh orchids. I wore them garlanded around me at a party friends gave for us that night, and a lot of people turned up to see us off. In the morning, we loaded the Mini with the children, our bulldog and the last of our possessions, and headed south.

It was the beginning of March 1970. In a few weeks I would turn thirty.

Chapter 13

Transition.

Moving from one place to another.

I hadn't known how difficult it would prove. I had never lived more than ten kilometres away from either my parents or the Morrinsville relatives. I had always known the people around me. I wasn't prepared for being cast adrift. Or that's how it felt.

Even coming here to Menton was hard at first, which sounds absurd, given the luxury of living on the Riviera. I've grown used to continuity. I stand on the balcony here in the evenings and everything is alien. All those old romantic lines from the *Golden Treasury* come back. Wine-dark nights and blood moons. A couple of nights ago there actually was a blood moon. It's hard to compare it with anything, although I thought of a lunar eclipse or the sunrises in the Australian outback, but really that doesn't describe it. What I can say is that, very late, after night finally set in (because in these summer months the light lingers on until well after ten), the colour of the moon intensified minute by minute until it was a darker, deeper, more disturbing red than anything I've ever seen. I found this phenomenon unsettling, frightening even.

Madeleine and Brian have been and gone and their visit settled me down. There were no startling new discoveries. We laughed a lot and drank rosé and ate fresh cherries bought from the daily market that opens beneath the apartment in the early morning. The men watched the World Cup football games on the little television on which we can otherwise get only Italian game shows. I saw some of the games too. I like soccer a lot and at home I often watch my grandsons play at the weekends. Madeleine read a book when I was looking at TV; she's never liked sport much, although after I left Northland College, and she went there, she was the school swimming champion. Her eyes are still navy blue. (I go on about eyes a lot, and I must admit different shades of blue fascinate me. My own eyes are a sort of muddy hazel.) She had an accident some years ago, and walks more slowly than me. I have impatient brisk footsteps, a lot like my mother's. I had to remember to slow down, and to arrange to catch buses back from town. The bus station is at the foot of the street where we live.

We went up into the mountains, and spent a day in Gorbio, which is one of Ian's and my favourite villages, reached by a bus that races around hairpin bends while the driver sings. There is a 300-year-old oak tree in the square, and a café by the bus stop where you can get a great lunch of fish, salad and bread, and a huge carafe of cold wine, for a few euros. The air is cooler up there, filled with the sharp scent of geraniums, their colours splashed in every window box. Menton looks like a toy town far below. Our friends Luc and Michel, and Michel's mother Madame Imbert, have a summer house there, which we reach by way of a cobbled path; theirs is one of the oldest of these ancient stone residences. Some nights we have dinner with them here, dark mountain faces on two sides, beneath us the lights of Monaco in one direction, and of Italy, in the other.

I had imagined that the four of us, Madeleine and Brian and Ian and I, would take the train to Nice—it's a journey of less than half an hour—and see Matisse's house, and the Chagall musée, perhaps travel on further to Cagnes-sur-Mer to visit Renoir's house. But nobody wanted to do that. I'll go there on my own, later on. I have to remember not to organise people's time so much. At home, in New Zealand, I make lists and stick to schedules. People think I'm efficient, but really I just need some kind of a blueprint to get me through things.

Being here, it's different. The sun beats down, the moon glows with the eerie light I've described, tides of people with oiled leathery bodies roll into town for the summer months, and lie packed hip to thigh on the hard white pebbled beaches for hours on end. (The population has risen by 50,000 for 'the season'.) I can't see the pleasure of lying on those beaches—the swimmers have to wear odd little plastic slippers to protect their feet—but the crowds are interesting to watch from beneath the vast straw-fringed parasols that line the sand. And the thing is, I don't have to hurry anywhere. I need to keep reminding myself of that.

The week after our arrival here the Deputy Mayor Luc Lanlo presented me with the key to the Katherine Mansfield Room at Villa Isola Bella. The ceremony took place in La Salle des Mariages (literally, the Marriage Room), a room at the town hall designed and decorated by Jean Cocteau in the 1950s. It is the only place in Menton where marriages can be legalised. Throughout the 1950s Cocteau was absorbed in the Orpheus and Eurydice myth, writing books and making a film based on the story. He chose to carry the theme over to this commission. I think he must have had his tongue firmly in his cheek, for it's a fairly brutal story to link with marriage: Orpheus, according to Greek myth, is the only person to descend into Hell and return. A player of the lyre and composer of charming odes, he falls in love with the nymph Eurydice and marries her, only to have her die suddenly from a snake bite. He follows her into Hades and, through his music and lyrics, persuades the gods to bring her back to life. The story goes on, none of it ends well, they all die. The legend is illustrated in murals that decorate the entire walls and ceiling of the Marriage Room. At the front of the room, like twin thrones, stand two chairs. These chairs and an altar-like construction are covered with red velvet. A carpet with a leopard skin pattern runs the entire length of the room to where it opens into a second portico stage that, with a final theatrical flourish, Cocteau lined with floor to ceiling mirrors. There, heavy doors open onto the street. When people are married bells ring, summoning the citizens of Menton to gather and hail the newly-wed couple.

As Luc is also the person who conducts marriages, Ian said, as an aside, 'You'd better marry us again.'

Sometimes Ian's jokes are taken seriously when he least expects it. By this time, I was armed with a large bouquet, and clutching the keys to the Katherine Mansfield Room, streaming with long blue and white ribbons, the colours of the Blessed Virgin Mary and the city of Menton.

Luc disappeared for a few moments. When he reappeared he was wearing the ceremonial blue and white sash he dons for weddings, and before we knew it, Ian and I had been sat down on the red 'thrones'. I sat in a daze through what was apparently my second marriage. When it was over we were turned around, marched down the aisle to the ringing bells and found ourselves blinking in the Menton sunshine while the assembled bystanders clapped and cheered.

If Cocteau's design seems a mildly cynical reflection on married life, perhaps he had a point. In the 1970s, Ian and I went to hell and back: it was a trip that a lot of people would take at that time. Death, divorce, drink, despair—there was plenty of them all to go around. Some would survive, but a lot didn't.

Naenae sits close to the wide Hutt River, some twenty kilometres north of Wellington. The streets run over a flat plain beneath a line of hills. It is a landscape that could be pretty, but is somehow depleted by the factories and row upon row of state houses that cover it. I would visit Naenae often in the years ahead, but I never found it easy to find my way around. There is a sameness that baffles me.

Naenae College, where Ian now began to work, had been built in the 1950s, as one of several responses to the 1954 Mazengarb Report. In the wake of two incidents, a wave of moral panic about the activities of adolescents had swept New Zealand. One was the Pauline Parker and Juliet Hulme murder case, in which two Christchurch girls had murdered Parker's mother; the other was what was described as 'the Petone incident', relating to the activities of 'milkbar cowboys' and reports of underage sex in the Lower Hutt area. The hastily prepared report on the moral decline of the young attributed these alarming developments partly to the proliferation of state housing.

If the town structure of Naenae was unprepossessing, the school was a place of hope, run on visionary lines by Derek Wood. Some see him, in hindsight, as an overly righteous principal, but if they had seen what Ian and I had in schools, they might have better understood his liberal and compassionate view of education. Although Wood set high academic goals, he believed, too, that if a community was struggling with its problems, the school couldn't operate in isolation from it. This would be one of the tasks he set Ian, to go out into the Naenae community and seek its co-operation with the school.

We set out with the intention of settling in the area and it was something of an accident that we ended up living in Wellington. I think Ian sensed dismay on my part when I looked at my surroundings. That, I suppose, does me little credit, although my willingness to move south had been driven by the opportunity to follow a life in the city. This was suburbia all over again, and a bit more downmarket to boot. As it turned out, Ian often said later that he couldn't have worked so effectively in Naenae if he had had to worry about my reaction to living there. We rented for a few weeks in the Hutt, while we looked for a house to buy.

The city was half an hour away by train; many of the students Ian taught at Naenae had never been to Wellington.

Besides, there was still, for Ian, the lure of Evans Bay, where he had lived with Tom and Doll. They had gone to live in Levin some years earlier, after the death of Doll's mother. The house where they all lived held no charm for Ian, but the front yard had been the playground of his youth. Evans Bay is at the end of an inlet running in from Wellington Harbour, the line of the Orongorongo hills in the background, the airport and Cook Strait beyond. Ian, who had been an air force pilot in his compulsory military training days, had always loved watching the planes coming and going. Until quite recently, flying boats had landed outside the front door of the old house.

Many friends he had sailed with on the bay were still around, including Clyde, who lived with his mother in the house where he had grown up in Hataitai, the hill suburb above the bay. One evening we drove into town to see them, climbing the long zigzag path from Rakau Road up to their house. The trees and houses were colourful and pretty, the air clear and Hataitai looked a much better proposition than the place I had remembered.

About ten doors along there was a house for sale. 'You could buy that,' Clyde joked, never thinking we would take him seriously. 'It's going for a song,' he added.

Ian decided we should look at it, and the next thing we were back down the path and climbing an even steeper flight of steps. The empty house, which clung precariously to the hillside dropping sharply beneath us, was a state rental, although it had been built in earlier times, with a gabled roof and leadlight windows. The last tenant had died after living there for thirty or so years at the equivalent of three dollars a week. The outside looked solid and well maintained, although we got the impression that the interior would take a lot of work to make it livable. Still, the outlook was glorious, and people we knew lived in the neighbourhood. Carole, the new friend who had visited us in Rotorua, was down at the bay. Ian said, 'Let's buy it.'

Before I knew it, we had agreed. It was the craziest thing. The inside of the house proved a disgusting tip, full of dried rat shit and rubbish, the carpet rotten and the wallpaper curling down between stretches of brittle match lining. The bareness reminded me of Kitty Slick's house, although at least that had been clean. But we were young and 'doing up' a house seemed exciting. What we hadn't considered, that pleasant summer evening, was how close we were to the hill behind us and how little sunlight there would be, nor that there was no space for the children to play outside.

I spent my thirtieth birthday moving into this house. Although we did a major clean-up the day before, we made only minor inroads into the filth. A lot of our furniture and possessions were still packed in boxes that had come from Rotorua. Now the movers began unpacking them. I had thought the packers up north a bit cavalier when they boxed up our stuff, one older man cackling over my 'pretties', meaning my underwear. Now I found that bottles of Worcestershire sauce and other kitchen condiments had been packed unsealed among the 'pretties'. Many of my clothes were ruined and much of our furniture was chipped. Our belongings looked like the debris from a war zone piled in the rooms of our 'new' house.

I sat on the steps and cried. 'I'm thirty today,' I said out loud; 'I'm thirty and look at me.' The children put their arms around me. We sat in a huddle until I pulled myself together. It was up to me to make the best of it. I think Ian and I were both in a state of shock, wondering what we had done. Even though the house was cheap we were still heavily mortgaged and we could see that the costs of fixing things was much greater than we had anticipated. We bought fish and chips and a birthday cake from the grocer's, because of course it had been Joanna's birthday the day before. She had turned seven, and it was time to sing happy birthday to both of us.

The next day Ian became a serious commuter between Wellington and the

Hutt Valley, something he would continue for more than thirty-five years. We didn't stay in that house for long but we didn't move far away either, and we have looked out on the bay and the strait and the hills ever since. But the early years in that house were indescribable. Until we got the place properly clean, we were often sick with stomach bugs and the wind whistled through cracks round the windows, making winter desolate.

I enrolled Joanna at the local primary school along the street. The headmaster, Mr Gladwell, had been there for a very long time. He and I didn't get along from the start. Our family name was the same as that of a former student who had been involved in an unsavoury 'incident' and nothing would shake his belief that we were connected to this person. I found Gladwell authoritarian. He let it be known that he expected women to keep their place. Hoping to placate him, and wanting to ensure that things went smoothly for the children, I said I would be happy to make myself useful at the school. Perhaps I could make myself available for the school committee (what we now call the board of trustees). Gladwell looked at me coolly and said, 'We don't have ladies on the committee but you'd be welcome to join the ladies' auxiliary.'

For some, he was the ideal headmaster. Hataitai, for all its charm, has remained relatively conservative over the years. To me, his methods seemed like turning the clock back to older, more unkind methods of keeping children and their parents in their place. But one of the things I did like about the school was the large number of Greek children who attended, bringing energy and vitality to the playground. Although most of the families have moved on, back then our 'village' bristled with the heavy moustaches of Greek men, and women dressed in black, from headscarf to toe, threading their way from shop to shop. The Greek widows reminded me of the black swans that used to glide over Lake Rotorua, steady, calm, dark.

When Giles started school a few months later, several Greek children began on the same day.

To Ian's and my astonishment, within a short time he became a fluent Greek speaker, the only one among the 'non-Greek' new entrants. As with Maori children in the old education system, their language was frowned upon in the playground, and before long English prevailed, but this early linguistic connection with his heritage has never really left Giles. At that time, I began to understand how important it would become for him to acknowledge his Greek identity.

That day, when I arrived back at the house from enrolling Joanna, the postman had been. A letter in a long envelope awaited me, my first mail in my 'new' house. It was a commission from Bill Austin to write another radio drama, only the commissioned rate was nearly five times what he had been paying me before. I stood staring at the letter, scarcely believing what I saw. I looked up at the house and thought, 'Right, we'll fix you.'

This was the beginning of a family life lived in two halves, Ian's in the Hutt Valley during the week, from six thirty in the morning until he arrived home towards six, and mine in Wellington. The weekends were filled with carpentry and decoration, and clearing landfill to make way for a bigger kitchen at the back. Ian never seemed to rest. During the school holidays, the children and I would frequently return to Rotorua to stay with my parents while Ian knocked down walls and tore out windows. The Desert Road became increasingly familiar territory. I came to know every bend and twist in it, learned the names of the staff in the truckie's roadside cafs, picked rosehips in the autumn from beside the road, occasionally glimpsed the wild horses that roam the territory. It is a wild area of open space, full of the unexpected, which I love to this day.

I wrote the play Bill had commissioned in a short, month-long dash. *Tell About Man* was a story about an intellectually disabled girl who is befriended by a man suspected of ill intentions towards her. In fact, he does her no harm and illuminates her life with a brief glimpse of happiness until it is undone when the pair are separated by well-meaning authorities.

Bill and Arthur loved it. Although they had paid for two of my plays, so far nothing had been produced. (It had been decided that *Martha* was too controversial to air, and it never saw the light of day.) Now they decided that *Tell About Man* would be my debut. They assigned one of their top producers, Antony (Tony) Taylor, to produce it. Ginette McDonald, who was only sixteen at the time, played the lead role, and George Henare, who would appear in many of my later dramas, had a role. Tony invited me into the studio for the week of production so I could learn more about the nuts and bolts. I loved what the actors brought to my script. The *Listener* took my photograph and there was a brief write-up in the magazine the week before the play went to air.

I wasn't prepared for how I would feel when I listened to the play on air. Radio drama is composed purely of words, sound effects, music and silence. As Arthur pointed out to me, a brief well-placed pause in dialogue can have all the significance in the world. It is up to the listener to decide what is in the silence. These pauses, and the music, were vital to *Tell About Man*. The production was so good, so subtle, that it made me forget for a time that I had written the play.

As luck would have it, Diane Farmer, the *Listener's* radio reviewer, had heard the broadcast. In those days, radio drama was treated with the same respect and critical interest that new stage plays receive nowadays. Her review was totally enthusiastic. Why had nobody warned her that she was about to listen to one of the best plays she had heard in years? I couldn't have hoped for better.

But if this was the good news, the bad news was that I was lonelier than I could have imagined. I hadn't prepared myself for knowing so few people. What I now discovered was another version of suburban life, lived high on a hillside, with nobody around during the day. I had lost the art of being alone. In the first year of living in Wellington, I was so afraid of the silence that some days I went out to the airport when I knew there was a plane from Rotorua coming in, just so

I could see familiar people. 'Hello,' I would say brightly, and they would say, 'Hi, what are you doing here?' and I would pretend to be meeting someone. Silly, crazy stuff.

Marjorie Brooke-White, and one or two people I had met on my visits south, were helpful, but they were older, and there was only so much they could do. After a time, Rena, from a nearby house, came along and introduced herself. She was several years older than me, but she offered meals during renovations when we didn't have a kitchen, and conversation at the weekends. Although this was kindness, it was a friendship forged in hell.

Rena drank copious quantities of flagon sherry, and introduced me to the habit. She always had a new problem on the go and her husband came and went in a miserable state of not knowing whether his wife was going to throw him out or not. As she often told me, she had enjoyed the war years when there were American Marines in town.

Needless to say, quantities of bad sherry made me sorrier for myself than I should have been. Rena had a tougher constitution than mine. I was up and down and all over the place in my moods. Ian tried to get me to distance myself but I soon became reliant on Rena. Her family babysat for us now and then so that we could have an occasional outing, and it was hard to argue with that. In spite of her ways, Rena held down a job as a receptionist in town, and dressed well. She was an excellent dressmaker and offered to make clothes for me at a modest price.

About a month after we arrived in Wellington, Tom Kidman died. Ian had been looking forward to seeing more of his father, on his terms, rather than the lengthy visits, now that we were living closer. But that didn't happen. On the day of his funeral, we travelled up to Levin. By now I had met my sister-in-law Mabel Porter, and, for the first time since I had met Ian more than ten years before, all his family were gathered together. Even his mother.

We stood at one end of the cemetery, and I saw a couple walking towards us. Immediately, I guessed who it was. At last I was to meet my mother-in-law, Ruby. I said to Ian, 'I'm going to meet her,' and ran down the cemetery path before it could be discussed. Ian followed more slowly. I've always sworn a stone angel on a tombstone raised its trumpet in salute. It was love at first sight for both of us. In an odd sort of way it was like meeting Ian again, as I saw the things that had drawn me to him, repeated in her. The rift wasn't healed at once—things like that never are—but it was a beginning, and Ruby and I became close. We have a fast-growing tree in our back yard that we planted in remembrance of her. We call it Ruby's tree and I never like having it cut back.

There was plenty of time for my work now. I was determined that the dreadful house would be transformed into something better. I set off to see a lawyer, chosen at random from the phone book, and asked him if he could help me raise a bank loan, as I would be earning money.

The conversation was startling.

He asked me what work I did. I said that I was a writer.

'A writer,' he said, in a tone of contempt. 'What sort of a thing is that for a mother to be doing?'

I said that it paid some bills.

'Oh, really,' he said, 'and I suppose your poor husband doesn't get his shirts ironed or a decent meal on the table?'

I reeled back in a state of shock. He did, I said. I did cook and iron.

'Who looks after your children? Go on, go off and look after your family,' he said as a parting shot.

I haven't forgotten this man. Over the years I saw his photograph in the newspapers, accompanying articles in which he supported civil rights causes. For a time he was a high court judge. I nearly choked when I read his self-righteous words. People wonder why women got angry in the 1970s.

One evening, we took a drive down to the port. A big passenger liner was about to leave, after spending a day in Wellington. People were holding streamers between ship and shore, just as they had when Jen left Auckland more than a decade before. I watched with some longing, as a band began to play. Alone among the crowd of passengers was a young woman who stood staring at the wharf as the ship pulled away. She was alone, pretty and weeping, and there seemed nobody to see her off. I couldn't help wondering what had happened to her, whether she had just been visiting for the day, and if so what had made her cry in Wellington, or whether she was leaving home.

That summer, back in Rotorua at my parents' house, I began work on a television play. Television had been operating in New Zealand since 1960, but there was very little drama. Bruce Mason had had a play produced called *The Evening Paper* and Alexander Guyan had written drama for the screen, but there was not much else. Now, the NZBC hoped to present local drama on a more regular basis. Bill Austin was appointed head of the new television drama department, a position he held jointly with his radio drama position. He decided that the best way to attract television screenwriting talent was to run a competition, to which Dame Ngaio Marsh agreed to lend her name. It was launched with a senior section, and one for people under twenty-five. I thought I might as well give it a go and began work on a play based on the girl I had seen on the ship. In the play, she spends the day in Wellington and meets an artist who takes her to his studio and shows her his still life paintings while they talk about life. A kind of *Brief Encounter,* if you like, though I don't think that was consciously in my mind as I wrote it. I called the play *Green Apples and a Jug.*

I had to wait some time for the result to be announced so, back in Wellington, I decided to fulfil my long-held dream of going to university. This had always been there, in the back of my mind, since Nat Pitcaithly had spelled out my bright prospects at Northland College. There seemed no reason why I shouldn't go and I felt certain that it would get me out of the black holes that I seemed to fall into more and more. By this time, I was not only writing radio plays and being paid for them, but Robin Dudding, who had succeeded Charles Brasch as editor of *Landfall,* had begun publishing my short stories. I enrolled for English at Victoria University.

Hundreds of people milled around me on enrolment day. I found my way to a queue, but when I finally got to the desk I was asked to wait until others had been processed. There was a query about my application. After a long wait, I met someone who conducted an interview of sorts, although I didn't really understand the drift of the questions. Apparently a professor had raised the matter of my publications. I wasn't sure, in the end, whether I was being asked whether I needed to start English at level one (on the assumption that I already had some papers), or whether I was being granted entrance to the university on the strength of what I'd written. The latter seemed more likely.

I was out of my depth from the beginning. It's easy to blame people for what went wrong but, with hindsight, I could have done things better. I found it hard that there were very few mature students. When I sat in the lecture theatre, I looked round at a sea of young people in jeans with rough hair, long muslin skirts, lots of beads and beards. I appeared too respectable, and old by comparison. In my tutorial group, I felt lost among the eighteen-year-olds, although the tutor was about my age. We all muddled along but I felt stupid every time I opened my mouth. The questions I asked were basic ones—all the young people seemed to know the answers. My first essay on Katherine Mansfield got a pass. But Andrew Marvell. Who was he?

I had been at university for about six weeks when some news arrived. *Green Apples and a Jug* had won the senior section of the Dame Ngaio Marsh Award for Television Writing. Paul Maunder had won the under twenty-five section, with a week to spare before his birthday. The announcement was made live on the news slot of the country's only television channel. I wore one of the long hip-skimming dresses that Ian had brought back from Hawaii and had my hair dressed up high, like a cross between Elsie Tanner in *Coronation Street* and Cilla Black. Rena lent me some long dangling earrings. The prize was presented by Major-General Walter McKinnon, chairman of the New Zealand Broadcasting Corporation. I was a celebrity. Everyone I had ever known could see me. I was interviewed, photographed and spoke on radio.

Then a newspaper reporter phoned when I was at university. My attendance there was something I intended to keep to myself as I was beginning to feel very diffident about my paper. But the children's minder that day answered the phone and said that I would ring back 'after I came back from university'. I returned the call and an appointment was made. The reporter turned up, and I was photographed with the children cosily on either side of me. When he enquired about university, I asked that this not be mentioned. I didn't say it in so many words, but I wanted to be known for my success rather than the failure I suspected I was facing.

The next day, when the article appeared, the caption under the photograph read: 'For a hobby Mrs Kidman goes to university'. I think I knew university was over even before I went to my next tutorial group. I was running late. Nobody looked up, except for the tutor who gazed at me for a moment or two, then said, 'Well, here's Mrs Kidman who drops into university for her hobby.' Everyone laughed.

For a long time I blamed this man. I don't now. I discovered later that he was a writer too, but his path had not been as easy as mine apparently was. Years later, he told me he was sorry for the pain he caused me that day. I had, by then, worked out that it was not a matter of age or gender, although it was perhaps my first brush with literary Wellington and the rivalry that can exist between writers. But the truth was, I had left school at fifteen. Had I really wanted to succeed at university I needed to have thrown myself into reading, catching up, paying attention. Instead, my mind was on other parts of my life, like worrying about whether Ian could get home to look after the children in my absences, and how Joanna would get to her drama lessons and Giles to his soccer practice, and if they would get their homework done. All that, and anxiety about writing for financial gain. We needed the money, and as far as the children were concerned, it was much easier to be a self-employed writer, setting my own hours of work.

I walked out of the university and that was that.

Nor did I involve the children in my publicity again. It may not have been the newspaper's intention to leave me open to ridicule but somehow the item had been skewed against me, and I didn't want them to be part of things going wrong like that again. Although we were outwardly a conventional nuclear family, I suspect that both my children would see their upbringing as slightly unusual. I decided that they must have private lives with space to be themselves. They have grown up to become highly individual, interesting and, in my view, successful people with their own stories. We are a family with intense bonds between us, but we are all different.

After I left university, I felt I was on notice as a writer. I never entirely got over the feeling that I had labelled myself as a 'commercial' writer who had failed when it came to the literary test. To this day, I do not feel altogether at ease in Wellington's university circles.

While I veered from one extreme to another, from triumph to ignominy, I met someone else who would influence my life. Bill Austin and Arthur Jones organised a weekend seminar for screen and radio writers, and of course I was invited along. So was another of their protégés, Witi Ihimaera. I was very aware of Witi as a writer, not just because Arthur had talked about him so much, but because he was publishing stories, as I was, in the Maori Affairs-sponsored publication, *Te Ao Hou*. (So was Patricia Grace but it was some years before she and I met.) Witi says he noticed me because of my clothes. I'd gone back to making statements with what I wore. This time it was a large squashy peaked leather hat, a mini and thigh-high white boots. 'How could I resist you?' Witi has said more than once.

We ended the weekend, sitting on the street with our feet in the gutter, talking with Tony Taylor and a number of young writers, including the playwright Robert Lord, all swearing undying allegiance to each other. When Witi has signed my books over all the years since that day, he has written, 'Darling, we are hitched to the same star.' In another year or two, he would make literary history by becoming the first Maori writer to publish a book of fiction, the short story collection, *Pounamu, Pounamu.* I was at the award ceremony when he was presented with third prize in the Wattie Book Awards, sponsored by the tinned fruit company magnate Sir James Wattie. Sir James came from the Gisborne area, as did Witi. 'Ah,' said Sir James, 'a lot of your people work for me, Mister, Mister er...'

'Ihimaera,' Witi finished for him. 'It's not hard, Sir James, it has the same number of syllables as Even Stevens.' Even Stevens was the name of Sir James's racehorse.

A quick wit, and a quietly subversive radical—that was how I knew Witi from the beginning. Before long, we were spending a lot of time with him and his wife Jane. Witi introduced me to another of his friends, Ian Cross, author of the phenomenally successful novel *The God Boy,* and recently appointed editor of the *Listener.* Ian was a big bear of a man, with bushy iron-grey hair, an infectious smile and a steely determination. He was used to getting his way. When I met him, he was seeking to put together a group of new talent on the magazine, and had noticed my work. He offered me a job as the magazine's television reviewer, on alternating weeks with Roger Hall. We started at roughly the same time that Rosemary McLeod began a weekly column and Tom Scott became the regular cartoonist and political commentator.

If I had quailed at the public exposure resulting from my plays, it was nothing compared with this. My photograph appeared at the top of my column and people in the street began to accost me to tell me how much they disagreed with something I'd said. I invoked a great deal of wrath for not liking a show Julie Andrews appeared in. A woman behind the counter of a department store refused to sell me a pair of stockings on the strength of my remarks. I decided to be nicer, although that was not really what the column needed. Cross by turn nurtured, cajoled and bullied us into doing our best work and, when we didn't, we would be invited into his office 'for a chat'.

One day he invited me in for a chat of a different kind. He had another idea up his sleeve for me. He was also the national president of the writers' organisation, PEN (NZ Centre), and he needed a secretary. PEN was riding high at the time. A year earlier, the group had persuaded Norman Kirk, Prime Minister of the third Labour government, to introduce an Authors' Lending Right (known as the Authors' Fund). This made New Zealand the first country in the English-speaking world to acknowledge that writers should be compensated for the free use of their books in libraries, in lieu of lost royalties on conventional retail sales. Cross, with Neva Clarke McKenna, had been largely instrumental in convincing Kirk.

PEN was (and still is) an organisation set up as an international voice on behalf of writers imprisoned or denied freedom of speech, but the New Zealand group was more focused on local writers' issues than most countries. There were not enough writers to make up the number for multiple organisations to defend what might otherwise be considered trade union issues.

As well as the Authors' Fund issue, Cross was keen to expand the New Zealand PEN Centre's role, actively seeking to instigate a separate Writers' Guild for media writers. There was plenty of work to be done. When he decided I would be ideal as PEN's secretary I agreed, not exactly with alacrity, but with a good deal of gratitude for my spot in the *Listener.* I was eager to please after my recent downfall at university; thus are literary handmaidens born. I've been on a lot of committees in my time. I don't regret most of them, but I think there are times when it's worth taking stock and asking yourself if you are achieving anything useful. Writing and committees don't always go together.

To begin my task, I was handed a cardboard carton of papers containing a large thick minute book, members' records and piles of their correspondence. When I fished out a pile of letters from Frank Sargeson, Janet Frame and other notable writers, it occurred to me that they should be stored in a safe place, rather than run the risk of being blown down Willis Street in a Wellington gale. I began squirrelling away papers from PEN and later of other organisations. By the 1990s, it would run to forty cartons of paper. The Alexander Turnbull Library eventually took them all away to deposit and store properly.

The committee met every month in the boardroom of the New Zealand Council for Educational Research (NZCER) in Willis Street, furnished with a long blond wooden table, blue padded chairs and a blue carpet. Cross, whom we all privately dubbed 'the godfather', sat at the head of the table. The composition of the committee came and went, although a core group was there for some years. Among them were the poets Alistair Campbell, Lauris Edmond and Bill Manhire, the latter looking like an angelic child; Anne French, who really was just out of school, with thick plaits wound in ropes around her head; Sam Hunt, briefly, because 'meetings weren't really his thing, you know, not my thing', although he provided memorable venues for some of the annual parties; the educators Dr Clarence Beeby (Beeb, as he was known, a wily silver-tongued old fox) and Jack Shallcrass; historian Michael King; short story writer Rowley Habib; screenwriter Michael Noonan; and the lexicographer Harry Orsman, full of raucous, energetic wit. We felt like the centre of the universe. That was proving to be something of a problem, because writers in other centres, particularly Auckland, thought Wellington had too much say in what was supposed to be a national body. They were probably right—our committee got to choose who the representative was on the State Literary Fund that gave grants to writers, and to nominate judges for various prizes. You could say that the great Auckland-Wellington divide between writers began about that time.

The meetings carried on in Willis Street pubs like the Abel Tasman for hours after the business was completed. We were often joined by the poet Louis Johnson who, with Rarotongan-born Campbell, had been part of a major 1950s movement of Wellington writers that included James K. Baxter. Marilyn Duckworth and Jean Watson, writers who had inspired me in the past, frequently dropped by for a drink. Scratch the surface, we were all human. There was never enough time to tell each other all the stories of the moment, over jugs of beer and bottles of wine.

Lauris Edmond and I were each other's great discoveries in PEN. Lauris was a tall bony woman, with a mop of blonde curls that she insisted on having permed and coloured until she was an old woman. She could have been a bit of a blue-stocking in her appearance, except for the hair and a full sensual mouth with a subtle curve that made her face instantly charming when she smiled. When we met, she was forty-eight, had a recently completed MA, spoke fluent French and was the mother of six children, five girls and a son.

Despite the difference in our ages, we had a lot in common, although Lauris's accomplishments were different from mine, in several ways. I had now been publishing in one way or another for some years, while she was just beginning to publish poems in journals and magazines. She was the recently appointed editor of the *PPTA Journal,* the magazine of the Post Primary Teachers Association. Her husband, Trevor, had been chairman of the organisation a few years before, so we both had schoolteacher husbands, committed to their work. While Ian was making his mark in the world of special education, and was often away from home, either taking part in or conducting professional workshops, Trevor had been a school principal at a number of rural schools, where he was revered by students for his radical teaching methods. Lauris and I were more familiar with small town New Zealand than the city, so, in each other's company, that experience began to seem like an adventure to share. For a long time our desire to become recognised writers, and our absorption in common histories of rural life, children and marriage, outweighed our differences.

Lauris and Trevor lived in Upper Hutt, nearly an hour's drive from town, so we would meet at the Western Park Tavern in Thorndon, to drink gin and tonic or brandy and soda at two o'clock in the afternoon; we felt it sophisticated. We were hugely preoccupied by the nature of love. We talked incessantly about our futures as writers, about publication, about the women's movement that was beginning to powerfully engage us. I had had close friendships before, but nothing like this in its intensity. Some days we linked arms in the street, and said things like '*What*would we do without each other?' All in all, we were on the brink of a friendship that would last for twenty-eight years, one that would rage up and down, come apart and be stitched together again, but that held fast until Lauris died.

And, just writing that made me stop what I was doing as a shiver passed through me, although it is such a blue Mediterranean day. Even though I'm living the past, in order to write about it, it has nudged me so hard today, that for the moment it is as if it is happening now, here in the Katherine Mansfield Room at Villa Isola Bella, where I come so often to work. Lauris actually lived here in this room.

After Luc Lanlo gave me the keys to the room in April, we came round here and I saw it for the first time. This house where Mansfield lived in 1920 is in Garavan, right on the Italian border. If you come by train, you walk down Rue Webb Ellis (William Webb Ellis was the man said to have invented rugby), turn left under the bridge, then hard right up Chemin Fleuri. Or, from the bus route, get off and walk up rue Katherine Mansfield. And here it is. Mansfield lived in the top two storeys of the house, which are owned separately from this room down below. I haven't met the mysterious residents above, who enter by a separate gate.

The room faces the railway lines, and beyond it you see the sea. In order to enter the white courtyard that separates the room from the road, I open a big wrought-iron gate, then pass through a second heavy door. I have to jiggle the key around a bit—the lock is not always easy to undo—then I'm inside the room. The walls are pale and creamy; there is silvery fluorescent lighting that flickers beneath the ceiling. Above the desk where I am sitting hangs a portrait of Katherine Mansfield and, alongside that, a sculpture of her head. There is nothing much else on the walls. A big red divan takes up one side of the room. It is very comfortable—you could sleep on it if you wished—and around at the back there is a bathroom, although living in the room is not encouraged, as the locals don't care for it. On your right, as you enter, stands a cabinet with drawers. Inside these is an assortment of odds and ends that show traces of those who *have* bedded down here: a blanket, a tiny gas burner, a frying pan with a folding handle, a bicycle pump. There is a table with a basket for fruit and some wine glasses.

On the left stands a big bookcase containing books by all of the thirty-five writers who have been here before me. It is a tradition to leave your books here, as well as ones you have been reading, because it's not easy getting your hands on English language books in Menton. They provide clues and links. Don De Lillo's *Underworld*—that had to be Ian Wedde last year. But who was reading Updike's *S,* and where did this or that collection of poems come from? Lauris's collection, *The Pear Tree,* is here, along with some other of her works. Fitting, I think, because these poems, mostly for her daughter Rachel, who died soon after I met Lauris, are to do with the central drama of her life, and how it was played out over all the years we knew each other.

When she wrote about the room, as almost everyone who comes here does, she noted in her diary, 'leaves across the windows—flax, good green New Zealand flax, at one, palm leaves like green fingers spread out at the other'.

I've never been able to find any flax; I guess the Menton summers, the heatwaves like the one we are experiencing now, have burnt up any New Zealand plants that might have been here. It was a long time ago that Lauris reported on the flax bushes, but the rest is all as it was then.

She also wrote of the room: 'There is no past and no future, only this island in time, light as a bubble and shining with rainbow colours'. She was right about this. How did I get so far from my own history, and when did I begin to reinvent myself?

Back in Wellington, perhaps, in the early 1970s, when I still had energy to burn, and at that time when she and I saw the adventures of our lives still unfurling before us.

Anyway, she was here this morning, saying my name with the breathy inflection on the second syllable that always meant she had some important piece of information to impart.

And it was from this room that Lauris would write me letters that began the process of mending a breach that had occurred between us some years before.

Chapter 14

So much work in all directions, I hardly knew which way to turn. Ian and I were leading erratic unpredictable lives. We would be flush with money one week and broke the next. But the house was beginning to take shape and we could start inviting friends to visit. And there were plenty of those. We were rapidly becoming party animals. Like me, Ian was developing his own trendy look: long sideburns, a white polo-neck jersey worn with a burgundy-coloured suit with flared trousers. We thought we were pretty hot.

Naenae College had its own circle, and soon we became part of their crowd as Ian's career flourished. His approach to teaching was strongly influenced by Beeb and Jack Shallcrass; now he had access to them and they were willing mentors. His community approach had won him friends and support from parents. Before long, he was invited up and down the country to give talks and lead seminars on the methods he was developing. A young film producer called Dave Gibson made a short documentary film, his first ever, about Ian. The school's guidance counsellor, Russell Bernstone, and his wife became close friends. They had children close in age to ours, which was a bonus, because we could do things together that included the kids.

We were also hanging out with the Littlefairs. Gordon was a Richard Burton-like character, in both voice and appearance, who claimed to be Welsh, although there was some doubt about where he really came from. His younger wife, Alison, was slim, prematurely grey, with a vibrant personality, and a great hostess. The Littlefairs' parties swarmed with trade union people, seamen like Bill 'Pincer' Martin, Bill Anderson, Gerry Evans and Press Gallery journalists. Some nights we put the children to bed there and stayed until the dawn came up. I remember us sitting looking out over the harbour as the first fingers of light touched the sky, and Gordon played *Finlandia* at full blast, the music rolling and billowing around us. We were all drunk (except for Ian), elated, emotional.

Another night there was a party at our house when Robin Dudding left *Landfall,* after an unhappy split with Caxton Press in Christchurch, and gathered up his family of six children, taking them up to Auckland to live. En route, he and Lois stayed over at our house, children asleep on mattresses in every available corner of the house. Witi and Jane, some of the *Listener* crowd and other writers who had grown close to Robin, gathered round.

I had particular reason to thank Robin. He had now published several of my stories, including the first in the long Bethany Dixon sequence. Bethany was a kind of alter ego of mine, an earthy disorganised woman who lived in a provincial town, separated from her husband, reading books, randomly falling in love and pleasing herself about what she did, something like the existence I had had in that last strange summer in Rotorua. She grew out of an image that had flashed before me as I drove away from the town with Ian, on our way south: Bethany, in the first story, sits on a verandah, breast-feeding a baby, surrounded by the leaves of a grapevine, her face turned to the sun. It was hard to explain where that came from, even to myself, but I think she represented a time of having children, being an ordinary young mother, not someone always pressuring herself to be this other person, this writer. Over the years, I came to recognise Bethany as the woman I might have been had I stayed. What I had yearned to leave, I sometimes wanted to go back to.

Now I did have some friends around town, although they didn't resolve all my problems. In the weekends, when Ian was home, if we weren't going out somewhere, or working on the house, I hung out with Rena, drinking her sherry, or with Carole. I wasn't surprised to learn that Carole's marriage was breaking up. Her husband had found the pressure of an autistic child difficult to cope with, and left her with the three boys. Our friendship seemed to be based on comforting each other, and helping with each other's children. And there might have been a hint of Carole in Bethany Dixon too. I followed

Bethany's life through fiction for more than a quarter of a century until her own book, *The House Within,* was published in 1997 and I was finally able to let her go. But, unlike Carole, Bethany was a survivor.

My mental health seemed to be on a permanent knife edge so I sought help for depression from David Minnitt, the local Hataitai doctor. He was a tall solidly built and quite plain man, yet he had a presence. He had come to medicine late, after a life in which hunting and shooting featured a lot, although, as I would later learn, he also had a deep love of good paintings and antique Oriental artefacts. David listened sympathetically, then prescribed tranquillisers. I was grateful at the time. I had no idea how addictive they were. Booze and pills—you could live a pretty high life on those. I met his wife Leigh, thirty years David's junior. She sometimes worked at the practice rooms, but at the time she was finishing her degree, so she was at university most of the time. Leigh's brown eyes held a wicked gleam; she had pale creamy skin and a brilliant thick mane of nasturtium-coloured hair. I've written about it more than once. She dressed with care, in the crisp linen style that made you wonder if she carried an iron in her handbag. Some days, under the careful make-up I detected smudgy shadows of tiredness. She danced attendance on her husband, ensuring that his life was comfortable, more like a servant than a wife, which was surprising, given that she was such a feisty woman in other aspects of her life.

Later, Leigh began work at the NZCER, so we came to see a lot of each other when I attended the PEN meetings. We would have a sly gin and tonic before I went off to take notes. She and David were well known in liberal circles, particularly supporting abortion law reform. Abortions were so nearly unobtainable in New Zealand that women travelled to Australia for them.

Leigh was one of a group of women who formed the Wellington group Sisters Over Seas (SOS), to help poor and desperate women from rural areas get to Australia. As well as helping with finance, SOS provided beds before and after their flights to Sydney. The pregnant women went out on the 6a.m. flight and returned at midnight, red-eyed and exhausted, minus their babies. I was drawn into this group and for a time had women to stay on their way back and forth across the Tasman. Various women were associated with the pro-abortion movement in some way, people like Di Cleary, Dr Carol Shand and Adrienne Morgan-Lynch, who became a close friend of mine, and of Leigh.

Around this time I was with Ian and the children at Wellington Railway Station seeing off a friend on the overnight train to Auckland. I saw a Maori girl asleep on a bench, her feet drawn up under her knees, shoes off, one hand clutching her bushy hair. She reminded me of my childhood friend Topsy, though it wasn't her. As we stood on the platform, the train ready to leave, a young man leaned out of a carriage door. He called out, 'Queenie, Queenie,' and, in response, the sleeping girl woke and rushed along the platform. She stopped by the carriage door and a conversation took place.

They looked like brother and sister. I watched the young man encouraging her to board the train. For a moment she considered it, then, undecided, she stepped back. He stretched forward to take her hand, the doors closed, she leapt at them but it was too late. She rolled over on the platform and picked herself up. Then a group of young people strolled along towards her, as the train pulled away. The girl didn't look back, but there was something lost in her face.

    Immediately I got home, I sat down and wrote a short story called 'New Shoes for Old', about a young man from the Far North who comes looking for his missing sister in Wellington: Bernard Gadd published the story in an anthology called *My New Zealand* in 1972 and, the same year, I dramatised it as a radio play for Arthur, this time calling it *Search for Sister Blue.*

> My name is Heta Rakete, me and my family are from up north ... I knew Mum would not be singing today. Every day this thing would happen between me and my father. At half past eleven we would

finish work for the morning and go up to the house real slow, pretending to each other that we weren't waiting for anything special, like say, Abe, in the rural delivery van, but when you're like us, a real family living close to each other, you know when people are pretending. And this is how it had been since my sister Queenie went away to the big city. In the first few months, there'd been some letters now and then, so it didn't matter when we said, very casual, 'Any mail today Mum?' because there just might have been. But that seemed a long time ago...

Heta finds Queenie only as he is about to leave, and the scene between them is played out much as I had witnessed the encounter at the railway station.

This is another of those stories where the narrator watches people as they leave on a journey. Sometimes when people ask me how to find ideas for their writing, I tell them they could do worse that spending time observing people saying hello and goodbye. One of the pictures I carry in my head is of a girl at the international airport, here in Wellington, clutching a huge heart-shaped balloon inscribed with the words 'I LOVE YOU' floating on a string above her head, and a red rose in her hand. After about a half-hour wait, her young man emerged from customs, and they threw themselves into each other's arms. The whole crowd waiting in the concourse burst into applause. The couple blinked and smiled. It was pure Hollywood.

Search for Sister Blue drew strongly on my time in the North, which still exerted a powerful hold over me. I often found myself in those early years in Wellington yearning for what now appeared the simple, more idyllic life I had grown up with. Of course, for the most part, it had been little of the kind. But the play brought together elements of those settings, my friendship with Topsy, with whom I had lost touch long ago, as well as the hours spent at St Faith's church in Ohinemutu.

I hoped to get scriptwriting work on the second series of a television drama series called *Pukemanu.* A year or so had passed since my prize for *Green Apples and a Jug,* which was, in fact, never produced. *Pukemanu,* devised by Julian Dickon, was set in a fictitious milling town in the Central North Island; the hub of the town's social life was the pub. The idea of writing about rural life, and characters who were mainly Maori, appealed to me. Actor Tama (aka Tom) Poata, whom I had met and was encouraging of my work, played a lead role in *Pukemanu.* The first series had been a major critical success, and seemingly set Julian on his feet.

All the scripts on the first series of *Pukemanu* were written, produced and directed by men and I sensed a growing culture of big money and male control in the industry. There didn't seem to be much room for women in the dawning new age of television drama in New Zealand. Nor, after his initial success, did it seem to have much room for Julian, who still lived in the country.

Word filtered back to me that I was considered Bill and Arthur's 'pet', who got all the work in radio drama. I heard, in a roundabout way, that I needn't expect to get a slice of the television pie. It probably didn't help that I was a television critic, although Ian Cross had by then moved me to radio reviewing. Arthur's view was that my writing worked for radio, and I kept to deadlines, which made his life simpler. I picked up a fair bit of work finishing projects which other of his writers had failed to complete. I was quick at adaptation work and turned a number of New Zealand novels into serial plays, including Noel Hilliard's *A Piece of Land* and Karl Stead's *Smith's Dream.* The latter, I turned into a four-part serial. I wanted to change the ending because it would have been difficult on radio to follow Smith's interior monologue without having someone else in the scene. When I contacted Karl to see if he minded, he said it didn't bother him at all. This was the second of the three endings the book had, as Roger Donaldson came up against similar problems when he turned the book into the movie *Sleeping Dogs,* although he came up with a different solution again.

The writers who felt threatened by the work put my way need not have worried about Bill Austin's role in the matter. He dropped dead of a heart attack in the street, a few minutes after leaving a doctor's surgery where he had been told that he was in his best health for years. I rang Arthur that morning around about eleven with a query. 'Austin signed off that contract of yours first thing this morning,' he said, in his best, clipped BBC accent. 'Died since then.'

Arthur began to fade almost as soon as Bill had gone; his heart didn't seem to be in the work any more. He asked me to take over a WEA (Workers' Educational Association) writing class that he ran. This seemed absurd, given that I considered myself still a beginner writer. My knees knocked the first night I faced the group, but they seemed to like what I had to say, and some of them remain friends to this day. It was Frances Cherry's first night at a creative writing class too, on the other side of the desk. She continues to publish books and teach. For me, this was the beginning of nearly twenty-seven years of teaching writing.

Arthur asked me then if I could write a serial based on an aspect of New Zealand history, which people seemed 'pretty interested in' these days. I knew very little about our past and couldn't think where to begin. Then it came to me. I suggested the story of Norman McLeod and Waipu to Arthur, who was delighted and promptly presented me with another six-part series contract. Apart from the fleeting trip for Jen's wedding, I hadn't been back to Waipu for eighteen years. I decided to go back there and talk to people about the migrations. Ian had come to accept that I needed to travel from time to time to do research, which proved fairly arduous in several respects because I didn't have real skills, although the years of writing feature articles had taught me how to ask questions. I took these trips during school holidays so that someone was home for the children. I think they enjoyed having their father to themselves. And I had developed a passion for travelling through the countryside, staying in small town cheap block wall motels with rooms smelling of antiseptic to mask old tobacco and people smells. I liked the anonymity, the sense of being an outsider looking and listening in.

    I went up north by bus in August:
One stark cabbage tree, fifteen hundred
above sea level, black
mists and driving rain, then
the long run down from the top of Brynderwyn
to the flat plains of the Braigh.
I rode into town on a Road Services bus,
Like the heroine of some Western movie,
The unknown stranger, who yet knew all.

It was deep winter, and the rain stayed with me for most of the trip. On the first morning, during a break between the showers, I took the long white road to the cemetery beside the sea. I felt that if I could get close to 'the Man' I might find out how to begin my task. The local gravedigger, who helped me to find the grave, had been there since I was a girl. We called him

'Clark Gable'; he lived in a shack surrounded by a collection of bottles and rags that he traded in. Nothing had changed. McLeod's headstone and the rusty iron palings were almost covered by rough scrub and paspalum, the moss-encrusted letters nearly indecipherable.

As I wandered around the headstones, looking at inscriptions that included details of the journeys, I was overwhelmed by a sense of what it must feel like to cross the world, knowing that you would never return. Like my great-great-grandmother at Brora. And, for the first time, I had an inkling of what grieved my father, and why 'home' seemed so far away.

I stayed for a week in the local hotel, and even there, I felt much like a stranger. Time spent at the excellent museum in the main street was profitable; in the evenings I read what literature there was available about the migrations, and fielded calls in my room from the gumboot tribe, who thought I might like to join them for a drink in the bar. Among the women I met in the village were girls I had gone to school with. They lived mostly on farms and had different lives from mine. They couldn't understand what I was doing there, living in the hotel and prowling about, and I was beginning to wonder too. Then I was rescued by Jen's father, Jim Gates, such a friend of my youth, who took me to meet Misses Myra and Hilda Lang, the last surviving Gaelic speakers in the community. They lived at Lang's Beach, in a weathered house overlooking the sea, delightful, sharp-witted old women, eager to tell me as many stories as they could, often with laughter and tears, over many cups of tea.

I returned also to the house of Kitty Slick, more dilapidated and tumbledown than when I left. The front door swung open, hanging by a single hinge. Inside were signs that animals had taken shelter downstairs. But upstairs, little had changed. This time, I collected some fragments of the newspapers covering the walls. I have them still. I stood at a window and looked out across the paddocks. The dark macrocarpa tree outside brushed against the wall. In my head I was asking myself questions, the old 'what if' ones that overtake writers now and then.

What if I had been the woman who lived here?

What would it be like to be absolutely alone at night, with nothing but the sound of that tree rubbing against the wall?

Would I have known that some people in the valley called me 'the witch'? Would I have looked up and seen me passing in the school bus when I was a girl?

I remember how cold it was, on that dull foggy afternoon. Perhaps, I found myself thinking, it is not madness or wickedness to be on your own, to be an independent thinker. The atmosphere of the place had taken hold of me. I knew I could write the play now, but I also knew that whatever I wrote, it would not be enough, that I had only touched one stage of the journeys from Nova Scotia. I wanted to know what the other places looked like, how the food tasted, the feel of old fabrics under my fingertips, what scents would be delivered on a spring breeze. When I wrote *Fire of the North,* the series

Arthur had commissioned, I understood that it was only the beginning, that I would, if I could, go to the other side of the world and find out more.

By the time I delivered the series, Arthur was very ill, and on the point of retirement. The serial was produced by a new young talent, John O'Leary, who loved the serial and gave it a beautiful quality sound, full of bagpipes and laments. Listeners loved it and it went on to play another three times.

I did end up with a television contract for *Pukemanu,* an episode called 'Who Needs Enemies'. Straight away the script came in for criticism from the editors for not being 'tough enough' and I finished up cowriting with Michael Noonan. Despite these rumblings, it seemed a great time to be in the thick of making television. We were filming in the old Waring Taylor studios in downtown Wellington; they were tiny, cramped and makeshift. The pub was the only static set, with barely room to turn around in. The rest of the sets were built and pulled down as fast as scenes were shot.

In my episode a couple was quarrelling in the pub. The wife, played by Glenis Levestam, had to say the line, 'Oh, for God's sake, Maurice.' The actors couldn't get this scene right, and because the set had to be changed first thing in the morning, it was filmed over and over again, throughout the night. Around about three in the morning, Glenis screamed, 'Oh, for Christ's sake, Maurice.' Take, shouted the director, it's in the can. 'For Christ's sake' was one of the forbidden expressions on air. When the show screened, I had the dubious distinction of being credited with introducing the term into broadcasting. There were howls of moral outrage, and I received a quantity of hate mail, the kind that comes unsigned in red and green ink.

It was in the green room during filming of *Pukemanu* that I came across a job advertisement in the newspaper: a group calling itself the New Zealand Book Council wanted a paid part-time secretary, for twenty hours a week. I looked at it, and wondered. I found the reviews, my only regular work, hard going: I didn't seem to have the stamina of the long distance columnist. And I had had hints that Ian Cross was beginning to feel I was compromised by continuing to work in radio and television; to an extent he was right. A regular half-time income would allow me to work on media projects I cared about, like *Fire of the North,* and let the columns go.

Around that time, several problems in my extended family were beginning to raise their head. In Rotorua, my parents' health was failing. You could say that my father had always enjoyed ill-health. As the years went by, he became increasingly absorbed by his ailments, real or imagined. Unless you had ten minutes to hear the answer, it was dangerous to ask him how he was. Now some of the illnesses were real and he had several trips to hospital. My mother was also sick with the acute rheumatoid arthritis that would dog her for the rest of her life. She, too, had long spells in Queen Elizabeth, the lakefront hospital that specialised in rheumatology. My father became helpless during the weeks when she was away.

As if that wasn't enough, the aunts and uncles had begun to die over the space of three years. I visited Margaret, the oldest one, with the quick tongue and acerbic manner, at her home south of Auckland when she was dying of lung cancer. She stood at the gate, a crumpled little figure, and said, 'I don't want to die, Fiona.' I didn't believe she would, I thought her indestructible. But she did.

Stewart would be the next. I didn't know this uncle as well as the rest of the family. He and his wife and my cousin Catherine lived on another family property that had survived the Depression in better shape than my grandfather's farm up the East Coast. At his funeral in Marton, I discovered the family cemetery where my mother's forebears lie, all the way back to my great-great-grandparents who came out on the *Oriental*. They lie together in this quiet cemetery that we reached after the cortège had wound through hills and valleys to the farm gate. Over the years since, I have gone there when I could, always meaning to take flowers but usually ending up plucking some rusty hydrangeas from the roadside to lay on my grandmothers' graves.

Then my beloved oddball Aunt Roberta died. She left me everything she possessed in the world: about eighty dollars, some silver vases, a gold bracelet she had had made out of strands of my grandmother's watch chain, other odds and ends purloined from family houses she had stayed in over the years, plus a sealed trunk that turned out to contain dozens of pairs of spectacles and many half-filled syringes of morphine. They must have come from hospitals where she worked. Jean and I stamped on them on her concrete driveway, before disposing of the evidence. Roberta had also left me all her diaries, only Jean had burnt them by the time I arrived to collect them—'I didn't think you'd want that old rubbish.' I had no reply to that.

I drove backwards and forwards to my family in all weathers, including snow and black ice across the Desert Road, when I was needed. Sometimes I took the children; often I went alone.

The experience with the Max Harris tour was in my mind when I went for my interview for the Book Council job. I was sure if I could do that, I could do this job, and I was hungry for it. I was interviewed by one of the prime movers in the new organisation, the bookseller Roy Parsons. He was a shrewd little man with a pointed goatee beard, his head constantly wreathed in cigarette smoke, an Englishman who had emigrated some years earlier and founded a left-wing bookshop off Lambton Quay. The New Zealand Book Council had been set up by the New Zealand Booksellers Association as a response to the UNESCO-inspired International Book Year in 1972. Its purpose was to link booksellers, publishers, writers, educators and librarians, to discuss and act upon book-related issues of common interest. The council also planned to reach disadvantaged readers through its activities, as well as pursuing the more commercial strategy of increasing interest in books and attracting higher sales. I have never had a problem with this concept: New Zealand needs a self-sustaining book sector if its literature is to survive.

At the interview, I was asked to comment on matters like this and I surprised myself with some of the suggestions I came up with. The practical side of me enjoys problem solving. The board had already committed itself to follow a research project called Operation Book Flood, which the appointed person would manage, to see how children in low-decile schools would respond to a large injection of books into the school; an academic study had been commissioned to analyse the results. I proposed that it might also be worth starting a Writers in Schools programme and that, to encourage adult interest in books, we could have more events where writers and readers met each other.

Roy nodded his head with increasing enthusiasm. He decided I would do for the job, although he was right to be anxious about my very rudimentary knowledge of bookkeeping, acquired in my teens in tractor garages. In this respect, he turned out to be a wise and patient counsellor.

In order to highlight its activities, the council invited one of the country's most distinguished historians to head it. This was Professor (later Sir) Keith Sinclair from Auckland University. Others on the board included Beeb, Patrick Macaskill, John Watson and David Wylie.

Keith swept into my life and changed the way I looked at the world. He was a short man, always seeming as if he were balancing on the balls of his feet, with a nervous twitchy energy that he could barely contain. His hair was a bushy grey mane, he had prominent intensely brown eyes that turned liquid over a bottle of red wine—and there were a great many of those—a swarthy complexion, a gold filling gleaming in one of his front teeth. Keith, a poet as well as an historian, was the first academic to sit down and talk seriously about my writing. My qualifications were never an issue; he'd read my work and treated me like a real writer from the start. We talked and talked—about writing, about how to run the Book Council—and he told me endless stories about himself, his family and New Zealand history, for he was nothing if not a raconteur. These conversations usually took place over lunch before the council's board meetings, at the old Woolshed restaurant on Plimmer's Steps, below Book House where the council met and I had my office. The Woolshed was a big pretentious barn of a place, the haunt of politicians, journalists and people who liked to be seen. In our case it was simply handy to work, but we were soon regulars there. By the time we headed to the office at two o'clock, we would both have drunk a fair bit of rough red and the meetings were often raucous affairs.

A number of eminent women, around my age, have told me similar stories about their friendships with Keith. If you were part of his charmed circle it was hard not to be half in love with him. He was a man who enjoyed the company of women, and liked to impress them. But he was also generous in the way he mentored them. In my case, he offered serious education in how to make sense of research material. When we first met he was writing a biography of Walter Nash, a former Labour prime minister. Nash had been an inveterate hoarder of papers, right down to bus tickets, and his vast collection was stored in an old warehouse in Vivian Street. Sometimes I would go down there with Keith, and he would show me the material he was working on.

Why would you study a bus ticket? I might ask. He would look at me sternly. A bus ticket, he declared, could tell you a great deal about a prime minister. Look at the date, the destination. Why was the Prime Minister of New Zealand going there, at that time, on that day? These were clues and fragments of history that I must learn to read if I wanted to unlock the secrets of lives, both public and private. These were the details that mattered. The technique served me well when I came to write historical fiction. Don't invent, until the truth is exhausted.

Ian and Keith seemed to enjoy each other's company, and sometimes, when Keith's new wife, Raewyn Dalziel, was in town, the four of us would head off for dinner or in search of company, which Keith loved. Other times, he and

I would set out together, looking for a party, disaster always at our elbow. He had a poor sense of direction and was afraid of the dark. We would go searching for parties in Wellington's hillside suburbs, Keith assuring me that he knew the way to the address, though he hardly ever did. These situations often ended in panic and finding a taxi, when it turned out the destination was only half a block away.

Another hazard of friendship with Keith was that he was frequently followed by the Secret Intelligence Service (SIS). Even though Labour was in power and Norman Kirk the prime minister, instructions lodged by the former National government weren't expunged by a change in power. A 'pinko' historian doing research on Nash, down Vivian Street, a trade union haunt and place of ill-repute in more ways than one, was definitely considered a threat to national security. The spies were particularly concerned because they had learnt that among the papers Keith had stored in the warehouse were some files about Dr William Sutch, a senior civil servant who, in 1975, was prosecuted, and subsequently acquitted, for allegedly passing official information to a Soviet diplomat. Nash had kept information that was supposed to be returned to the SIS. It was a particularly sensitive period and there was almost invariably someone on our tail. You could tell the 'spooks' easily: they were almost laughably stereotyped in their black suits, with briefcases and rolled newspapers in hand. Keith knew who they were anyway, but just sometimes they seemed a bit close for comfort. One afternoon, at the airport, Keith's bag fell open, spilling papers all over the place. You could almost feel the collective surge of the men in black.

Keith's *Walter Nash* was published by Oxford University Press in November 1976, and launched at Parliament. Keith signed the book 'With love to Fiona and Ian Kidman' and then Bill Rowling (briefly a Labour prime minister) and John (Jack) Marshall (prime minister for a short time for National), who were standing alongside, offered to sign it too. Rob Muldoon, by then the incumbent prime minister, stood glowering in a corner. We didn't offer the book to him. We should have, perhaps, but you had the feeling he wanted to be the only prime minister in the room.

With all these people filling the spaces in my life, my concept of friendship began to change. You could love friends, care about them as you did members of your family. And close friends could be men. This had never occurred to me before. Men were people women thought of as 'mates' or boyfriends, potential lovers, husbands—and brothers, though I hadn't any experience of these. But friends? That was different, and I liked the new dimension it brought to what one could talk about, laugh over, gossip about.

Witi. Keith. Alison. Leigh. Later, Sharon Crosbie. Michael King. Lauris. These were the people I loved then, the people I think of when I recall Wellington in the 1970s. I loved our passionate exchanges, the conversations, the causes we believed in. Several of them have died. There are days when I would like to be able to reach back in time and bring them back, just to carry on where we left off our last conversation. I have only to sit quite still for a moment in this room here in Menton, and I hear one or other of them.

Chapter 15

For a long time I had been drawn to poetry. I kept bumping my shins against it, even though there wasn't much around in my early years, not even at the library. But, although it's easy to dismiss my education, here and there, teachers like Terence Buxton and Eileen O'Shea had made a difference. Frank Gee, at Rotorua Boys' High, and Max Harris from Australia had wanted to talk about poetry. Before I left Rotorua I came across the work of American poets Elizabeth Bishop and Louise Bogan. It was Kit who mentioned Bogan to me, the last summer before I left the town. Still inconsolable about the loss of Len, she had turned to poetry, surprising herself, because she had always preferred fiction. Bogan's work has never been widely discussed in New Zealand, or not so far as I know, but I liked her spareness, her understanding of form and design, her plangent female voice, which spoke in quite formal ways about the nature of love and the difficulty of being a woman artist. I liked the intensity with which she described coming across the idea of writing poetry herself, in her mother's hospital room, where a vase of marigolds had offered her an exact image of light and contrast. She believed, too, that women had to help themselves rather than expect to be rescued.

When I arrived in Wellington, I began to meet poets but, before that, in the first months when I had felt so isolated, I began searching the library shelves for a wider range of books. Wellington Public was a satisfying hunting ground, crammed with good collections. I began to discover New Zealand poets, never a good topic with Kit, who thought Baxter 'a frightful man', whose books she wouldn't have in her library. I came across Robin Hyde's work and instantly fell in love. Her poem 'Words' struck a great chiming chord:

> *But I tell you this, I,*
> *Who have shaped my word while the fools have bungled ten,*
> *Words should be hard old lamps, and white of wick,*

And the right flame rises then.

I once went to a Bethune's rare book auction and spent most of a month's housekeeping acquiring all the first editions of her poems. Then I met Keith, and he was a poet. His collection, *The Firewheel Tree,* had just been published and he was full of pleasure at having won for it the Jessie Mackay Prize for the Best Book of Poetry. He quoted whole poems over lunch, and later sent me some new pieces. Suddenly there were poets all around me and I began to dabble with the possibilities of writing poetry too. I sent some to Keith in response to his; he liked them and persuaded me to send them off to *Landfall.* By the time I met Lauris, I had begun to call myself a poet too.

Irene Adcock, the mother of Fleur Adcock and Marilyn Duckworth, had started a Poetry Society that met at her house, and later at the old Settlement café in Willis Street. There was a gallery upstairs where the meetings were held, and the gatherings just got bigger and bigger, with poets coming from all over the country to read their work. Then there were gatherings at Battle Hill, where Sam Hunt lived with his partner Kristen Wickens. He had had a celebrated sojourn in a boatshed at Pauatahanui, in an inlet he renamed Bottle Creek, for all the obvious reasons to do with his celebrated drinking habits. Now, further round the inlet, he and Kristen lived in a huge creaking old farmhouse. We had first grown close to Sam and Kristen when they lived directly across from us in Rakau Road. Kristen was expecting a baby, and on Sunday evenings the couple often ate at our house with the family. Lauris, Alistair Campbell, Rachel McAlpine, Marilyn Duckworth, a whole host of us, gathered out there, overlooking the water, drinking apple cider and reciting poetry far into moonlit nights. At Sam's place, I first met Vincent O'Sullivan with whom, over the years, I have fallen into a close and easy friendship. His wit was so quick and rapier sharp that I was a little afraid of him; since then he has lost none of his wit but I have gained confidence. One night, when it got cold, Sam led a procession to light a bonfire of blazing logs in the paddocks. He presided over the proceedings, wearing his drainpipe pants, winkle pickers and colourful jerkins, his strange rasping voice exerting an odd magic over us all.

Later, I did some touring with Sam. He was still publishing books of poems, but performance was taking over his life, and I could see that his love of oratory, his affinity with landscape and the easy way he got on with people who weren't poets, were leading him away from the 'established' forms of poetry—for this, read the 'establishment'. I shared some of these views.

I also found myself in a disreputable scrape at a house where we stayed in Hawke's Bay. After the reading, there had been a gathering at a big elegantly appointed residence in the countryside where the poets and some artists were being billeted. As so often happened, it ended up with a few too creatively drunk people. I went off to sleep in the room allocated to me, a children's nursery decorated with murals and delicate chimes hanging from the ceiling, and containing two beds. Sometime later, I heard Sam's voice urgently whispering at the door. 'Fiona, Fiona, d'you mind, I mean, would you actually mind, Fiona, if I slept in the other bed, because I can't stand that drunk man in the room where I am. He's throwing up, throwing up, can't stand it.'

I said it was fine by me, and it was. In the morning, I woke and saw that the room was full of sunlight filtered through an oak tree at the window. Sam was lying in his bed reciting Dylan Thomas, and worked his way from there through several chapters of the Bible, and then some Yeats. It seemed peaceful and harmless, lying there listening to him.

At breakfast, the farmer's wife slammed down some tea and toast, her face stony. Her special displeasure was directed at me. I understood how offended she felt, and imagined her fumigating the room of evil before her children returned there to sleep. It seemed pointless to try and explain. Unintentionally, I had joined the ranks of badly behaved poets.

Through Lauris I became involved with Denis Glover's circle at the University Club in Featherston Street, although, as it happened, Denis and I had met earlier. Denis, and Allen Curnow in Auckland, were considered the two most distinguished living poets in New Zealand. In some ways, Glover had a touch of Max Harris in his history, with an early flowering of outrageous talent, strong left-wing views and a literary scandal to his name, plus a burning desire to change what he saw as the bland and pretty poetry of his time. But there the resemblance ended—with his frequent irritating put-downs of women's writing, it could hardly be said that he shared Harris's enthusiasm for female emancipation.

As a student at Canterbury University, Glover, along with Ian Milner, who was the editor, had produced the magazine *Oriflamme* in April 1933 and provoked widespread anger by publishing an essay by Patrick Robertson entitled 'Sex and the Undergraduate'. Later that year Glover was sacked from his student reporter job at *The Press*, Christchurch's daily newspaper, on account of the scandal. But print and poetry, not journalism, were Glover's passions. He collaborated in early printing press experiments with Bob Lowry, set up the Caxton Press and, after distinguished naval service in the Second World War, established *Landfall* with the support of a group of friends that included Rex Fairburn and James Bertram. He called on another friend, the high-minded poet Charles Brasch, a man of independent means, to be editor. Glover particularly loathed the poems published in *Best New Zealand Poetry*, the only major outlet when he began writing. At that time, Curnow was his long-time friend and they encouraged each other in this effort to establish a new literary environment. Glover saw to the publication of much of Curnow's early work. But once Glover had achieved his goal of providing this alternative forum, he succumbed to his alcohol addiction. At Caxton he had taken on a business partner, Dennis (Dinny) Donovan, the former office boy, who tired of Glover's drink-fuelled mismanagement and had him removed. Glover moved to Pegasus Press to work with sailing companion Albion Wright. Although the business relationship didn't last, the friendship did.

By the time I met Denis Glover, he had become a kind of godfather of New Zealand writing. Although much had changed at *Landfall* since Robin Dudding replaced Brasch as editor, and the scope of what constituted literary value had been more broadly redefined, it's fair to say that if you wanted to get a foothold in the literary periodicals, it helped to get along with Denis. The work I had already published in Noel Hoggard's *Arena* stood me in good stead. Hoggard and Denis were also colleagues.

When I got to know Denis, his friendship with Curnow had long since soured. I think an element of competitiveness had entered the relationship and that Curnow, with his own reputation, admirers and adherents, had overtaken his early mentor. Denis frequently spoke of Curnow with a snarl, as 'the parson up north'. (Curnow was the son of an Anglican vicar and, in his youth, had trained for the ministry too.) At Auckland University, Curnow had an academic career and respectability, while, in Wellington, Denis led a kind of swashbuckling vodka-fuelled life as writer and man about town. His curling red nose, constantly dribbling with snuff, almost met with the pointed tip of his upturned beard. He had a habit of addressing anyone young as 'my de-ah girl' or 'my de-ah boy'. Even if he was not overly sympathetic to women's writing, Denis did seek women's company. Certainly he liked Lauris, whom he chose to edit the letters of his contemporary, and great friend, the poet A.R.D. Fairburn, who had died in 1957. For myself, I often found Denis's habits disagreeable but I did like his hard, bleakly funny, often passionate work dedicated to the sea, landscape and men alone in the countryside, like the Arawata Bill and Mick Stimpson sequences. I found, on the whole, that I could forgive his worst behaviour, although from the outset I was tested by it.

My earlier encounter with him had been when Michael Frayn, renowned columnist, novelist and playwright, visited as part of my newly established

Meet the Author programme at the Book Council. The British Council had agreed to my request to fund Frayn to come to New Zealand en route to a speaking tour of Australia. Ian and I picked him up from Wellington airport in the Mini, after he had flown non-stop from England. He was so tall his knees almost touched his chin in the front seat of the car. The British Council had arranged a dinner in his honour only an hour or so after his arrival. Fortunately, he was young and resilient. We took him to his hotel to drop off his bags, before setting off for the residence in Oriental Terrace where the dinner was being held. I can't remember all the people who were there that night, perhaps not more than half a dozen local guests, including Denis and his wife Lyn, and about as many again of the British Council contingent. I don't know why Denis had gone, for he loathed the British and didn't mind saying so. It was probably just because he could never resist invitations of any kind. He was furiously drunk and made several anti-English jokes throughout dinner, not that he consumed much or any of it. You never really saw Denis eat, just extract his hip flask while others ate.

As we finished the meal, Denis glowered around him. 'Poms,' he shouted. 'Lily-livered *Poms.*'

Dessert was hurriedly cleared away and our hosts stood up. They nodded to each other, and as one, moved to some seats near a bay window overlooking the harbour. Apparently, there was an important cricket match on, and one of them produced a transistor radio. For the next hour or so they sat with their backs studiously turned towards the New Zealanders. And Michael Frayn. After one or two bewildered glances, Frayn had decided to throw in his lot with our end of the room. He could hardly contain his mirth as Denis ranted on. I've sometimes wondered whether he got some ideas for his later more farcical plays from that night. *Noises Off,* which I first saw in Halifax, Nova Scotia, and again in Wellington, remains one of the funniest plays I have ever seen. Around eleven o'clock, Lyn turned to Ian and me with a pleading look. Denis called her Pixie, and certainly she had the appearance of an elderly otherworldly creature, with big eyes and an urchin haircut. 'Please could you take us home,' she implored.

This was fine, except that we had promised Michael that we would return him to his hotel too. When we said we were leaving, our hosts nodded. Nobody budged from the transistor, and it was clear we weren't going to get any help there.

A long flight of steps leads from Oriental Terrace down to the Parade. There was nothing else for it. Ian and Michael picked Denis up, one on each side, and carried him down. They then poured him into the front seat of the car, and Lyn and I crawled into the back, me more or less sitting on Michael's knee, while Ian drove the Glovers home. At the other end, there was another flight of steps, so the two younger men carried Denis up those as well.

'Oh thank you, de-ah boys, thank you,' Denis managed, before he passed out.

In those days, I didn't know that some famous touring writers might expect special treatment. And famous Michael Frayn was, even then. He had already won the Somerset Maugham and Hawthornden Prizes. I am glad I didn't know, because we might have missed out on a wonderful and funny ten days with him. Sometimes when I see writers behaving like prima donnas at festivals, I think what a lot they miss out on. I have never believed in the cult of writer as super celebrity. Instead of being cloistered away, protected from the country he had come to visit, Michael tramped and sailed with Ian and his friends and often joined us in our barely restored house for meals at night. One day, Ian and David, one of Marjorie and John's extended family, took Michael on a tramp through the Orongorongos, and David played his recorder as they climbed.

During this stay, Michael took a plane trip up to Rotorua and stayed for a couple of days. I had to lend him some money for his fare, as a bank draft he was expecting hadn't come through, and the Book Council didn't have the funds to cover it. On the last night in Wellington, Michael gave a talk and then, with various invited guests, left for a party at the home of one of the university's leading academic lights. He had promised the money he owed me that evening, as I wouldn't be seeing him again. Assuming I was invited to the party, he allowed himself to be whisked away by his hosts in their car. As it turned out, I wasn't invited, but I followed him there anyway. The host wasn't pleased to see me. After some time, he said, 'I can take Mr Frayn to his hotel.'

'Stay,' Michael hissed at me. Comic he might have been, but he was also a gentleman. He wasn't, as he explained later, going to give me the money in public.

'I suppose you want another drink, do you?' the host enquired, in a chilling tone.

I could have left then, but I was worried about the money. 'I'll have a glass of water,' I said. 'If you don't mind.'

Eventually we left. 'Why did you do that?' I asked.

'I wasn't having a good time,' said Michael. 'You might have left me there with those dreadful people.' He was laughing so hard he could hardly stop as he counted out a handful of money. 'I so enjoyed the look on your face.'

I was buying vegetables at our corner greengrocer late one Friday afternoon, when I ran across Michael Noonan. Since Bill Austin died, Noonan had a role in commissioning scripts. I hadn't had any television work since *Pukemanu,* but I knew that Noonan and a producer called Tony Isaacs were commissioning a drama series called *Section Seven,* based around the probation service. I liked Michael and Tony, but although they both treated me with respect, television was rapidly being captured by other men I considered ruthless, self-seeking and hungry. I had been disappointed not to get a commission for this particular series because I was sure I could do a good job, and had an idea in mind. However, by this time I had been given to understand that the series was complete and about to be shot, so I had given up on it.

Over the silver beet and peaches, Michael asked me what I was up to. I said I was very busy, which was true. To my surprise, he asked me if I could write a play to fit the *Section Seven* series.

'How long have I got?'

'Till Monday morning,' he said. He filled me in on a few brief details, and walked off.

So that was that. I had two days to write a thirty-minute drama. I guessed that, somewhere along the way, an episode had fallen over. The idea I had was about a Pacific Island woman who is wrongly accused of a crime, and a female probation officer who becomes emotionally involved with the case. I didn't sleep over the weekend, but on Monday morning I was able to ring Michael and tell him that I had a play ready. The play was accepted; I was paid handsomely, and flown to Auckland shortly afterwards for the filming of 'They Called Her Elizabeth'. The lead role in the series was taken by London-based, New Zealand-born Ewen Solon, the Shakespearean actor who had been coached in his youth by the same

Terence Buxton who taught me at Northland College.

At the wrap party on the last night, Ewen said, 'You write terrific drama. Why don't you take yourself off to England? The BBC would snap you up. You could make a fabulous living.'

I explained that I had a husband and young family in Wellington.

'Well, tell them to shift too,' he said.

But by that time the die had long been cast.

It was a night of drama. The director had had a serious love affair with a beautiful young violinist, and this was their last evening together before she left for England. I found myself crying inconsolably with Tony on the back doorstep of the house where the party was being held. I had no real idea why at the time, but I suppose it was because life was full of choices, and some of them were hard, even the ones with obvious answers. Tony ordered a taxi for me and I made my way back to Niyaz's place in Remuera, where I was staying.

Niyaz had left Rotorua and her marriage some years before. Her life had been difficult since then, involving long separations from her son. Although she had felt like a captive in her marriage, her freedom had a bitter tinge to it. All the same, she had acquired an MA in political science and a teaching job in Auckland. We sat up until morning, talking about the way we led our lives and what to do about them. All around us, people's lives were falling into various states of disrepair.

Lauris's life was in turmoil and she was thinking of leaving Trevor. Ian and I were having less to do with the crowd at Naenae as damage spread among our friends. Several marriages had broken down, and others were on the brink. The parties we went to often had a tense atmosphere. I had become close to Alison Littlefair, but Gordon had a destructive personality. As well as making her life hard, he liked setting other couples up against each other, as if it were a sport. He had already told me that I wasn't worth Ian's time. There was a spectacular night at a house in Goldie's Brae, when Gordon was baiting an old friend of his from university days in England, throwing in some political angst along with the personal. Joe, a gentle pink-faced man, ended up with a plate of spaghetti on his head, the strands dripping down his shirt collar. I used that scene in a later novel, *True Stars.*

Could I have gone off to England to make my fortune? No. That was never the issue. But although I was working so hard, running in so many different directions at once, there was something I couldn't see, a contentment I couldn't put out my hand and touch.

As it happened, the deal from *Section Seven* couldn't have come at a better time. When I got back to Wellington, a call came from a neighbour two doors along the street. He and his wife were selling their house, and remembered, rather belatedly, that we had expressed interest in buying it if it ever came up for sale. They had actually moved out; the house was standing empty and an offer on it was due to close the following day. It was really just a courtesy call to cover their memory lapse, not an invitation to buy.

As I put the phone down, Ian and I looked at each other. Although we had made our house comfortable, I had never been happy there. I spent as much time as I could away from it. The total absence of sun was a major problem, much like living under the macrocarpas in Rotorua. I often thought that if I could just get away into sunlight, my life would be better. Living so close to Rena was difficult too; as her problems mounted up, I was called along the street more and more to hear the various tales of despair, most of them, in my view, self-inflicted. But she didn't do me any good either.

Ian said, 'Come on, let's go and look.'

The house was just along the path: we didn't even have to go down to road level to reach it. But it was round the corner, and the clifftop there reaches a promontory so that the house is exposed to both the south and north in a wide-angle sweep. From the front window you can see not just across Cook Strait and Evans Bay and the boat marina, but right back across to the city and the harbour. It was a beautiful clear moonlit night, the sky like an immense starry cave above us, a hint of frost in the air. In the past, I had visited the elderly couple who owned the house, and I knew where they kept a spare key. Sure enough, it was still there so I collected it and opened the door. The gas was connected, though not the electricity. We turned on the gas fire in the empty sitting room and watched it glow into life. Then we walked from one empty room to another, in our minds filling them with our presence.

Finally we sat on the floor in front of the fire, like two joyful thieves. I said, 'I have to live here.' Ian agreed.

In the morning, I saw the agent. I said that I had come to make an offer on the house. 'You can't do that,' he said, 'it's already sold.'

'No, it's not,' I said, 'because the owner has told me that the deal doesn't close until five o'clock tonight. Whatever has been offered, we'll go higher.' This was reckless talk on my part of course, but the *Section Seven* money was burning a hole in my pocket, and we didn't have to go very much higher. By the end of the day, we had signed for the house. A few weekends later, the school rugby team came and shifted our furniture along the path. The young couple who had lost out to our bid bought our old house. Another family along the road bought their house. Like an army of giant ants we moved our belongings from one house to another.

We have lived in that house for more than thirty years. Things began to change for the better as soon as we moved in. One of the many things I loved was that I could see the school grounds from the house. I could watch our children, and sometimes hear their voices called. I felt a comforting sense of being able to watch over them, as if I might keep them safe. There was space at home for them to play when they got home, and a huge ngaio where Giles built a tree house. The house has grown around us, with rooms added here and there, windows taken out, and larger ones put in place. A small cable car installed on the side of the cliff enabled my mother to live with us years later, and will allow us to stay there until we are old. Or that is the hope.

The sun shines into the house in the mornings, and in the garden in the afternoons. Both our children have held their weddings at that house. Some of it is antiquated, and we won't change anything much else now, but I know it, every groove and corner.

House, I said, when I left to come here to Menton, house, I'll come back. Whenever I leave it for any length of time, I do the same thing, going from room to room, taking the feeling of home with me.

I mentioned the poet Robin Hyde, but I haven't said much about her. She was born Iris Guiver Wilkinson in South Africa in 1906 and came to New Zealand as an infant. When she was a teenager she was stricken with poliomyelitis, which left her permanently crippled. Her life was short, eventful and tragic. As a prolific journalist, novelist and poet, she emblazoned her name across New Zealand's literary landscape. By the time she left New Zealand for London in 1937, she had had two children out of wedlock, one of whom had died. She suffered often from depression. Like me, she loved the

North, and I am familiar with places where she lived up there. Her signature novel was *The Godwits Fly,* about the migration of New Zealanders abroad, like the famed round-the-world flight of the bar-tailed godwits that begins and ends every year in New Zealand. Another novel, *Check to Your King,* about French adventurer and self-proclaimed monarch Baron de Thierry, was set in the Hokianga. Hyde travelled to England via Hong Kong, but then visited China during the Sino-Japanese War of 1938, where she went into the battle zone and was captured. After reaching London, she died in August 1939, by her own hand. She was thirty-three.

I tell you all this because her framed photograph hangs above my computer on the faded apricot wall in my study back home in New Zealand. Her eyes are dark and heavy with sadness, but you can't help but be struck by the handsome profile, the strong jawline, the dark hair swept back in a loose bun. She wears a striped cotton dress, the sort my mother and my aunts might have worn at the time;

she was roughly the same age. I was given this picture after I had opened an exhibition at the National Library, about Hyde's life and writing. She is another of those women whose lives haunt me, another one who took the road less travelled, one of those I might have followed, but didn't. I had thought about leaving, but I stayed. I look at her every working day of my life when I'm at home. Sometimes I think I should take her picture down. After all, I survived. But I like her there.

And sometimes, here in Menton, I think of her too. I cannot help but believe that Hyde had a great yearning to follow in Mansfield's steps, and although their deaths were different, one ordained by illness, the other by suicide, there might have been a sweet temptation for one to emulate the other. Towards the very end, Hyde wrote a poem called 'Katherine Mansfield'.

> *Our little Darkness, in the shadow sleeping*
> *Among the strangers you could better trust,*
> *Right was your faring, Wings: their wise hands gave you*

Freedom and song, where we had proffered dust...
Dust is the unthrown wrestler at our gate.

Dead young writers and artists. This morning I made one of my pilgrimages to the higher part of the old cemetery here in Menton. Before I left New Zealand, Vince O'Sullivan told me about Aubrey Beardsley being buried at Menton, something he had first learnt from Lauris. An elderly woman who lived in the town was going away for a while and, during her absence, she asked if Lauris would take flowers to Beardsley's grave every week, as she was in the habit of doing. Apparently Lauris did this, although it was not something she and I had ever talked about. In the 1890s Beardsley produced dark, perverse and deeply erotic posters and illustrations for literary works, which drew heavily on history and mythology for their inspiration. Of him, Oscar Wilde reportedly said that 'he had a face like a silver hatchet, and grass green hair'. He died from tuberculosis in Menton in 1898, having hoped, I suppose, that sunshine would heal the deadly ailment. He was twenty-five.

We came across his grave by accident during one of our explorations of the cemetery. Ian likes visiting graveyards and taking photographs. The best route to the Menton cemetery is on the Number 9 Pont Saint Louis bus, which takes you high around the town, through narrow streets and alongside some of the town's most dramatic friezes, which decorate the houses beneath the eaves with fruit and flowers, birds, griffins, butterflies. Although it's quite a long ride, this bus takes you fairly close to the cemetery gates. We came up that route this morning. We were looking at an ornate mausoleum, and I stepped back, just avoiding a plain flat slab tomb—Beardsley's. It was easy to miss. Nobody had put flowers on it for a very long time.

I don't go every week; it's a long climb up the twisted paths and rapid flights of steps, beneath the sun and the Wedgwood blue sky. It's worth it, though, to see Italy over to the left, the ancient spire of Saint Michel and the town of Menton curving away on the other side. But when I do go I lay a little bouquet on the tombstone. I like the connections: Vince, who's alive and well and sending me sardonic notes from New Zealand, Lauris, writers.

And here's another thing. Katherine Mansfield's silk shawl was stored in a cardboard carton in the city's municipal buildings for more than seventy years. Helen McNeish had located it in the mid-1970s, but otherwise it's been shut away for all that time. Some local historians have included it in an exhibition of the city's collection of Mansfield memorabilia. It's in a glass case at Hôtel d'Adhémar de Lanagnac, an historic house with a small exhibition space just off the main street.

Yesterday, Luc phoned and asked me to come down and see the shawl with him. And there it was, glowing in the filtered light of the room, a rusty soft red, patterned with green. Luc took some pictures of me beside the glass case. Then, on a sudden impulse, he asked the attendant to open the case.

Non, she said, *non,* not possible.

But might prevailed—Luc is, after all, the Minister for Culture for Alpes Maritime—and to the accompaniment of many protests, the case was opened, and the shawl taken and thrown around my shoulders. And then he marched me out into the street and took my picture among some palm trees. The attendant, a very pleasant woman, looked quite anguished.

But here's what got me. Not just the soft fabric floating across my arms—I swear I smelled Mansfield's famous scent. Vince once told me about it, Genet Fleuri, made from gorse flowers I think, much derided by Virginia Woolf. A heavy loitering perfume like a summer afternoon up North, where I come from.

Chapter 16

In 1974 I was asked to judge the Wattie Book Awards (now the Montana New Zealand Book Awards). My fellow judges were Tom Fitzgibbon, a noted educator and expert in children's literature, and television celebrity Dr Brian Edwards, famous for grilling politicians until they fried. Tom was the convenor. I was surprised Edwards had accepted. He was well-known for his frequent public dismissal of reading, which he said was a boring activity. And look at him. He had a PhD without reading a book. Or so he said.

He stayed true to form. The judges were scheduled to meet and arrive at their verdict at Le Normandie, one of the best restaurants in town. Tom and I fretted over the menu, waiting for the third member of the team to arrive. Eventually he turned up.

'Hello, I'm Brian Edwards,' he said. 'I've just come by to wish you well in your deliberations. I don't read books.'

'Well,' said Tom, 'why are you on the panel?'

Clearly, Edwards had waited for this moment. 'Ah,' he said, with obvious relish, 'I wanted to prove that you didn't have to be able to read books to be invited to judge them.'

He declined to stay for lunch and Tom and I carried on judging on our own. The three finalists were Witi Ihimaera for his first novel, *Tangi,* Tony Simpson for his documentary account of the Depression, *The Sugarbag Years* and geologist Graeme Stevens for *Rugged Landscape.* In those days there were no categories for the finalists.

The ceremony to announce the awards was due to take place at a lunch in Christchurch. A day or so before the date, Tom fell ill, so I was the sole judge left to put in an appearance and make a speech.

As it happened, all three finalists lived in Wellington too. It was raining hard when I turned up at the airport, where publishers and writers were clustered in the leaking old aircraft hangar that used to serve as the departure lounge. Christchurch airport, we were told, was closed by fog and likely to remain so all day. A publisher on the organising committee came over and said it looked as if most of them would miss the lunch, but it was important, from the sponsor's point of view, that the winners and a judge be present. A light plane had been chartered for Witi, Tony, Graeme and me. We were to fly to Blenheim, hire a car and then 'drive like hell' until we got to Christchurch. There was one spare seat on the plane and as Witi's wife Jane was there it was decided she would come with us. I was charged with getting everyone there for the lunch. We might be a bit late, but I was assured the people down there would keep the proceedings going until we arrived.

We leapt into the tiny plane waiting on the tarmac, and headed for Blenheim. Graeme Stevens's book was, as its name implied, about the rugged geological structure of the landscape and mountains we were crossing. He was a quiet man, whom I never met again, but in the drama of the moment, he opened up to give us a running commentary on the journey, scaring us silly about what might happen in an earthquake, if the land shifted.

In Blenheim, there was not a rental car to be found. Finally, one was discovered in Nelson but we would have to wait an hour for it to be delivered to us. We sat in a coffee bar and counted the time passing while the streets of Blenheim ran with one downpour after another. About eleven thirty, we were able to leave for Christchurch. Tony offered to drive. A pale man, wearing an elegant dark hat with a wide brim, he was well known in trade union circles. He had seemed a little aloof until then, but once behind the wheel, he thawed. We all knew by then that we weren't going to make it for lunch. I had rung the organisers from Blenheim and told them what was happening. At that point I learned that Christchurch airport had cleared about ten minutes after we left Wellington, and everyone else had arrived on time. Just keep coming, was the decidedly terse message.

The whole undertaking had been miscalculated from the beginning. On a good day, the journey takes about four hours. We might have made it for a late lunch if all had gone according to plan, but we would be lucky to make it by afternoon tea at the rate we were going. Large slips had come down with the rain, and the edges of the road melted away beside us as we crawled past several washouts. But along the way we had some amazing conversations, not least, the announcement that Jane was expecting her and Witi's first child. Everyone in the car described a journey they had taken, or a country that interested them. I didn't have one to describe; even the landscape we were passing through was new to me. As I would write later, in a poem called 'On Going Missing for the Wattie Awards', 'I am lost in time and space/Being no traveller that I could ever boast/Except the countries of the heart', lines that still have a certain resonance for me. I know it felt strange that day, listening to this conversation among a group of people I had judged, and yet knowing so little of a world that seemed easy and familiar to them. And knowing that I alone knew who had won.

We rolled up to the venue at five o'clock that evening. There were still a lot of people there, many in various stages of inebriation. All the champagne had run out. A television camera was pushed in front of Witi's face. 'Mr Ihimaera, how does it feel to have won the top award?' he was asked.

Witi turned to me with a look of total astonishment. 'Have I won?' he said.

I was proud of myself. Spotting the winner on the day literary prizes are given out is an old Wellington game. You wait until the day itself to strike, doing a bit of needling here and there at those who might be in the know. I had been caught the previous year when I was a judge of the Feltex-sponsored television prizes and, over a long champagne-fuelled lunch, let it slip to a major contender that he wasn't in the running. He didn't turn up at the awards ceremony and I'd vowed never to let it happen again.

Tony looked around for his publisher, Alister Taylor, who was nowhere to be seen. Taylor had collected the cheque when the announcements were made at lunchtime, and gone back to Wellington.

Inside the venue, a large pink-faced man with ample jowls and girth, and shrewd eyes, stood leaning against the bar. 'Albion Wright,' he introduced himself. 'Have a gin, dear.' This was the man with whom I had an assignation of my own. I had rung him the previous week and asked if I might bring him a collection of my poems. I thrust my envelope containing the manuscript for *Honey and Bitters* into his hands. He sniffed loudly, and looked resigned.

The following Monday morning, he rang to say Pegasus Press would publish the book the following year.

I think my poems had a certain vitality that suited the times, and that Albion had seen that. He had chanced his arm with a number of women writers when other publishers were not interested, writers like Janet Frame with *Owls Do Cry,* Jean Watson with *Stand in the Rain.* But he didn't publish much poetry by relatively unknown writers and I was proud that he had taken so easily to my work.

Lauris and I had been talking about a possible joint publication of our poems for a while, but we had gone off the idea. In my heart, I knew that she understood more than I did about what made a good poem. Her poems, although immediate and personal, were at the same time measured and distinctive in their voice. When she read, her audiences were drawn to her, at a very personal level, as well as to the work itself. My poems were raw, fairly unstructured, and increasingly influenced by American beat and feminist poets, a shift away from Bishop's and Bogan's more formal structures, which had attracted me earlier on, and which I struggled over. Critics would describe my poems as 'confessional' and I suppose that's what they were, although I've come to question the glibness of that definition. It seems to me that most poems give away something of the poet who writes them. But I hadn't really grasped the art of drawing experience into the small fictions that move a poem beyond 'what happened to me' or 'how I feel'.

I had been getting some advice about shaping the work from Alistair Paterson, who mentored several younger poets. From him, I also learned how far I still had to go. It was Lauris who had pulled away from the idea of joint publication and I, too, could see it might not work. We needed to stand on our own feet. I had a niggling feeling that, in the close confines of a single volume, my work would suffer by comparison and that that would be difficult for both of us. With Albion's acceptance of *Honey and Bitters,* a reversal of this scenario began to unfold.

Delighted, I rang to tell Lauris the news. I heard a sharp intake of breath, followed by a pause. When she spoke, she sounded withdrawn. I suppose I was a bit full of myself. I knew she had already submitted the manuscript for *In Middle Air,* but when pressed on Albion's response she had brushed the matter off. Some weeks later, she mentioned that Albion had accepted her book. At that point, all difficulties were apparently swept aside. What I didn't know until years afterwards, was that Denis had intervened and persuaded Albion to publish *In Middle Air.* Denis was right, of course: Lauris was the true poet. As things turned out, Albion had no cause to regret publishing either book. *In Middle Air* went on to win the Jessie Mackay Award the following year, and Lauris's work began to be published internationally. In 1985 her *Selected Poems* won the Commonwealth Poetry Prize.

We decided that we would hold a joint launch party for the two books at the University Club. Nineteen seventy-five would be International Women's Year and we saw our double celebration as part of this event. In fact, word had flashed around publishers that women's poetry was the happening thing, and before long nine books of poems had been signed up for publication for that year. They included work by Marilyn Duckworth, Fleur Adcock, Peggy Dunstan, Christine de Beer, Elizabeth Smither, Rachel McAlpine, Jan Kemp, Lauris and me. In the whole previous ten years, there had not been as many. As well, Riemke Ensing set out to collect New Zealand women's poetry for the first time, in an anthology called *Private Gardens.*

All of this was still to come, the day I set off for the Wattie Book Awards. Nineteen seventy-five would be a year crowded with incident.

I was infinitely happier in the new house. Things were falling into place. I felt as if I was conquering some of the old demons. True, life wasn't always good for my friends. I had seen Carole through some difficult times. She had a new relationship but it was not what she wanted, so she ended it. The man ended his life.

But I now had a job, a circle of friends and two books lined up for publication. When Albion accepted *Honey and Bitters,* I already had another small book in preparation. Publishers A.H. & A.W. Reed had approached me to see if they could include *Search for Sister Blue,* the radio play about Heta Rakete and his sister Queenie, in their educational series for secondary schools. This little book was produced with a fine Ans Westra cover photograph that exactly matched the mood of the play. We had a party at our house. Ray

Richards and David Elworthy from Reed's and Ian Cross and a crowd from the *Listener* braved a southerly to send the book on its way. Craig Harrison came down from Palmerston North as well. Concurrently with my book, Reed's published his play *Tomorrow Will Be a Lovely Day.*

From time to time, I made some calls I regretted. One of these was at the children's school. Ian and I often crossed swords with the principal, Gladwell. We didn't believe in his disciplinary methods and said so. Nor had I recovered from his offer to serve on the ladies' auxiliary, which I had never taken up. I spoke to a few women in the neighbourhood who were equally uncomfortable that the school committee was 'men only', but they didn't see what they could do to change the situation. Ian and I decided we would do something.

This took some planning, but when the triennial elections for the committee took place, we were prepared. Leigh Minnitt shared my views. Although she didn't have children, as the wife of a local professional she felt entitled to express an opinion. Her friend Sue Edwards agreed to be nominated to the committee. Sue lived within the school's area, although her children attended another school. She knew she would probably lose, but was willing to put herself on the line for the principle involved. I spent an afternoon ringing around, and whipped up a posse of local supporters, some of them grandparents of children now at the school, all eager for change. Teachers' training college lecturer Patrick Macaskill, who also served on the Book Council, was among our group.

As the meeting got under way, we saw that Hataitai's conservative element was well represented. Nominations were called for, and almost as quickly closed, but not before I had nominated Sue from the floor. There was a stunned silence. Gladwell called for a show of hands. Ian, armed with the regulations, pointed out that if there were more nominations than seats vacant there had to be a ballot.

'We don't have ballot papers,' said Gladwell, by now appearing apoplectic.

'Well, I do,' said Ian. 'I brought some in case you needed them.'

Our supporters demanded that the rules be followed, so the ballot took place. When it was completed, Gladwell offered to count the votes. By now his supporters were in a sullen mood. A guest speaker was supposed to address them, and it was nearing eleven o'clock.

'No,' said Ian, 'the regulations require that you have an independent scrutineer.'

Leigh was the only person present who qualified. At some stage during the counting, Gladwell approached her to see if the result could be hurried along. Leigh threatened to call the police. As we expected, Sue was not elected. But at the next election a woman was, and later several women were, and the cycle was broken.

Did I ever regret this? Of course. People have said that it took courage to do this, that we were before our time. But it didn't feel like a triumph. Our children had to pay for our principles and they had less power over their lives than we did. School was always difficult after this, until they moved on to high school. This event shaped some of my views about the morality of inflicting personal choices on those who might be disenfranchised by them. Although I have joined a number of collective movements over the years, I also believe in individual responsibility. I have learnt that the greater good is often a big muddy moral quagmire.

I was, by then, caught up in the women's movement in New Zealand, not that I had consciously thought my way into it. I don't want to seem artlessly naïve about the role of feminism in my life. Over the years I had read the books—Simone de Beauvoir's *The Second Sex*, Betty Friedan's *The Feminine Mystique*, Germaine Greer's *The Female Eunuch*. I had heard Greer lecture in Wellington some years before, and marched in protest when she was taken to court for saying 'bullshit' in public. Of course I knew what it was about. And yet, there was an accidental element to my becoming a feminist. This wasn't a role I had sought or deliberately planned. What I wanted to be was a writer, always that, but so often I was writing about women's lives, and about poor and disadvantaged women. I couldn't help but notice inequality, and more than a few times in my life I had felt disadvantaged by being a woman myself.

But even if I understood what the women's movement represented in 1975, nothing had prepared me for the New Zealand United Women's Convention, where I had been invited to speak about writing. I don't know what I had been expecting—perhaps a gathering of people in a room, much like one of my evening classes. The convention was to be held in the Wellington Show Buildings in Newtown. On Friday 13 June, the sky burst apart and an immense deluge soaked women as they made their way to the convention. The rain would continue for most of the weekend, the noise on the roof all but drowning out the sound of speakers' voices, except in the main auditorium area where there were microphones. More than two thousand bedraggled women crushed together, trying to find their way to different workshops. My site was right in the middle of the main hall, and I had an apple box to stand on. At least two hundred women had joined my workshop. With the noise overhead, the steam of bodies, the upturned faces, I suddenly began to understand the magnitude of the movement and my own part in it. Over the previous five years, my name had become well known and, in a time when it was still difficult for women to get their writing published, I was perceived as successful. These women waited anxiously for me to tell them how to unlock the key to their own creativity, how to be published, how to find time to write in the middle of their domestic lives.

What did I say? Be like me? Be single-minded, driven, often manic in your determination to work? I might have said, be an only, often lonely, child with a mother who lived partly in a fantasy world of soap opera and Maori voices from the past, and a father with a doubtful history, and you've got a good brew for the imagination. That wasn't enough, of course. I tried to tell them about setting targets, making space in their lives, giving themselves 'permission' to work. 'Permission' was the key word, and it seemed to be useful. Afterwards, I was mobbed by women wanting to tell me their experiences, and some of them were harrowing. I heard from women who had been beaten and abused, who had lost their children because they were lesbians, women who worked liked slaves for pittances or nothing at all. My own life experience seemed limited by comparison.

Now and then, I have been celebrated for holding feminist views. But over the years I have also been heckled, abused, accused, ostracised, had my family insulted, my sexuality called into question. More often than not, the term 'feminism' is used as a pejorative in New Zealand. It's shorthand for 'this woman is opinionated' or 'who does she think she is?' or 'we think she's difficult'. I have been forced, on occasion, mostly in order to protect my family, to define my brand of feminism, although this goes deeply against the grain. Believing what I do is part of the person I am, and it is troubling to be asked to put belief into boxes. Making utterances about not being 'extreme' or 'radical' seems apologist. But my views have been consistent ever since I became seriously involved in the women's movement. I believe that women are equally entitled to receive education, adequate health care and recognition in the workplace. I believe, too, that women have the right to choose their sexual partners—that means not being forced or coerced to have sex—and to have control over their fertility. Women are not human chattels.

That's all. I don't think women are 'better' than men. I was mentored and supported in the development of my career by several men. I haven't forgotten. It's neither here nor there, but I've never attended a single encounter group in my life, nor gone to speculum parties to inspect vaginas. I have never slept with or been intimately involved with a woman. Do these things matter? Not really. For some women it was part of understanding themselves. I respect their courage, but there were aspects of the women's movement that were simply irrelevant to my own personal growth as a woman. I think we were, all of us, passionate and brave and strong. From this distance, I can see that we probably looked faintly ridiculous at times, but that doesn't make us wrong. Most of us were fired by the genuine belief that we were making the world a better place for women, and that doesn't seem like something we should have to apologise for.

When I explain my own basic philosophy of feminism, most people nod their heads and agree that this argument is about human rights, rather than pitting men and women against each other. More than once, I have heard Margaret Atwood offer similar views to mine, when heckled from the floor, and her voice is tinged with a certain note of weariness that I hear in my own responses. How many times do you bang your head against a wall without becoming unconscious?

Lauris was missing throughout much of this time. Earlier in the year she had spent several weeks with her third daughter Rachel, who was being treated for schizophrenia in Ward 10 at Auckland Hospital. I had only met Rachel once, at the Upper Hutt house during university summer holidays. She was a pale gentle girl, her smile much like that of her brilliant vibrant siblings, but different in some indefinable way. I remember her sitting on the grass, beneath a tree, plaiting flower stems, and talking about how to make japonica jelly. Lauris wrote to me regularly from Auckland. In her first letter she explained that the situation was much more serious than she had suspected and she could only stay with Rachel until she seemed reasonably safe. I walked straight into a nightmare when I came to see her on Sunday morning, Lauris wrote. I was in a car, being driven to the hospital when I saw her—a little pale wraith walking along the footpath. A week or so later, Lauris described her time spent in the ward, staying all day and eating with the patients and family who had joined them, as she had Rachel. One of them was Hone Tuwhare, who was staying there to support a relative. He was, she said, 'a great genial bear of a man' who had encouraged people to write their own poetry and read it aloud. When he left, he had handed to Lauris the job of keeping the sessions going.

Lauris, then, was living a totally different life from mine. After she returned to Wellington, we continued to meet and talk, and plan the launch of our two books later in the year. She seemed optimistic about her daughter's recovery, but Rachel came back to Wellington and her health continued to deteriorate. When most of the women poets who were being published that year gathered one evening for a reading at the Settlement, word came through that Lauris wouldn't be there. Rachel was very ill; the family was at her hospital bedside.

I rang the next morning and learned that Rachel had died. Immediately I went to the Upper Hutt house, where the family was gathered. Lauris seemed pleased to see me but the funeral would just be for family, and I left soon. It was to be some time before I saw Lauris again. I realised that however close to Lauris's life I had thought myself, I was not part of this. I wrote a poem for Rachel, called 'Winter Roses'—'I have only some winter roses,/bought from a flower factory,/to lay beside the wounded earth'—but the truth was, the flowers didn't get delivered.

After the launch of our books, Lauris and I began to pick up the threads, or so I thought. In the interval, since Rachel's death, other appalling tragedies had struck. No fewer than five of my friends' daughters died suddenly within the space of twelve weeks. I felt as if I was becoming a sort of ubiquitous mourner, without a tragedy of my own, thankfully. And yet, as a mother, I was overcome by a numb and helpless horror. At nights, when the children slept, I walked around our new house and touched their sleeping faces, overcome with dread.

At times Lauris cried; at other moments she appeared overtaken by a wild gaiety. She insisted we go ahead with the launch at the University Club. Denis launched *In Middle Air* and Sam spoke for my book, *Honey and Bitters.* It was during his speech that Denis made his infamous comment about 'the menstrual school of poetry', confirming the view of many in the packed room that he was an elderly misogynist. He did himself a disservice because his deeds were kinder than his drunken words. About 300 people had turned up, many of them uninvited. The gatecrashers included members of the Press Gallery and a number of Labour politicians. We felt like the centre of our universe. Nobody had mentioned to Lauris and me that publishers usually paid for launch parties. Albion arrived beaming from Christchurch, behaving as if he was the host. Afterwards we counted the cost of our largesse.

Often I seemed to fail quite simple tests of friendship with Lauris. I'm sure I was inadequate, but the ups and downs of that year, and the volatility of our friendship, were beginning to make me feel isolated and uncertain again. She had decided the Edmonds should move to town, and enlisted my help in looking at houses. I don't know whether her family was aware of the role I was playing in its future, but at least it felt as if I were doing something useful. We looked at dozens of places together, and then, all of a sudden, Lauris settled on a house I hadn't seen. I thought it an outlandish choice, a 1950s L-shaped house nestled in a hollow halfway up Grass Street in Oriental Bay. It was within walking distance of where I live, but there were hundreds of steps to be negotiated whichever way you approached it. It was a suntrap though, and she was enchanted by the bush that surrounded the garden, and by the inner harbour view.

Despite the change, she and Trevor were constantly in despair with each other. Their marriage was in its last crumbling stages, although it would totter on, presenting an agonised face to the world, for some years. In fact, although they separated, they never divorced. Much has been written about their relationship, both by Lauris herself, and by their son Martin. None of it seems very conclusive. My own view is that, although Lauris appeared to move away from the marriage, and wrote about the relationship in the past tense, Trevor and she were the real loves of each other's lives. There is a poem of hers called 'The Mountain', which begins:

> *Oh love let us learn our love*
> *Now there is no more laughing in it–*
> *Let us remember the mountain*
> *When we woke to the frost*
> *And ran with our clothes to the kitchen...*

The mountain was Ruapehu and the kitchen was at Ohakune, where Trevor and Lauris had lived when the children were small. That mountain, and what it represented, seems so central to what she would write in the following years, so crucial to her emotional life, that I can only conclude that she could no more put the marriage completely behind her than Trevor could. He moved out and went to live in Greytown, soon after Lauris returned from Menton in 1981. They continued to see each other, Lauris frequently visiting Trevor until he died. It seemed to me that, although she had a number of relationships, she never found anyone who measured up to her and Trevor's youthful romantic selves. Perhaps she half wilfully drove the others away, because none of them endured, although she did have a long deep friendship with Beeb, to whom she became close in our years in PEN. But at the end of 'The Mountain', she recalls how she and Trevor had stood on the tiny porch at the Ohakune house and shook and gasped 'in the mazarine dark' before going indoors and shutting the door on the cold 'and the mountain's terrible closeness'. This seemed to echo the way their lives, once so close and wonderful, had become 'dark' and 'terrible', overwhelming them as the mountain had done.

The 'terrible closeness' of almost anyone was apparent at this stage in her life. There were fractured times with her family, and with some of her friends too. As one of the closest, I came in for frequent criticism, and before long Lauris declared the friendship over. She summoned me one afternoon in the summer and some hard words were spoken. In her opinion, I was unduly influenced by some of my other friends, or that's what she told me. In particular, she and Leigh, whom she encountered often in the workplace, didn't get on. Nor did she like the way I was conducting my professional life. Of course there were things I didn't know about, the day we quarrelled, but I was aware that some kind of rivalry was involved. I did understand that she had leapfrogged ahead of me, immersed now in her lifelong commitment to poetry, while I moved restlessly from one form of writing to another. Perhaps, if such disaster hadn't befallen Lauris in the shape of Rachel's death, we would have sorted it out more easily. That summer afternoon, I remember walking home awash with tears and a feeling of utter rejection.

Nearly five years passed before we behaved as more than civil acquaintances. It was here, from this room at Villa Isola Bella in Menton, that she started to write to me again, began to stitch our abandoned friendship back together. We would be the closest of friends until she died in January 2000, only it became friendship of a different kind, as we shared work ideas, took pleasure in each other's successes and commiserated when things didn't go well. At Grass Street, we would regularly put the world to rights, with a phone call most days, and frequent visits.

Chapter 17

All that, and still 1975 had not run its course. My time at the Book Council was close to an end. Joanna fell ill with suspected tuberculosis. This turned out to be an easily treatable infection, but rest was ordered. Ian and I were beside ourselves with worry. Ian had had tuberculosis as a child, and the spectre of the disease in his family hovered over us. Not only had his father spent so many years in the sanatorium, but Ian's aunt had died in her twenties of the same illness. I took leave from my job to be at home with Joanna. It was a beautiful spring and early summer that year. Joanna, quiet and reflective by nature, had grown into a tall slender girl with dark hair falling nearly to her waist. I was grateful that we had a garden filled with sunlight and shade, where she could spend her days in a deckchair. She passed the time writing stories and poems of her own.

This hiatus provided me with more time to be with both the children than I had had for some years. Giles wasn't happy at school, and often spent his days riding the buses with a Maori driver called Bunny. The school didn't seem to care, and when we met Bunny we decided that he was a positive influence on our son. Some weekends, he and his family would take Giles on spear-fishing expeditions around the coast. It seems odd now that we let this happen, but Giles was a popular quick-witted boy with many friends. Although he didn't enjoy school, he didn't want to leave his mates behind and shift school either. I realised he enjoyed having me at home, and he was more settled when I was there. This time couldn't last, but it was good for all of us.

Our existence was still very hand to mouth. Old Wellington houses can suck money up remorselessly. There was rewiring and all manner of repairs to be done, and now I was saving for a new roof. My work at the Book Council was twenty hours a week, although I often put in forty, and the wages were modest. I loved the job and was proud of the programmes I initiated. The Writers in Schools programme was under way: the first writer to talk to students was Noel Hilliard, who visited a group of Rotorua high schools. Margaret Mahy and Joy Cowley were enthusiastic, and plans were made for them to begin touring. Meet the Author was mainly dependent on overseas writers who, like Michael Frayn, were on their way to Australian festivals. I found it uphill work attracting audiences to hear New Zealand writers, despite the flourishing poetry gigs the Poetry Society was already running.

These Book Council initiatives were big concepts and if they were to grow, they needed total commitment from whoever was running them. When Roy Parsons employed me I had said in my interview that I wanted to write, 'although I never expected to write a great New Zealand novel'. Putting myself down. A part of me believed it, but I wanted the job badly at the time. I had put aside serious consistent writing for a long time, but the hope of writing a novel still lurked.

Then Michael Noonan and Tony Isaacs came to discuss a proposal with me for New Zealand's first television soap. The crux of their idea was a serial based on the daily lives of a family who lived in the upstairs flat over a grocery shop in Hataitai. They asked if I would like to be in on the action. We tossed around some ideas, and suggestions for the name of the serial. I think it was Tony who said, 'It should be something that feels really close to home for viewers.' And Michael said, 'That's it, close to home.' This was how *Close to Home,* the long-running serial, was born. It employed scores of writers, editors and actors. I would work spasmodically on it over the next few years and Joanna acted in several episodes while she was still in high school.

So that was an option, but even before the serial was up and running, I could see it being hijacked by the same powerful group who had moved in earlier. A proposed staff contract didn't eventuate, so it wasn't a real job prospect. Meanwhile, two of my early stories had been selected by Phoebe Meikle, now editing at Longman Paul, for a collection called *Ten modern New Zealand story writers.* It would include

Witi, Patricia Grace and me, as well as Maurice Duggan, Maurice Gee and C.K. Stead. This was a more important collection than any I had been included in so far. Phoebe was a hard taskmaster. Although she had chosen my stories from the many available, she thought they could be better. She behaved like a schoolmistress, reminding me frequently of the principles of grammar, punctuation and clear narrative story telling that I had lost sight of when I left school. My report card from her always read 'could do better'. It was one of the best things that could have happened to me. I began to look at all the work I had done, and think about how it could be improved.

I started incorporating Phoebe's 'lectures' into my teaching. I had moved on from the WEA and taken over weekend courses for Victoria's University Extension classes. These had been started by Christine Cole Catley, then carried on by Michael King. Michael was moving north to be near his children, after the break-up of his marriage, and the job fell to me. I was surprised at how well the teaching was going. More and more students came flocking to the classes, held in an old Wellington house that had been converted into a lecture facility in Fairlie Terrace. Some began travelling from other parts of the country to participate. I tried to create a friendly constructive environment, and to equip the students with skills to criticise each other's work in an honest but not threatening way. By then, I had had several instructors of my own whose advice seemed worth passing on. I also began to receive letters from people who wanted advice. For the most part, I had to let them down gently.

There just wasn't enough time to answer all these letters, although I did begin a correspondence with a young man in Mount Crawford prison. One Saturday afternoon I took myself off to visit him. The visit wasn't a great idea. I was horrified when I was searched: it had never occurred to me that I would be seen as anything other than a friendly visitor. I was so ignorant of prison life and the loneliness of criminals that I hadn't realised how reliant this man might become on my correspondence, or that his feelings for me might develop into a romantic fantasy. I stopped writing to him after a while and felt badly about it. I did think that he had ability. Meanwhile, as I worked alongside my students, I found myself thinking more and more about how I could return to the writing I had set out to do when I was in my twenties.

Something else was bothering me too, which I was keeping to myself. The rumour mill in Auckland was busy and, although I never met Frank Sargeson, I had heard that he was a gossip. I was told that he was linking my name too closely with Keith Sinclair's. Then, one evening I went to a poetry reading at the Settlement with Keith, where there was a gathering of poets, all young men, who had been students at Auckland University and had been published in the student magazine, *Freed*. Perhaps they had felt slighted by Keith in some way, and wanted to extract revenge, or just thought it funny, but the next issue of *Freed* carried a gossip column that linked us as a couple. So the rumour was in print, and I was devastated. This was unfair and untrue.

I did talk about it with Keith. He thought that the matter should be ignored, given that our friendship had been misconstrued. But it was clear to me that it could not continue in the same uninhibited way, if it was not to pull the Book Council down with it. Keith and Ian were good friends; we all enjoyed being together when Raewyn was in Wellington. There seemed room for unfortunate misunderstandings. One morning I woke up totally clear about what should happen next. I rang Keith and told him I was resigning. He tried to talk me into changing my decision, but I had made up my mind. By the end of the conversation, my job at the Book Council was over. Happily, the friendship was not. Keith continued to support my work for a long time afterwards.

Earlier in the year I had written a radio play called *Angel,* commissioned for International Women's Year, taking the abuse of women as its central theme. The central character was based on Carole and her difficult journey of self-discovery and survival, although the events in the play were not her story. It was just that Carole was always up against things, often overwhelmed by the hardships associated with raising three boys by herself, including one with a disability. For a time she worked at one of the embassies, where she met a group of journalists who liked her wild energetic humour, and determination to overcome obstacles. But although she was bent upon improving her situation, something usually got in the way. Since the death of the man she had been seeing, she seemed to fall in and out of liaisons that went nowhere. She was always looking after people who, it seemed to me, took advantage of her generosity. When I visited in the weekends there were frequently oddballs there of one kind or another, addicts and misfits and dropouts who took hospitality from her, giving little in return. I would take small food parcels when I could and leave them in the fridge, and she and the boys would come to us for Christmas. If we were hard up, they were much worse off.

Sometimes when I visited her, she would pick up her car keys and say, 'Let's get out of this. Let's have a picnic.' Once we were in the car, there was no stopping her, as we tore round the bays at dizzying speeds. Eventually she would pull into a lay-by and order me to open the boot of the car. ''Ello sailor, look what we've got here,' she'd shout, and I'd find the cask of wine. It only took me a couple of these trips to realise that she was on a different plane. I didn't do drugs, never had, and these road trips frightened me. In her company, there was a real sense of things spinning out of control. I felt, too, that Carole was tired, as if somehow the struggle was wearing her out.

When I wrote *Angel* I was thinking about the two sides to her nature: the loving person who would do anything for anyone, and the wild child. I loved Nina Simone singing 'Angel of the Morning', and threaded it through my play. This was my first radio drama for a while, and there was a new producer, Fergus Dick. He didn't like the play much, seeing it as too issues-driven. I think he was right to an extent, although I felt the character had integrity. Fergus is a flirty funny man, full of wry self-mockery. He and Lauris got on well together, and later, in the 1980s, when Lauris and I had been reconciled, the three of us would meet for rowdy afternoons filled with laughter and gossip, that most infectious Wellington pastime. (There is, I should say, gossip and gossip. The first sort is the cold-hearted rumour that destroys people; the second, humorous takes on conversations and who said what to whom, is not seriously unkind. Fergus has always practised the second kind as an art form, with a flair for mimicry.)

For better or worse, the play did draw me back into the radio circle. And I had some moving letters from women who had suffered abuse in their lives, saying that the play had 'spoken' to them, and they felt as if somebody understood. Tony Groser, also an actor, and John O'Leary were now running radio drama. I found myself with two work offers: one a small part-time job to produce a new programme about books on the Concert Programme, and a half-time job as script editor in the National Radio drama department. Tony had devised the idea of offering work in six-month blocks, hoping to find fresh ideas and an extra pair of hands, as well as mentoring to provide a regular income for selected writers. I'd already accepted the Concert Programme job when the second offer came up. I was persuaded to take them both.

I started the drama department work in a broom cupboard at Aurora House on The Terrace. The room, with a slanting ceiling and no windows, had been the storeroom for the big building's cleaning equipment. There was a dank smell of stale polish. Now it was cleared to make space for the three script editors: our desks touched each other. I shared this tiny space with two young men, Chris Hampson and Simon Carr. Chris dated back to my library days in Rotorua when, as a child, he used to come in with his mother to change his books. I remembered his library card number as soon as I saw him, and we fell quickly into an easy bantering relationship. Simon had come to New Zealand with the Oxford Union debating team a year or so earlier, with Simon Walker, and both men liked New Zealand so much that they stayed on. Simon (Carr) was sandy-complexioned, thin and so tall that I had to step over his legs to get past his desk. His immaculately tailored hacking jackets had been made in England, and he tilted a tweed hat over one eye while he read scripts, or simply while he feigned sleep if he was bored, which was quite often after I arrived. He and Chris had sharp funny tongues, and a rapid flow of running black gags, but I could tell Simon wasn't happy at having a third person in such a confined space. Because I was a woman, and older than him, he clearly felt the need to curb his language now and then, and, although I never commented, I could tell he felt inhibited.

On my second Monday morning, I brought flowers in to brighten the place up. The next morning they had turned blue—the old osmosis trick of ink in the water that kids do when they are about ten. I said as much, and that we could either get on or not, it was over to him. I was feeling reasonably confident when I looked at the work put in front of me—I knew at least as much as Chris about what constituted a good radio play, and a lot more than Simon, although he was a good reader. Things improved after that. I wooed the pair of them with sandwiches and cakes for morning tea, and it worked, although Simon left after a couple of months. By that time we had moved to a proper office, and in the meantime I had written the radio play *Mandarin Summer,* which Simon liked very much.

Throughout the early 1970s, I had managed to make a number of trips back north, since my return to Waipu. The year after that journey, I had gone up to Kerikeri for a week, staying in the old Homestead Hotel. I went on the pretext of work, but also because I couldn't get the North out of my head. If Waipu had exerted such a profound influence over me, how much more did my imagination owe to Kerikeri? When I went back that year, one beautiful day followed another. I didn't make myself known to people, except to catch up with Michael Gross. There was the same dizzying breathless humid perfume I remembered from my childhood, the banana passion fruit hanging heavily from the hakea hedges, the air full of butterflies, and dragonflies skimming the rivers. The blue gum trees had grown taller and denser. I went back to the waterfall and it was just as I remembered it.

Finally, I went back up Darwin Road to where our house had stood. In its place was a smart new bungalow, oozing prosperity. I knocked on the door and introduced myself, asking if I might have a look around the place. I soon discovered the old army hut, moved further back along the paddock, under a hedge. My old lean-to bedroom had been moved with it. I sat on the step and wept. All the old memories of sitting on the outside looking in overwhelmed me.

The following year we made a family trip up there so that I could show the children where I had grown up. I don't think the reality of the 'house' sank in; I wondered if they thought it was my playhouse. We were heading over to the Hokianga to join up with our old friends from Naenae, the Bernstones, and their children, and we didn't talk about it again. Russell wasn't well that summer. He had begun a long decline into terminal cancer.

When I sat down to write *Mandarin Summer,* it was time to draw on this stored material about the North that I had carried around in my head for more than twenty years. I wrote about a child who goes north with her parents at the end of the war, to a strange household of old China hands who torment each other in various ways, until the house goes up in flames. There is a beautiful pianist and a distraught wife and an overbearing decorated soldier. Yes, all of those. The words fell onto the typewriter in a white heat, as if the story was burning me up as I wrote. It took less than a fortnight to get it all down.

I left it with Chris and Simon one Friday afternoon, feeling as if a load had been lifted from me. I didn't really care what they thought about it. On the Monday morning, there was a new sense of respect in the air. Simon had written a glowing report, except for a comment about a few passages of 'vile lyricism'. He was right and they could be fixed. We all went across the road to the 1860s pub to celebrate. The 1860s, facing onto Lambton Quay, was another red-velvet haunt, so beloved of the 1970s. The drama department often met there for liquid lunches.

Some days, Leigh would come down the road and meet me there. Long after, I wrote a story about her called 'Nasturtium', only I called the character Vree. It began:

> 'Life is better than death. Well at least it is more alive,' Vree would say, and order a gin.
>
> Vree had hair like nasturtiums. When Tess went out to meet her she'd be waiting for her somewhere in the street, always in a place where the light struck her amazing shock of hair. It stood out in a shining halo, and it was so full of electricity Tess could feel it bristling in the air between them when they went inside the pub and took off their coats.
>
> Usually Vree would have her dog Malcolm X with her. He was as dark

as a seal. He looked at her all the time with strong intelligent eyes, his body fretful. When she went into the pub he would sit outside and wait for her.

'It's Vre-ee here,' she would say when she rang. She was one of those friends who you waited for to ring first, or she was at the beginning. Later, if you loved her, you had to call across spaces.

I had guessed for some time that she and David had trouble in their lives. They had been at Golden Bay, where they owned a holiday house, when David had taken ill one stormy night. He was able to diagnose himself as having had a heart attack, and Leigh got him into the car and drove him across flooded streams to Nelson Hospital, where he stayed for some weeks until he was well enough to return to Wellington for open heart surgery. She wrote to me often from his bedside, a more sombre Leigh, not knowing what the future held.

I wrote a fictional version of this letter in my story 'Nasturtium'. It says some of the things she had written to me, but also reflects how I saw the character of Vree.

It's hard for people to understand about us. I know they think he's a father substitute and it's true, I'm afraid of my life without him. He gives me space to do the things I want. I think I can change the world, which of course is silly, but at least I can try ... I sit here in the hospital, and outside the trees are dark red and the air is cold and I know that there is the smell of snow around the mountains. It's there at nights when I walk the dog, and I watch him sleeping and know that I don't want to do these things alone. I don't know whether this is good feminist philosophy, but if we cannot find someone to love, what's the point, why do it, and for whom?

She was right to be concerned. After his surgery, David changed. His manner at the surgery became abrupt and a consultation with him could be difficult. He had shown me extreme kindness on occasion, even if, looking back, I don't think his medication regimes did me much good. I began to wish for a change of doctor but I didn't follow through because it all seemed too awkward. Then one lunch hour at the 1860s, Leigh asked me to go into the women's toilets with her. There, she showed me bruising on her body, dark purple welts administered by a belt. David. I was shocked and made all the obvious suggestions about leaving him. Her eyes filled with tears. She still loved him, she said. In time, she was sure things would improve.

'You can't love him,' Tess said, when they had ordered another drink.

'Love, what's love?' she said, dropping her head. She was on her fourth gin and it was half past twelve ... 'Don't you see,' she said, her eyes haggard, 'he needs someone to look after him.'

I had begun my job in the Concert Programme as producer of the *Writing* programme, at first broadcast monthly. I was working under the direction of the departmental head, David Delaney, who sent me on some production and voice training courses. Soon it was time for my first programme.

I was dispatched on assignment to a hui for the first Maori Writers Conference, held at Lake Rotoiti, near Rotorua, over Queen's Birthday Weekend 1975. My attendance had been negotiated by the Maori Programmes Department, which included Bill Kerekere and Hirini Melbourne. Bill was planning to go and said he would give me whatever support I needed. I drove up in a second-hand car I'd bought the week before, and stayed with my parents.

The weekend started badly. My mother's health was deteriorating and she was miserable with joint pain. I had brought Giles with me, and although they were delighted to see him, it was mid-winter and there was little they could do by way of outings while I was out at the marae. When I announced proudly that I had joined the Labour Party there was a frozen silence in the room. My mother turned away. 'I suppose it was to be expected,' she said, 'marrying into the family you did.'

My father-in-law had worked for the Labour Party for many years.

But this had had nothing to do with it. I knew hardly anyone in Wellington who was not inclined to the left, and my parents' and relatives' politics had become anathema to me. This, apart from marrying Ian, was my biggest act of rebellion. It meant something then. I'm not sure that it does now. At any rate, my mother and I had one of the few quarrels, and certainly the worst, we ever had.

I don't remember as much of the hui at Rotoiti as I should. I had expensive new microphones and equipment to operate, and I was distracted by the technology. Bill Kerekere was sick and couldn't come, so I was on my own. Hone Tuwhare was there, but a lot of writers, including Witi, who was Burns Fellow at Otago that year, were absent. There were several Pakeha there, however, people on the fringe of writing and the arts. A group of them told me that they had come to give support to Maori writers in their struggle with people like me who wanted to steal their voices.

If I was taken aback by this direct attack, it was not a total surprise. I was aware that criticism was growing of Pakeha writers who spoke with a Maori voice, and had been considering my position for some time. I had started to write in a state of innocence about the things I knew, as writers are so often advised to do. So much of my early life had been associated with the Maori world, and I had married someone of Maori descent, that the criticism didn't seem to be about me. But lately I had begun to wonder if it was, and I had simply chosen not to hear what I didn't like.

Already Michael King and I had talked about the issues. By then he had edited *Te Ao Hurihiri,* a collection of essays by Maori writers, and, with photographer Marti Friedlander, published *Moko: Maori Tattooing in the 20th Century.* But already he was feeling some chill winds of disapproval. Michael spoke Maori and, through his time covering the Maori round on the *Waikato Times* and, later, his relationship with Irihapeti Ramsden, he had close links with Maori royalty. He and Irihapeti had lived in our street together during a brief and sadly fated affair. They lived with Irihapeti's children in a brown box-like apartment with low ceilings, at the edge of 'The Zigzag' steps that linked Hataitai and Rakau roads. We visited each other frequently. Things didn't go well for long, and Irihapeti returned with the children to their father, although she and Michael maintained an affection for each other until the end of her life. Michael would call on us on his way to visit her in Hataitai, during the last months of her life.

I was willing to listen to those who criticised, but what I didn't like that wintry weekend, was that Pakeha people were pointing their fingers at me. Nor was that the reason I had come to the hui at Rotoiti. Even as their attacks began, I was being greeted by familiar Maori faces from Rotorua days, embraced and exclaimed over as if I'd never been away. I stood my ground but I was shaken, especially when one of the opposing group hissed at me: 'How can you can call yourself Maori? A honky with a tape recorder.'

Of course I had never called myself Maori, nonetheless I felt angry and humiliated. As I left, I knew I would have to address the problem eventually. Later, when I did begin to explore the matter in a calmer light, I started to consider the implications of writing as if Maori didn't exist, and that seemed as big a problem as the one I stood accused of. If I left Maori voices out of my work altogether, surely I would present the face of a monoculture that was, in its way, a form of reverse racism? This was something I wasn't prepared to contemplate. I would have to learn to do it differently. But, as a first step, I decided never to adopt a first person Maori voice in my work again; rather, I would regard the relationship from a Pakeha perspective, in which the characters had equal weight. After all these years, it interests me that none of my friends in the Maori or Pacific Island writing communities ever appeared to waver in their friendship. Witi, Pat Grace, whom I have known for thirty years now, Albert Wendt—they have all been constant. If they had private views on the matter, they did not express them; I think they understood some of my inner conflict, and trusted me to find my way through it.

As I drove away from Rotorua, I was feeling troubled on several other counts. Before I left, my father had taken me aside and asked me what I could do to help them leave Rotorua. He and my mother were lonely in the Hannah's Bay house, and my father had never been good at coping with other people's illness. My mother's frequent extended trips to Queen Elizabeth Hospital were taking their toll on both of them. Nearly every time I left them, he would say, 'This may the last time you see me.' It never made departure easy. This time, he said, 'Get me out of here.'

I drove down the Desert Road, the landscape bitter in the rain. Giles and I were both pleased to be on our way home. Every tyre on the car punctured before we got back to Wellington. At first it was something of an adventure for Giles, who already had a handy knack with everything practical and helped me to change the tyres. About ten o'clock, the last one to go blew out on the Mangaweka hills with an explosive bang. 'I'm frightened, Mum,' he said, as we sat in the black night air, swirling with mist.

'So am I,' I said. We were picked up by some passers-by and given shelter for the night in their farmhouse at Hunterville.

The first *Writing* programme went to air and received a mixed reception. Some writers down south were outraged that a nationwide programme was being run from Wellington, declaring that it should appear on a province by province basis. A critic wrote that I had a curious, hollow voice, or words to that effect, and should let someone else voice the programmme. Delaney took me off air, and although I produced the programme for five years, I never voiced anything again. This meant that the programme carried the cost of bringing in other presenters and interviewers. These included Michael King, who returned to Wellington from time to time, and, for the most part, Elizabeth Alley, who had had a high profile career in broadcasting before having children. At the time, she was out of the permanent workforce. The Concert Programme position was one of those situations I should probably have walked away from, but ten hours' work a week was better than nothing. I had hoped that the position in the drama department would lead to something permanent, but although I loved the work and was good at it, Tony Groser's plan to rotate writers was firmly in place. I couldn't argue with that.

I tried to compensate for my shortcomings on air by being super efficient and by drawing in a wide diversity of writers for the programme. My desk, which I occupied for two afternoons a week, was on the second floor of Aurora House. There, I quickly discovered a new friend. Sharon Crosbie's office was next door to mine. She was to be found there in the afternoons, after she had finished her *Nine to Noon* morning programme, planning the following day's stint with her producer, Maree Corbett. Sharon was one of the most vibrant human beings I had ever met. At first, I was totally in awe of her, as was the whole country. There was no competition from talkback then and she had the airwaves to herself. If Europe stops for a siesta, in those days you could say that New Zealand took its daily break while Sharon was on air. Witty, sharp, relentless in her probing interviews, and ferocious with politicians from either side of the House if they tried to lie to her, Sharon was one of the most influential women in New Zealand. Yet underneath this ran a beguiling warmth, a sweetness in her nature, that kept her in touch with real people. These are the qualities that I still find irresistible in her company. She has always been an insatiable reader, and although she had guest critics, she read everything that was reviewed on her show. Having a favourable review on her programme was the New Zealand equivalent of appearing on *Oprah.*

Soon after my arrival on the second floor, she invited me in for a cup of tea. Her office was a scene of organised chaos—two phones ringing all the time, piles of paper everywhere, people banging on her door. After our first few afternoon teas, the callers would often be told, 'Go away, I'm having tea with Fiona.' Sometimes I wondered why. Perhaps it was just that I wasn't given to prolonged bouts of awe. Sharon wanted to be a person as well as a star and we began talking about our lives as other women do. When I introduced Sharon to Keith during one of his visits to Wellington there was an instant rapport between them. The three of us started having late lunches together when he was in town, which helped to dispel some of the slight awkwardness I had felt after my abrupt departure from the Book Council.

My hours for the *Writing* programme increased the following year but I was still working on part-time contract when more work on *Close to Home* came up. I hadn't entirely given up the hope that I would be offered the once promised staff contract, which would have solved my employment worries. The work didn't last long and ended in a deeply shaming episode. The commissioning script editor decided to hit on me, often asking ask me to lunch in the cafeteria at the new Avalon studios, where *Close to Home* was shot, when I delivered my scripts. There was something creepy and unctuous about this man. I didn't want to be rude to someone who was employing me but I made excuses to hurry away. One day he asked if I could drop by his house with my script, as he would be working from home.

When I arrived, he opened the door and invited me inside. Straight away I felt uncomfortable about this, but we were work colleagues and it seemed churlish to refuse. And anyway he stood inside so that I had to step in and hand him the script. Immediately, the door was slammed behind me as he pushed me against a wall, hands under my dress. As I tried to fight him off, his phone began to ring, and kept on until he decided to knock it from its cradle, allowing me to make my escape.

The next time, I was asked to deliver the script to the studio on a Sunday morning. Guessing there wouldn't be many people around, I asked Ian to go with me. He sat in the car park below and waited. I told him that if I didn't come back within ten minutes he was to follow me. In those days there were no security guards on duty. There wasn't a soul to be seen in the building, except the editor. Straight away he jumped me, only this time I was ready for him. I told him that Ian would be here in a minute or so if he didn't let me go.

In the 1980s, I would work in the screen industry with a private company, but as I left Avalon that morning I felt pretty much finished with television. I learned shortly after these disgusting episodes that some of my scripts had been found in the department with obscenities scribbled all over them. As women often do in situations like this, I felt guilty and ashamed. I knew that the man had abused his position but there were no other women working in drama, nobody I could tell. I couldn't see any recourse. This man is long dead. Although I have never, once, hated men in any general sense, I hated this man.

I had had enough. I was exhausted by the years of piecemeal work, erratic hours, frustrated ambitions. I decided that, whatever the cost, I would write a novel. Nothing else would save my sanity.

I took a chance and sent off an application to the State Literary Fund, asking for a thousand dollars. I didn't expect to get it but in one of those miraculous serendipitous moments, a letter came to say that my application had been successful.

One thousand dollars was exactly the price of a new roof. And when a reporter phoned to ask me what I would do with the money that was what, in a state of euphoria, I said I would be buying with my grant. Some letters of indignation appeared in the newspapers, demanding what the state was doing handing out money to a writer to spend on a roof. In hindsight, they were hilarious.

The contretemps more or less passed me by. I was a writer who was going to write a novel without water dripping down the back of my neck. I was pretty happy.

I had come to the point of writing this novel by a long and difficult road. It was not the first one I had attempted, but this time I knew it had to work, or else I needed to get on with my life, find a steady job, stop looking back over my shoulder and yearning. I had decided to write about the lives of the women I knew who had somehow muddled their way through the past decade or so, and survived. I had the title in my head as I shoved the first piece of paper into my typewriter. I was ready to begin *A Breed of Women.*

Chapter 18

This morning I got up at five thirty. I don't know what woke me, perhaps one of the trains that rattle across the bridge over avenue de Verdun, coming and going to Italy.

I went out onto the balcony and stood looking in the greenish grey light of dawn towards the sea, to where I thought I might see Corsica. An earlier fellow had told me that if you looked at this time of day, it was possible to see the island lying on the horizon, although I suspect you have to be higher up in the mountains.

After a while I went back to bed and fell asleep. When I woke, Ian had gone out and the day proper had begun. Before long, I spotted him coming along the avenue, which is filled with buckets painted cobalt blue and crammed with chrome-bright zinnias. The public garden spaces are planted with vegetables, peppers, tomatoes, maize. Why don't people steal the vegetables? we asked Luc the other day. He laughed. They know that the dogs have already pissed on them. Well, that makes sense: there are dogs everywhere, even with their own seats at restaurant tables, where they sit with their long coiffed hair falling over their eyes, just like the old ladies who inhabit this Riviera resort.

Ian was loaded with fresh fruit and croissants, and had an English language newspaper under his arm. He goes out every morning to the markets to buy fresh supplies, before it's too hot. A heatwave has developed over Europe. The temperature has soared beyond that of the desert train stops in Australia. It's too hot to go backwards and forwards to the Katherine Mansfield Room, easier to write here in the apartment. Soon after we arrived, I discovered that the card table beside the door to the balcony unfolds to reveal a perfect work surface covered in green baize. This is where I set up my notebook computer. We open all the doors and, because we are a little way above the town, up the mountain, a breeze slips through the apartment from time to time. At lunchtime, I stop work, drink ice-cold rosé and eat fresh rosy peaches. All my life I have been unable to bite a peach. Like my grandmother Small, on my mother's side. Now it is not a problem at all.

I watched Ian turning into Montée du Lutetia, the steep little street where we live. He half raised one laden arm in salute, as he walked towards me. This is the story of my life—Ian walking towards me, never away. There were times when he might have. I don't know whether anyone else would have stayed.

Memory can be difficult sometimes.

In the beginning I was so consumed with the pleasure of writing that I didn't consider the implications of going on and on until something was finished. Some days I'd wake up and begin to write with such freedom and spontaneity that it seemed effortless, and there are still days that are like this. I'm happy when I'm in this state, and when I haven't been writing for some time I become unhappy in some deep subconscious way. But as the early years passed, I began to worry that I didn't have the staying power to finish a major work. This was partly why it took me so long to begin my second attempt at a novel. I hadn't written my first by the time I was twenty-eight, as I had once hoped, and if I didn't do something about it, it wouldn't happen by the time I was forty. I'd kept on writing all those things that could be completed in short bursts to meet deadlines, followed by a little celebration and meeting people. In essence, I'd forgotten how to be alone.

About the time I set forth yet again to write a novel, I discovered a book that actually did change my life. *Working It Out: 23 Women Writers, Artists, Scientists, and Scholars Talk About Their Lives and Work* was edited by Sara Ruddick and Pamela Daniels, and had a foreword by Adrienne Rich. The contributors all talked about the working life of the creative mind. An essay by a psychology professor called Virginia Valian held the key for me to making good use of limited time. As she identified, it's often not the time a piece of work will take, but the fear of being cut off from the world that puts people off writing. When she was young, Valian had faced real problems with completing work. She would try to concentrate on work she had set herself, but the hours stretched ahead of her, hours she believed she must fill in a significant way, and she couldn't face them. So she didn't begin work at all. She then began experimenting with breaking time down into small, quality chunks, what she called 'doable, imaginable' acts. In short, she proposed that by working for, say, fifteen minutes, without interruptions of any kind—no trips to the kitchen for a snack, or to the bathroom, no phone calls, just work—it was possible to achieve a surprising number of words on the page. The writing didn't have to be complete or polished, but it was a confirmed act: it existed. Most people, she reckoned, could survive fifteen minutes of work. If they were having a good time, they might like to keep going. If they weren't, they should stop. This was the difference between quality time and unimaginable quantities of time.

Valian showed me that what I had been doing, ever since I began to write seriously, was, in a sense, a method, and one particularly suited to a woman with a domestic life. All those early mornings, the snatched minutes and hours when I worked as if my life depended on it, had been to some effect. What I needed to grasp was how to work consistently on one continuous project without stopping. Her words persuaded me to 'work it out' for myself. To find my own system.

And this is it. I figured out that it was not so much the time, but the amount of work that I could achieve each day on a regular basis that counted towards my finishing something. Earlier, Keith Sinclair had mentioned something along these lines. I remembered him saying that if a writer writes a thousand words a day, it's possible to work out roughly how long a project will take. Treat it like a job, until you've finished, he said.

As it happens, a thousand words a day is about right for me. I can write more, but writing is physically and mentally demanding and if I write too much I get too tired to begin again the next day, and the routine is lost. Because I know there is tomorrow, I'm generally excited about what the next day will bring, rather than being frightened of it. Later, after the early novels, I began to do a rough plan, using a board in my study with notes pinned to it, showing an outline of where the book was heading, so that I didn't have to stop and struggle with the structure in the middle of what I was writing. That, at least, was something I learned from television, to storyboard efficiently. Not that I did this for *A Breed of Women.* Rather, when I was back home, writing my book, I remembered that I had once been accustomed to solitude, that it had featured in my life for much of my childhood, and that I had survived it. More than that, I had often been happy in my own company. As I wrote I began to like myself again.

In many ways, *A Breed of Women* fell into place as if it had always been there, although not without some lost direction at the beginning. There were some decisions to be made. The characters had some strong resemblances to women I knew, and to their lives. To my own, too, as it happens, although, as I have often told people, I am not Harriet Wallace, the central character. When I look back, I can see that I was naïve if I expected people to believe that she and I did not share exactly the same stories. Harriet grows up in the North in a tiny township called Ohaka. It means 'the place of the dance', and so far as I know there is no such place. It is a nice name for a town and I'd like to think there could be a real one some day.

When Harriet is a teenager she goes to live in a small North Island town with an aunt. I wrestled for some time with what to call this town. In the end, I invented Weyville, because it sounds so much like other small towns in the North Island—Hunterville, Morrinsville ... Harriet has a brief disastrous marriage to a young Maori man called Denny which ends when their baby dies at birth. The couple divorce and, after a second marriage and the birth of more children, Harriet and her husband move to Wellington, where she writes poetry, becomes a television presenter who gets sacked for putting on too much weight, and develops a drinking problem.

So the bones of my own progress from rural to city New Zealand are there, but of course the journey is laced with events that never took place. For a long time I was asked about my 'first' marriage, and about the process of divorce.

I was drawing on the experiences of a number of women for the novel. As I wrote, I felt their voices at my shoulder, as argumentative and real as if they were in the room. There was one crowd of friends saying 'No, no you can't put that in, everyone would know it was me.' Others urged me 'not to leave it out' or said, 'You've got it wrong, it wasn't like that.' I wrote 70,000 words before the magical transformation between 'what happened' and fiction took place. It's a mysterious alchemy, almost impossible to describe, yet a writer knows when it has happened. It is not the blunt pickaxe of 'the characters taking over': I don't really believe in that kind of automated dictation. Ultimately, I like to be in charge. But there is a moment when something happens that arises entirely from the character's experience or personality. Then you know that the characters have achieved a life beyond you or the people you know. At that moment, you sit very still and listen to what they have to say to you.

And this is the commitment you enter into in a novel: to be willing to do a good deal of listening, to talk to your characters when they talk to you, to keep track of what they tell you, even when you're not writing. I keep a pen and a small notebook with me at all times, because I don't always remember what I've been told, and have to write down straight away what I hear. This is what happened when I was writing *A Breed of Women,* and it wasn't until that moment of listening occurred that I knew how to write the book. I took the first 70,000 words down the garden (because of course they were written on paper then, not a computer), dumped them in the incinerator and set fire to them.

I have never done anything so drastic with a manuscript since, but then it was the right thing to do. I began the book all over again, listening to the voices of Harriet and her friend Leonie, and all the people they encounter along the way.

The subject of rape arose in the book, because that was something my friends and I talked about, the forced casual nature of sexual encounters in our youth, and what constituted consent. Since I had written *Angel,* and my own close brush with a would-be rapist, I had thought about it a lot. At a dinner party in *A Breed of Women,* a man suggests that rape doesn't occur because people would hear women screaming if they were being raped. Harriet suggests that all the guests shout 'rape' as loudly as they can. When they conduct this experiment, nobody comes, and the dinner party continues, point proven.

In order to write this scene, I conducted an experiment of my own. I went through the back fence and saw my elderly neighbour to warn her what I was about to do. Then I went back to the house and shouted 'rape' at the top of my voice for five or ten minutes. I opened the doors and windows and shouted and still nobody came. I rang my neighbour and asked her how it had sounded. 'Oh,' she said, 'have you done it? I didn't hear a thing.'

The women in my book have love affairs, and quarrels, and they drink a lot. I had wanted to write about that because, for many of us, the 1970s sometimes seemed like a decade of blurred vision. Perhaps, reading this, you will wonder if I used only my imagination and other people's experiences, without ever having to feel remorse or regret of my own. Well, of course not. You couldn't get through those times without making some mistakes. I made some of my own. One of Harriet's is rather too close for comfort, a night when she has been with friends and had too much to drink. She gets in her car, drives in the opposite direction to home and finishes up on a dark deserted beach some thirty kilometres from home, having travelled over a steep and winding road. She sits in the dark at three o'clock in the morning in a state of sudden clarity and absolute horror at what she has done. Something like this did happen to me while I was still writing the book, and the episode was painfully etched on my conscience.

I had been persuaded by Leigh to come out of my self-imposed exile for the sitting in Parliament to pass the Contraception, Sterilisation and Abortion Act, which would enable women to obtain abortions for other than medically life-threatening conditions. The previous five years or so had seen intense political activity in the abortion debate. In 1975, under Prime Minister Bill Rowling, the Labour government had established a Royal Commission of Inquiry on Contraception, Sterilisation and Abortion, which sat for twenty-one months. In the same year Air Commodore Frank Gill had introduced a bill that sought to restrict abortions to public hospitals (known as the Gill Bill), but it had been defeated. Although the royal commission report was very conservative, it was introduced, with many amendments, by the National government. On 15 December 1977, it was decided to pass it in one all-night sitting, with the House under urgency.

This, of course, was a campaign that Leigh and David had long championed, along with other leading figures in the movement. I had had to bow out of providing accommodation for Sisters Over Seas. Both our teenage children had friends staying either on a semi-permanent basis or as regular visitors, and most nights there wasn't a spare bed in the place. Giles's best friend Boydie, who had migrated from a settlement on the East Coast, was living with us, and Vannessa Ternent, a school friend, used to stay over at the weekends. There had perhaps been an element of relief in letting go of this arrangement with SOS. I found I had a divided heart over the predicament of some of the young women who stayed with us. Most of them wept through the night, both before and after their secret shameful flights to Sydney. Some of them wanted to keep their babies, but could see no way of doing so. At least one of the deaths of my friends' daughters had been due to the 'shame' associated with an out of wedlock pregnancy, and her subsequent pain over giving her baby up for adoption.

Although adoption worked for us, I was increasingly aware that this was not the case for all families, and certainly not for all the children who had been adopted in the past, or for the many women who had been scarred by giving up their children. There was now a groundswell of opposition to adoption, which I understood, although I was often discomforted by those who felt bitter towards women who had adopted. I saw my own role as being part of a movement towards wider options. The Labour government's 1974 introduction of the Domestic Purposes Benefit, to provide support for single mothers, seemed singularly enlightened legislation, although it took a few years for it to catch on as a way to deal with unplanned pregnancies.

However, my views on women's right to choose remained unchanged and this night in Parliament was such a momentous one that I agreed to go along with Leigh. A big group of women was camped out in the office of the feisty young National MP, Marilyn

Waring. The House was sitting under urgency. Gin was being poured by the tumbler. Every now and then Frank Gill came to the door, red-faced, to stand shouting and jeering. At one point, he lurched into the office, raising his fists in a threatening manner. He and Waring were both members of the same party, but they couldn't have been more opposed to each other's views.

Marilyn faced him squarely. 'Get out of my office,' she ordered.

Gill looked as if he was going to refuse and blustered about his right to be in that part of the building. The mood in the room turned ugly as the women readied to throw him out bodily. Soon after that I left. I found the enraged politicising over women's rights and bodies an unhappy spectacle and I'd had enough of the aggression. I wasn't there when the bill was passed. Some time in the early hours of the morning, I got in my car and accidentally headed for Makara, in the opposite direction to home.

Anybody who does something as stupid as that doesn't deserve the right to forgive themselves unless they vow not to do it again and mean it. I did, and so does Harriet Wallace. The novel, then, allows for redemption in the face of folly. In many ways, like the character of Bethany Dixon, Harriet was an alter ego, but a much raunchier, more upfront one than Bethany. Harriet stands up for herself and says what she thinks. Not everyone admires that trait in a woman, even now. But, for the times, it was a declaration about what women could do if they set their minds to it.

Almost as much as the characters in the book, the town of Weyville was a place that readers would identify with, as if they lived in it themselves and I was simply writing their town in disguise. People from Whangarei to Gore claimed it as their own. They insisted that I could confide the truth to them because it was so obvious. I've kept the place in several stories, but like a mad town planner I've been able to put in whole new subdivisions, and redesign its town centre. As its population has risen, only its essential nature remains the same—a central North Island town, with shining blue or thundery grey days in summer, biting cold, clear frosty light and a rim of pink over evening hills in winter.

I finished the book early the following year. On the last day, I began early and typed with furious haste. There was a function at the Book Council that evening, and I had decided that if I could finish the book in time I would go. I'm a fast two-fingered typist and I broke all my own rules, typing 6000 words that day. When I got to the party I met Michael King at the door. 'You look as if you've seen a ghost, Fiona.'

'I've seen the end of my book,' I said, 'and I reckon it's going to work.'

I did some revisions, paid a friend to type up clean copy for me, and sent it off to Ray Richards. Ray had been the managing director of A.H. & A.W. Reed when *Search for Sister Blue,* which sold well for years, was published, and had since set up as a literary agent. In his forty odd years at Reed's, he had 'discovered' many notable authors, including Barry Crump and Mona Anderson. His original intention as an agent was not to take much fiction but, as a gesture to the past, he agreed to look at my book.

A couple of days later the phone rang around six in the morning. 'Ray here. I've been up all night. I've just finished your book, couldn't put it down. I'll find you a publisher.'

The publisher he found me just a week or two later was Brian Wilder at Harper & Row in Sydney. Brian was a powerful man on the Australian publishing scene, an English immigrant who, nonetheless, looked a lot like Rolf Harris, with a similar gung-ho jovial approach to life. I liked him and his wife Helen straight away when they came over to visit for Brian to eye up his new talent. He was a smart businessman with a great marketing sense. It would be nearly two years and a good bit of rewriting before the novel appeared in 1979.

Chapter 19

In all, I spent six years working in radio broadcasting. That was never my intention, but some things happened between my finishing *A Breed of Women* and its publication that changed everything.

The health of both my parents continued to spiral downwards. On a trip north I called to see the Morrinsville relatives. Robert, not well himself, took me aside and had a word. He was worried about my mother and felt he should do something for her. It weighed on his conscience, he said, that he might die without having offered help. I pointed out that the worth of the tiny Hannah's Bay house up north was very different from what it would cost to buy a house in Wellington. He assured me that, if I could get my parents to Wellington, he would provide financial help. Then Jean wanted to chip in too. She had looked after my grandmother without complaint, seeing herself as chosen for the task. In my case, as there was nobody else, she took it for granted that I would take this role upon myself too.

Shortly afterwards, I found a house in the next street down from us in Hataitai. The rooms were large and well proportioned, and sunshine flooded the dining room, while the back door opened onto a pleasant sheltered courtyard. I could see its roof from the bay window at the front of our house. There was a lot of work needed to tidy it up but it was sound and Ian and I agreed we would do as much as we could ourselves. One way and another, however, there was still a big financial shortfall. Nevertheless, with Ian's agreement, I borrowed the money and went ahead. Almost on cue, David Delaney offered me full-time contract work in the Concert Programme. As I had to find regular work again, I decided it might as well be that. I didn't tell my parents what I had done, and they moved without knowing. My father never knew. Given his past relationship with my mother's family, I understood that it would have humiliated him. But I had run out of ideas.

So, near the end of the most active decade of change in women's lives, I had become a dutiful daughter. During the day, I went to work to pay my silent debt. Each evening, I went to check that all was well with my parents and attend to their daily needs.

Did I regret it? At the time, not really. I am at the end of that generation of women who were expected to look after their parents as a matter of course. And I loved mine, in spite of my odd, incomplete relationship with my father.

What would I tell women now, faced with this dilemma, of choosing between independence and the care of their parents? Or rather, what would I say to their mothers? Deep down, I would have to say, prepare to be alone. This is not why we bore daughters. It was hard, and I fell back into unhappiness, my old difficult ways that can have been little consolation to my parents after the upheaval of their move. All the same, my mother loved the house I had bought, and her illness eventually went into remission for some years after my father's death. I am glad that she had the pleasure of a house she truly liked. No, I don't regret what I did. But I wouldn't want anyone to do it for me.

The contract I had with radio extracted the maximum of work for the minimum of pay. I was now required to produce the *Writing* programme on a fortnightly basis, and a weekly talks programme of my own devising. At first I worked with a producer called Lynne Alexander, but she left soon afterwards. I considered the men I worked with lazy and inept. One of them had a cruel tongue; he took months to produce programmes of his own, but often verbally sliced mine to pieces. The other was no better. He held strong misogynist views and had unpleasant personal habits that included taking his Roman sandals and long socks off in the summer, and using the office scissors to cut his toenails, foot up on the desk while he performed this unsavoury task. Both of these men were on regular staff, and senior to me, so there wasn't much I could do. Not all the men on our floor were unkind, although they worked in different departments: men like Peter Downes and Haydn *In a Mellow Tone* Sherley were gentlemen broadcasters who gave me friendly professional advice when they could, but there was nothing they could do about the situation in our office.

I was saved from sheer desperation by three remarkable women. One of them of course, was Sharon next door, who could make me laugh on even the worst days. Then there was Helen Young, manager of the Concert Programme, who had a formidable background in music. She had the most immaculate appearance, never a blonde hair out of place, make-up flawless every day, elegantly cut clothes. Of more importance, she had a generous spirit and stood up for me when things were difficult in the office. Her father had delivered me in Hawera, which was neither here nor there, although there was a sense of family in Concert from Helen's point of view, and she and I were not the only Hawera-born people on our floor. There was also a young woman called Anne McCarten, who had come from the country, a calm sweet-natured person who did the typing and administration in our office and managed to instil sanity into our dysfunctional environment.

If I didn't produce the programmes I was contracted for, I didn't get paid. This prompted me to devise a number of programmes in series. I never failed to deliver and I am still proud of some of the work that I did. When I first joined the Concert Programme, a few inquiries revealed that the entire national archival system was in poor shape and that tapes were regularly recycled. There were, for instance, only four recorded minutes of James K. Baxter, and very little Glover. I set about recording every living poet I could and playing them on alternate weeks to the *Writing* programme. Through this, I met several poets whose friendship I would value far beyond that initial recording session, people like Elizabeth Smither and Michael Harlow.

Elizabeth is a New Plymouth poet whose work has attained an international reputation. Although I had arranged for her to record some poems, when the day came I was away for some reason or other, and production was done by one of the senior producers. I think he unnerved her because, not long afterwards, Elizabeth rang to say that the recording session had gone badly. Then the producer told me the tape was unacceptable for broadcast. I listened to it and thought that some hesitations in the reading could be easily rectified by tight editing, and music run beneath would make the flow of the words sound more relaxed. As I recall, I chose some Schumann, and the recording sounded delightful. Not long after the broadcast, the artist Michael Smither, Elizabeth's husband at the time, sent me a card with a small drawing of his to thank me. I launched Elizabeth's book, *The Sarah Train,* a few months later and we continued to see each other for many years.

Like me, she also became a close friend of poet Michael Harlow, who is another of the writers to have occupied this room here in Menton. Originally Michael Haralambópoulos, and known to his friends simply as Harlow, he is an American-born Greek Ukrainian who has lived in New Zealand for close to forty years. He is one of the few people

I know who still prefers letters to emails, so I look forward to cards and envelopes from Harlow dropping into the letter box at Palais Lutetia.

Because Harlow has lived in various parts of the South Island for as long as I've known him, and Elizabeth in New Plymouth, the three of us would often meet for weekends in Wellington. The first time we all got together was for lunch on a sunny day at a café on Oriental Parade, where we spent the whole afternoon discussing D.M. Thomas's *The White Hotel* with wild enthusiasm, a conversation that carried on until evening. About halfway through the afternoon, I decided to buy a dress at Memsahib's, then a fashionable boutique next door to the café, and the talk was interrupted long enough for everyone to troop in and view the garment while I tried it on. A soft silky black dress splattered with rusty gold and dull red flowers, it appears in one of my Bethany Dixon stories. I gave the dress to Bethany as well as to myself.

I devised a major series called *Looking Back,* recording the memories of older New Zealanders who had made significant contributions to art and education—always, of course, with the help of guest interviewers, because of my voice. I organised the recording of educators, like Beeb and Max Riske, and the last interview with the artist Olivia Spencer Bower, and a whole host of others, on tape. Elizabeth Alley went down to Christchurch and recorded the last interview with Dame Ngaio Marsh, who forgot Elizabeth was coming and went upstairs to take a nap at the appointed hour. As Elizabeth told it, she stood forlornly on the doorstep, ringing the bell. Eventually she managed to rouse the sleeping crime writer, and the result was a great interview. She and I also recorded several hours of Denis reading his work, and talking about his life. We brought some vodka into the studio to help him sit still for the required length of time, and I took in a glass every hour or so. What I hadn't realised was that Lyn had sent him off with a hip flask of his own. In his moments of clarity, he was a great subject and raconteur. I found myself wishing I had known him before he became such an addled reprobate.

The archival system didn't improve during my time in broadcasting, although change was afoot round the time I was leaving. I was afraid these precious recordings would be wiped. You only had to leave a tape on a windowsill and someone would collect and recycle it. I wasn't the only one to take them home. I stored dozens in my wardrobe. They would later find their way to the Alexander Turnbull Library, along with my hoarded cartons of correspondence.

Ian and I were working incredibly hard. His school commitments had expanded still further and, as well, he got the children up and took them to college with him every day. We had decided that Naenae was the best co-educational school available. They were usually all out of the house by seven. Up until then, I had been able to fit freelancing comfortably into my life, but now housework was a struggle. The washing machine went on every morning as soon as I got up, coloured one day, whites the next. Weekends were taken up with shopping and preparing meals in advance. I looked in awe at the rapid demolition of Sunday roasts I'd spent hours over. I had the new responsibilities of my parents in the neighbourhood, and all the people who lived in our house to feed at the end of each day. I was still teaching for University Extension one weekend a month. That was Ian's weekend to take over the household.

At the same time, I had tentatively begun to write *Mandarin Summer,* a novel based on the earlier play, at the weekends and in my lunch breaks. I was trying to follow the routines I had learnt from reading Valian's essay, about making the best use of even small amounts of time.

Since the success of the play on air, I knew *Mandarin Summer* was a story I wanted to hold onto. Much as I loved the medium of radio, I regretted the way the best stories would melt away in time. Besides, I couldn't leave the North alone. Now that my parents lived close, we often talked about the past and our time in Darwin Road. They were still divided over their view of

Kerikeri. For my father it was a place where things might have gone well but for a little more luck here and there. For my mother it was a nightmare of servility and poverty. And for me, it remained a place where the exotic was mingled with solitariness and a fractured family life. A place where I had felt damaged. Some nights, when I lay awake, I would see sunlight, sticky summer paspalum grass, ripe pendulous fruits hanging in the hedgerows in the heat. And oranges, glimmering among their jade-green castles of leaves. I often slept restlessly or not much at all. A dark corner would turn over at the edge of the picture. I could never quite lift it. Nor, in this fragmented way that I was writing, could I see how to shape the book. I struggled this way and that trying to work out points of view and who would tell the story.

When Albion Wright published a second collection of my poems, *On the Tightrope* in 1978, there was no launch party, but I decided to cheer myself up by organising a party at the house anyway. Everyone was there. Except Lauris, who had quietly brought out the elegiac and haunting collection, *The Pear Tree,* a month or so earlier, poems that reflected considerably on the death of Rachel. But there were film producers, editors, publishers and writers all crammed into our small house, the rooms overflowing. Chris Hampson and his then wife were there, as were Sam and Kristen. Chris and Sam had been collaborating on the publication of some beautifully designed books for their own private press, Hampson Hunt. This press didn't last long, but the books they did produce, such as the 1977 *Drunkard's Garden,* are collectors' items. Beeb was there, as usual, demanding to see our resident Botticelli Venus, as he called Joanna. Alison Littlefair, now on her own and saddened by the end of her marriage, Alistair and Meg Campbell, Noel Hilliard and his wife Kiriwai.

There was something in the air. Ian's friend, a Greek psychologist, went through our pile of records and came across Ian's beloved collection of Gregorian chants. 'Gregorian chants anyone?' he yelled. 'How about a bit of Gregorian?' What started out well enough quickly assumed a troubling edge. People drank too much too fast. Men began dancing together in ways that were unusual at the time. A poet mooned, inviting women to paint faces in lipstick on his buttocks. At some point, writer and bookseller Chris Else and publisher Bob Ross got involved in a good-natured but riotous farewell on our steps. Ian suggested they leave more quietly because he was getting worried that the party might attract the police. Michael Noonan came back inside and announced that Ian Kidman had thrown Chris and Bob down the steps. It never happened, as all three men would say, but it was a rumour that persisted for years. Then, in another quite separate incident, a man left the party and was involved in an incident that required Ian and me to spend the rest of the night at the police station. You could say it had all turned to shit.

In the morning, Ian was grey-faced as we surveyed the damage. He looked at me and said, 'I can't do any more of this. No more parties.'

I had to agree. What happened hadn't been fun. In the early days of Wellington, Ian had enjoyed the sparkle and novelty of being in the swim with well-known people. But he didn't drink and, lately, he had begun to see these nights from a different perspective, as messy affairs leaving clean-ups and regrets in their wake. Our children were used to writers streaming through the house, but they no longer wanted to perform for them. We were approaching middle age; it was time for their parents to grow up.

So that was it. I still loved to socialise but the parties at our house were over. There have been many gatherings of friends and family at the house, but that was the last time we ever allowed chaos to rule.

We turned our energies back to work, and also confronted the fact that Russell Bernstone was dying. We visited him every night at the hospital for many weeks, until the end. He wasn't even forty.

Neither was Carole when she died.

As we were getting ready for work one morning, we heard on the seven o'clock news the report of a car crash on Wellington's southern coast. Carole was named among the dead.

I hadn't seen much of Carole the previous year, as she had bought a house further away from us, the first she had owned since the break-up of her marriage nearly a decade before. But on International Women's Day, the previous year, Lynne Alexander had made a special programme of women telling their life stories, and I had suggested Carole. The recording was strong and poignant. She spoke of failures in her life, and about the unpredictability of the future, the way she took things a day at a time, and what gave her strength—small things like milestones in her children's lives, her belief in friendship, and giving what you had to others, even if it was just the time to listen.

On the recent occasions I had spoken to her, she seemed happier, although I knew that some of her old hangers-on were still around. After she died, a friend who had been in jail produced a letter Carole had written a few weeks earlier, in which she predicted her own early death. Yet she had had no part in the accident that claimed her life. A friend had called with his son to show off a new car, and invited her and her second son for a ride around the coast. It was a black night with high winds and rain, but the friend let his son drive, and the two sixteen-year-olds occupied the front seats, while Carole and the friend sat in the back.

The car leapt out of control over the cliff beneath the Pines Cabaret. The two boys were injured, although not critically, but both the back seat passengers were killed. Before she died, Carole crawled on her hands and knees across the rocks to say goodbye to her son and leave messages for the others.

> *Carole friend*
> *named in fact after that silvery*
> *cataclysmic blonde*
> *who took such an unruly*
> *unexpected plunge*
> *into a warring sea*
>
> *so you too taking*
> *to the indecipherable dark.*

The symmetry seemed too unlikely to be true, but it was. Carole's mother asked me to help arrange the funeral service at the local Anglican church. The vicar was a man with a cold manner. I told him that there was a tape of Carole speaking about her life and that I thought it might help the family if they heard her voice at the funeral.

'I don't want any funeral service I conduct turned into a 2ZM roadshow,' he said.

'Well,' I said, 'that may be so, but I think she's still got something to say.'

So, after the last letter had been read aloud by one of the friends, the packed and hushed church was filled with Carole's voice on a crackling speaker, explaining that life had been hard, bits of it gone astray, but how, knowing where she had come from, she understood better how to face the future.

Carole's mother asked if the mourners could gather at our place after the funeral. There were sad little farewells, not just to Carole but to the family. The son who had been in the accident was in hospital, where he stayed for several months; his older brother was going off to live with relatives; and the third boy was collected by his father and placed in institutional care.

A decade or so later, Carole's mother mailed me a framed picture of Carole before I knew her, holding her second child in her lap. I opened up the package, and there she was, with that same zany grin at the corner of her mouth that I knew so well. Only she was younger in this photograph, and she was wearing a twin-set and pearls. That was the Carole I never really knew. Perhaps it's the person she would have liked to have been or set out to be. The picture still stands on a desk in my study.

Chapter 20

I was still struggling to write *Mandarin Summer*. Help came in an unexpected shape. I came across Ruth Prawer Jhabvala's Anglo/Indian novel *Heat and Dust*, which I liked immensely, particularly the way she captured the exoticism of her setting and the contrasting reality of life within it. I liked, too, the structure of the novel, in which alternating points of view were presented. What I didn't realise was that Jhabvala was also a screenwriter, part of the famous Merchant Ivory group that later made a number of period dramas, including *Heat and Dust*. The choppy style of the novel was very filmic and I identified with the similarities to screen writing. This was the answer I was looking for, and offered a way forward for *Mandarin Summer*.

Like the play, my novel explored the voice of the child Emily, who goes north with her parents. Of course it is an autobiographical novel, more so than any I have written before or since. As in the play, too, the pianist, initially a casual visitor, becomes a semi-permanent resident, the fire proves lethal, and the child lives in the house when it happens. None of these things was true, but the story of Constance and Luke Freeman and Emily essentially belongs to my family.

Unexpected help came, too, from Anne McCarten, who was widely read and well informed about books. With her good degree and interest in literature, I could never quite work out why she worked in the typing pool and looked after our troublesome office, but I was very glad that she did. I had even more reason to be grateful when she offered to type up clean copy of *Mandarin Summer* in the weekends, and read and reread parts of the manuscript as it was done, offering sensible comments along the way.

When *A Breed of Women* was finally released, I figured I would have a second novel ready to offer Brian Wilder.

Breed was launched in 1979 at the old Alexander Turnbull Library in Bowen Street, the first launch party in the building since the Turnbull had been shifted to its new National Library premises. To me it seemed like hallowed territory, as it was to the crowds who turned up, used to its quiet atmosphere and book-lined walls.

Sharon had agreed to launch the book. A day or so before, I had taken delivery of my advance copies. I was at my desk in broadcasting when they arrived. Immediately, I took an extra copy through to Sharon. Keith had dropped by for a coffee and I gave him a copy too. We finished up in my car driving through town with Keith Sinclair and Sharon Crosbie leaning out of the windows waving copies of *A Breed of Women* and shouting the good news that there had never been a book like it, and encouraging me to toot the horn.

On the morning of the launch, I woke up at five. I pulled on my dressing gown and went out to the sitting room where I can look over Evans Bay and across the harbour. In the clear calm dawn the faintest breeze ruffled the sea. In the quiet, before people were up, I could hear the chink of rigging on the boats anchored below.

In a moment of premonition, I saw my life ahead and knew that it would never be exactly the same again. There was no turning back from what I had done.

I was due to be interviewed on Sharon's programme later in the morning. When she came on air after the nine o'clock news, she said, 'Darlings, I've got the book we've all been waiting for. This book is about us. We're *all* in it.' That night she made another glowing tribute at the launch.

Again, everyone was there. The family. My parents. Politicians. Journalists. All the old Book Council crowd, including Keith, and masses of broadcasters. Shona McFarlane and her husband Alan Highet, the Minister for the Arts, sat drinking champagne on the steps. We don't have launches like that any more.

Leigh was there too, looking tired and distracted as if she wasn't quite part of the celebration. I knew that she had all but given up on the struggle to live with David. The changes in him were so profound that it was hard to keep love alive. I knew too there was someone new in her life. I could hardly blame her.

The next week the book sold 9000 hardback copies. I lost count of how many it sold over the years, but I think it was about 40,000. The reviews were very mixed. The *Listener* was decidedly ho-hum. The critic in *Landfall* wrote, 'Sigh! The thinking woman's Mills and Boon.' It didn't seem to make any difference. People bought and bought it. I was all over the newspapers, the most interviewed woman in the country at the time, everything from the lightest women's magazines to the feminist journal *Broadsheet*. Foolishly, I told one interviewer that I had bought a pair of French stockings for the launch. The ensuing article described me as 'a plump housewife in French stockings'. It was true. Like Harriet, I was decidedly overweight at the time.

A rumour circulated that I was about to be sued by someone who believed they had been caricatured in the book, but nothing ever came of it. It was surprising the number of people who believed they were portrayed in the novel. One day I was walking down The Terrace with Michael King when he said, 'Fiona, you don't know how embarrassing this book of yours is for me.'

'Why?' I asked.

'Well,' he said, 'ask yourself—Harriet's boyfriend is called Michael. People just assume it's me.'

I burst out laughing. 'Oh vanity,' I said. Good friend that he was, the thought of him as a romantic hero had never crossed my mind.

I tried to explain that in fiction you made things up, but he didn't see it. 'Anyway,' I said on a cross note, 'even if he was based on a real person, I would hardly have given him his real name, now would I?'

I suppose that was the difference between us, why Michael was a non-fiction writer and I was a novelist.

As well, the book was banned from many school libraries, including the one where Ian taught. I knew he was embarrassed by this, in the same way that he found it difficult to mix with people who assumed that every detail of Harriet Wallace's life reflected mine. We became socially withdrawn for a long period and neither of us would answer questions in each other's company about the book. But, outside of home, and much to my astonishment, I seemed to have become a feminist icon of the times. When I stood up to speak, people began to clap before I had opened my mouth. Fame and notoriety stalked me hand in hand.

Such a radical shift was bound to create some ripples. Although we had fallen quiet in each other's company, Ian and I hung onto each other for dear life. I might have had a glimpse into the future, but I had had no idea that the changes would be so profound. I learned, with dismay, that some of my mother's family were not willing to give house room to the book. I had thought I could do no wrong in their eyes, that I would be forgiven whatever I did. But now I saw that I had gone a step too far. To my surprise, however, my father seemed to take it all quite well, as if scandalising his wife's family wasn't such a bad thing. My mother set her face resolutely and defended me. She would always accept my books for what they were, not what her family would like them to have been.

Now and then I would be pleased by someone who told me that *A Breed of Women* had made them laugh. I had included some moments of comedy, black perhaps, but funny all the same. Most of the public had taken the book with such deadly seriousness, an earnestness I never intended. When someone glimpsed an element of mockery, it changed the way they read the novel. But perhaps that was the real problem for the many men who were so troubled by its contents, and why it caused so many extreme reactions.

The worst response happened when I was scheduled to appear on a television programme designed for family entertainment. David Hartnell plastered me with a heavy layer of make-up. Then I was left to sit for some hours while the rest of the show was pre-recorded. Finally my turn came. The compere didn't look quite like the Mister Nice Guy of the screen.

'What about the morals of this woman, this character in your book? What about her drinking?' he thundered. 'What sort of example are you setting the women of New Zealand?'

The audience laughed, titillated by this humiliation. Finally I was released, to stumble over a pile of cables in the half dark. I was refused tissues to remove the garish clown make-up. Of course, the item was never shown, nor, I realised, had it ever been intended that it should. I was the comic turn, the extra. This unsavoury tale graphically illustrated the way in which, at the most extreme end of the scale, men had decided to deal with women's experience—through calculated laughter and ridicule.

Apart from these personal costs, there were other, later repercussions. Women often asked me for advice about separation and divorce but I had none to give. One woman approached me at a reading and said, 'You owe me twelve thousand dollars.'

Of course I asked why.

'Well,' she explained, 'I read *A Breed of Women* and thought, yes, women can take control of their lives, so I got a divorce. But twelve thousand is what it cost me.'

'Are you happy?' I asked.

'Absolutely, it was the best decision I ever made.'

'In that case,' I said, 'I think it's you who owe me twelve thousand.'

We both laughed and agreed to leave it at that.

Then I had a letter from a man up north, a quiet reflective person, who I'd met on one of my writing courses. He was, he said, grateful that he'd read the book, and that it had made some things clearer to him. A few weeks later a letter came from an acquaintance telling me he had taken his life. I often wondered whether the letter and death were linked, and was deeply troubled by the possibility.

My relationship with the men in my office had become more difficult through all this blaze of publicity. Helen and the other women in the department were proud of me, and often said so; the men hardly spoke at all. Unhappily, around this time, I had also fallen foul of the management of the drama department. The New Zealand Writers Guild that Ian Cross had long advocated, and involved me in from the beginning, had come to fruition. I was part of the first negotiating team who met with the various media organisations to negotiate better rates of pay for drama: the only woman in this new union role, and the only person to represent specifically radio interests. The television rounds had gone surprisingly smoothly but the radio round turned bitter and personal.

When I think back, my roles as both an employee and a negotiator were probably incompatible. I didn't see it that way at the time, as I wasn't working for the drama department and felt that it was in the interests of radio to retain its writers, who were simply melting away to television. Although I had enjoyed good rates of pay, they hadn't shifted in eight years.

I began to understand just how far I had fallen from grace when various staff members met me in the stairwells and, at first, tried to persuade me that I was simply mistaken, and later expressed anger. Tony Groser never recovered his goodwill towards me. As it would turn out, it would be at least ten years before I was employed by the drama department again.

On the off chance, I applied for the annual Scholarship in Letters, the major writers' grant awarded by the State Literary Fund. I had repaid my debts and if I could get some serious financial help now, the way ahead might be clear for writing.

Not that I really expected to win the scholarship. Despite the immense popularity of *A Breed of Women,* the muted critical acclaim didn't bode well, nor had it shown up well in the new annual New Zealand Book Awards, designed to complement the more commercial Wattie Awards. Neither of the two men judging the fiction section was renowned for their sympathy for women's causes. When a shortlist of seven was announced, my book wasn't on it. I was fairly taken aback. I hadn't built my hopes around winning the prize but I thought, given the interest in it, the book might at least have been a finalist. If I kept my thoughts to myself, Denis Glover was not so sanguine about his omission from the poetry prize list. He sat hunched at the back of the award ceremony when Curnow went up to win the prize, shouting insults. 'Fraud! Imposter!' he called. But I was standing close to him, and saw that he was close to tears. Denis died suddenly, within weeks of the ceremony. With Elizabeth Alley's help, I took a retrospective tribute to his life and work to air the following evening. Curnow spoke at his packed funeral in Wellington's Anglican cathedral.

My consolation prize was a trip to Sydney. *A Breed of Women* had been around for a year, but Brian Wilder decided it would be a missed opportunity if the book wasn't promoted properly in Australia.

I was forty and had never set foot outside New Zealand.

As I walked into the Harper & Row office with Brian, his secretary was holding a phone. 'It's for Fiona,' she called, although we hadn't met. 'It's Mike Willesee. He wants to talk to her in person.' I could feel the hush around the office.

'Who's Mike Willesee?' I asked. The next morning I would be on the biggest television show in Australia. I did twenty-eight interviews in Sydney and Brisbane that week. On the last morning, I was interviewed on television for *Good Morning Australia* by a woman who asked me, in all sincerity, what I would do if my children married Maori, like the character in my book. I said, 'But my family is Maori, that's who they are,' and she looked shocked and the interview ended. Later that afternoon, I was in a radio station where I had a sudden moment of feeling like a split personality and actually 'saw' a woman who looked like me, in the empty chair opposite, mocking the repetition of the story I had told so many times. It felt troubling and I asked if we could beg off our last appointment. But no, it was *Cosmopolitan* and far too good an opportunity to pass up.

Sydney was crowded and teeming with rain as we threaded our way into the building. At forty, I was very aware of my weight, and I was feeling dreadful. We were hustled into a room where a photographer was organising his gear. 'Take your clothes off and get on the couch,' he said, without turning. He tossed a leopard-skin bodysuit over his shoulder.

His face fell further than mine when he turned around. He had been expecting their centrefold girl of the month. As it was, a discreet head and shoulders turned up in the magazine with a caption 'career girl of the month'.

While I was in Sydney, I learned that Brian didn't want to publish *Mandarin Summer.* I had sent the manuscript on ahead to him. It was, he thought, the kind of strange little book that might go well as my fourth or fifth novel, but not my second.

The day after I arrived home, David shot and killed Leigh.

I had been worried about her for a long time, of course. A week or two before I went away, she rang me to tell me that she was planning to leave David soon. I had rung the house before I left but there was no answer. I arrived at midnight from Sydney and rang Leigh as soon as I got to work next morning. When she answered, her voice sounded strange and hollow. She had gone away with the man she was in love with, but a phone call from one of David's relatives had persuaded her to come back and see him. The previous morning he had roamed the garden, carrying a gun and threatening to shoot himself. They had spent hours talking to each other, without reaching any conclusions. He had poured her several strong gins, and then told her she drank too much. That morning, before he had gone to the surgery, he had given her some Hemineurin to take, which would make her throw up if she drank. It had also made her sleepy and now she was going to lie down.

'Leigh,' I said, 'what has he done with the gun?'

'It's downstairs in the gun cupboard,' she said.

'Are you sure of that?' I felt very frightened for her.

She assured me that the gun was not in the room.

'You should go now,' I said. 'Leave today.'

'I can't, I'm just too sleepy.' Her voice trailed away. 'I'll ring you tomorrow,' she promised.

As I prepared for work the following morning, I heard a news bulletin. A man had been arrested at a 'residence in Kelburn, a plush inner suburb of Wellington' where a woman had been found dead of gunshot wounds. Police were now guarding the entrance to the property. I knew straight away. This was the second time in as many years that I had learnt of a friend's death on the morning news. Ian, for some reason, was late going to work that morning. He took me up to Kelburn and we drove past the house. Sure enough, the police were there. When I got down to work, I rang the newsroom to confirm the name of the person who had died. It was Leigh. Then I rang Adrienne Morgan-Lynch, our mutual friend, and the whole surreal nightmare unfolded:

> When Tess woke the next morning, Vree was dead. Her husband had shot her through the back of the head while she sat on the end of their bed. Later, in court, he told the judge that she had said terrible things to him, and compared him with Clicks. He had

taken the gun, and she had fallen silent. 'She bowed her head, and then I shot her,' he said. Of course he wouldn't have missed, the women said, he'd been a good hunter. One of her teeth was pinned to the floor with the bullet. He smoked a cigarette and called the police.

Only the names, as they say, have been changed. Leigh was thirty-nine when she died. I waited for the police to come and see me while they conducted their interviews, but nobody came. I went to my lawyer and asked him to help me make a statement. I was, I believed, the last person to speak to Leigh. He listened to me, took down many notes, and advised me not to go to the police. There was, as he pointed out, nothing I could do to bring Leigh back. And, by that time, David had a high-profile lawyer. I had been David's patient, and my lawyer thought that if I had any private issues I might prefer not to have raised in court, it would be wise for me not to appear. I saw what he meant.

In the end I did nothing and the matter rested uneasily on my conscience. I didn't go north to the Waikato for the family funeral, nor did I go to demonstrate when David's court appearances turned ugly. I had supposed, in a naïve and silly way, that David would plead guilty to manslaughter on the grounds of insanity. I was wrong. In court, he said that the gun was in the wardrobe, and that in a fit of rage at things that were said in a quarrel, he had grabbed the weapon and shot her without thinking. Worse, Leigh's character was painted into an ugly corner. She drank and smoked dope, it was said, she had a lover, a dirty mouth, her underwear wasn't as clean as it should have been. He pleaded manslaughter on the grounds of provocation and got away with it. Within five years or so he would be practising medicine again.

Crowds of women turned up at the court bearing placards to protest at the way Leigh's character had been portrayed. I felt simply numb with grief.

Some time after this, a memorial service was held for Leigh and finally I surfaced. I wrote a poem for her. One of the men I worked with tried to have me sacked because I asked Anne to type it up for me in the lunch hour, but the complaint was dismissed. I stood up and recited the poem at the service. All kinds of people spoke, including human rights campaigner Rosslyn Noonan, various people from the pro-abortion lobby, a politician and Edelgard, her hairdresser. A group of string players played Leigh's favourite music, and television turned up to film her 'supporters'. I didn't feel particularly heroic. To be honest, I felt as if I had failed a friend, though I couldn't say exactly why:

> All of them had known that Vree was in trouble, and nobody had done anything to save her because, in the end, they were afraid of her husband. They were afraid of his authority, afraid of making trouble, afraid of losing their causes. I did what I could, Tess comforts herself. I have mortgages and regrets, just like everyone else. But hers is a writer's problem. She has got to close top the action, like a

photographer in a war zone, and the edges have become blurred and she can't stop pressing the shutter on and off.

Twenty years later, I went public with my view of what really happened when Leigh died. I would like to have let it rest, as I am sure most people would. But the case against Leigh became a standard line when 'men's rights' were being argued. She was used more than once in the media as an example of the lengths to which a 'bad' woman will drive a man. One day, that line drove me to sit down and write the other version. Of course it hurt people, and of course it changed nothing. But Leigh was a person who deserved to be remembered better.

At the time, though, it felt as if a cause had turned into a war.

Chapter 21

I now had the task of finding a publisher for *Mandarin Summer*. Apart from anything else, I wanted to put *A Breed of Women* behind me. Although I had had so many letters of appreciation for the book, and it finally moved from the banned list to being taught in some secondary schools, I didn't open it again for close to twenty years. When I did, I was surprised. The person who wrote that book wasn't a very polished writer, but she had a passionate and youthful energy that I couldn't help but like. Was that really me?

I went to Auckland and saw my agent, Ray Richards, who arranged a meeting with David Heap at Heinemann's. A few days later came a call from his chief editor, David Ling. He had read the book, as had Michael Gifkins, a freelance editor who did most of Heinemann's reading. They were wildly enthusiastic about the book and had agreed to publish. These two men would be my editors for nearly a decade.

The book puzzled readers when it came out. As Brian had predicted, it was a disappointment for those who loved *A Breed of Women*. But the book created a new readership who saw in *Mandarin Summer* an odd little 'cult' novel, something dark, a trifle sinister, and exotic for New Zealand. I hadn't named Kerikeri, partly because I was not ready, when I wrote the book, to acknowledge just how much of it came out of my own family's life, and partly because I had wanted to create the sense of the big house—Carlyle House in the book—as an isolated and singular backdrop for the mysteries of the story. The novel is long out of print but for many it remains one of the most interesting I've written.

And some good news was on its way. I had been awarded the Scholarship in Letters. I could go off my radio contract for a year to write, and my job would be there waiting for me at the end of it. But as I cleared my desk, just before Christmas, I made a decision. I was not coming back to broadcasting. Ever. And I was never going to take regular work again. I had proved I could manage; I knew I could get work despite my lack of training for pretty well anything. But for nearly twenty years, I had juggled with a variety of jobs and family and writing, searching this way and that for a way to find balance in my life. I had seen other people self-destruct. I felt worn out, not just from my job, but from the griefs and losses of recent years. From now on I would live by my words and some teaching. This was it.

I remember a summer afternoon a few weeks later. I was digging in the garden at the back of the house. There was not a sound except the singing of cicadas. Shadows fell around me through the ngaio tree creating sunlit patterns on the grass. I couldn't remember ever feeling happier.

Eventually, there was no dodging the issue of where *Mandarin Summer* was set. Towards the end of the following year a television crew wanted to make an hour-long documentary of my life in the North for the *Kaleidoscope* arts programme. A week was put aside for filming and, once I'd agreed to the deal, it became clear that much of the documentary would be set in Kerikeri. By then, I was sixteen kilos lighter and had had my hair Afro-styled. I had looked at a picture of myself at Alison's wedding when she remarried (she is now Alison Morgan), and knew that I didn't want to be that exhausted, overweight woman any more.

There was a crew of three on the film shoot. The presenter and director was a woman called Katherine Findley, whom I met when we both worked on the *Listener,* and there was a cameraman and a sound technician called Owen. Over a week in Northland, we formed those strange connected bonds that develop on movie sets. You get to know, after a while, that these are illusory friendships, and in a year or even a month, you will hardly recognise one another in the street. Even the place where we stayed served as an unreal setting for our long late-night conversations: a rambling motel, deep in the country, with suites decorated as the Hollywood, the Las Vegas, and Roman Nights. Katherine was installed in the Arabian Nights room, which invited 'sheiks and slave girls to enjoy the deep purple splendour, the desert stars twinkling in the ceilings'. Outside, cows scratched against the fence posts and moaned softly to themselves. I reached out one night in the Las Vegas suite, looking for the light switch. It was a large wooden dice fixed to the wall with Blu-Tack.

Only the backdrop for my life was not a set, I told myself, it was real. It was at the end of Darwin Road.

The owners of the property that had once been Goathland Farm allowed access to our crew. Katherine and I sat outside the remnants of the old army hut that had been my home and talked about the life I had lived there, while the blue gums rustled sweetly in the background. There were some things I might have said but didn't. My parents were still alive. I felt I hadn't known the person my father was back there, what was true and what was not. When he died, the year after the programme was shown, I still didn't know.

He died one Sunday afternoon. The family had come to accept his melancholy ways and long expectation of death as the way he was, rather than something to take seriously. One day he will be dying and nobody will notice, we said to each other. But my father's life, which had been so full of small twists and reversals of fortune, turned out to have an ultimate irony about it.

In another room of the same hospital, his first great-grandchild, Joanna's daughter Amelia, lay sleeping. She was two days old and he had longed to see this baby just once before he died. I confess that somehow between the joy of becoming a grandmother, concern for Joanna, and the anxiety of daily visits with my mother to see my father, I had not really prepared myself for his death. He had lost his voice completely a week or so before, his throat either closed over by his cancer, or perhaps a constriction from going cold turkey. An earnest young intern had decided he must give up cigarettes when he entered hospital, although he had smoked them every day since he was fourteen. A few days earlier, I had given him a notebook and pencil, begging him to write a note if there was anything he needed to tell us. In a faltering hand he picked up the pencil and wrote his last message: 'Nothing to say'.

That Sunday afternoon, I went along to the maternity ward and asked that our daughter and the baby be taken to see my father. The staff refused because he was in the chest ward, classified infectious. Indeed, it was a dingy four-bedded room where there had been two deaths that week. Across the aisle from my father's bed, a wizened old jockey shouted reports of my father's condition to passers-by, in an excited falsetto.

At five o'clock we left him. Giles would be with him at six. Before we left, my father took my mother's hand and bit her thumb hard: *remember me.*

Amelia's father was with us. He was a Spaniard, something which had interested my father. Over the last years, he had tried to teach himself Spanish from one of those old yellow covered Teach Yourself books. At the door, I turned.

'Say something to him in Spanish,' I said to Amelia's father, walking behind with me. He turned back.

'*Todo está bien. La niña es hermosa. Te veré pronto abuelito,*' he said. Everything is fine. The baby is beautiful. I will see you shortly, Granddad.

Somewhere between five and six, a nurse decided to prop my father up on a chair and feed him his tea. Between spoonfuls of custard, over that last horrible supper, he stopped breathing.

My father had become something of a legend in life. So, too, he was in death.

Last week, we went to Ireland. We boarded a plane at Nice in the South of France, just half an hour's drive away from where we live. To get to the airport we catch a bus at the bottom of our street, which whirls us through the dazzling Mediterranean seascape, past Roquebrune where my distant kin, the Empress Eugenie, lived when she was old, past Beaulieu and Villefranche, stopping here and there to pick up passengers in Monaco, before dropping us at the door of the terminal. When the Aer Lingus flight took off, I began to cry. This was not what I expected of myself. I learned to control tears in public places long ago. My father always said that it showed a lack of breeding. But I couldn't help myself. I wept all the way to Dublin. I'm going to Ireland, I said over and over again as the plane swept over mountain ranges and the green valleys of France, over the sea and past Land's End.

In my handbag was a precious bundle of papers. As well as letters from my grandmother to my father, including her last, there were others from my grandfather and my great-aunts, Poll and Sal. These later ones told different versions of the story familiar to them all: the apparently sudden death of my grandmother. They contained descriptions of the last days and hours of her life, the people they knew who brought cakes to the house, and short graphic descriptions of life in Ireland during the Troubles. Included in the letters were promises of money and better times to come. One called my father Nip, another called him Lofty, another by his given name Hugh. Of equal importance, the letters included the address of the house on St Patrick's Quay where my greataunts had lived all their lives, and where my grandmother, Ann O'Hara, grew up. It was time for me to find out whether any of it still existed.

We caught the train from Dublin to Cork, down past the estuaries and tidal flats and through the green landscape, the abandoned farms, the little houses. At Cork, we caught a bus to Bandon. It is a pretty market town, more prosperous-looking than some I had seen. I thought first to call at St Peter's Church, where the death records were kept. The graveyard was a wild overgrown place, full of falling down tombstones and rusted railings. A curate, new to the town, was in charge while the vicar was away. He had such trouble opening the safe where the record was kept that he had to call in the sexton who had been there 'for a long, long time'. At last I held the book in my hands. And there, next to each other, were the names of my two great-aunts, Poll and Sal, or Margaret and Sarah to be correct, who had died just five months apart in 1949.

'So now,' I said to the sexton, 'would you be kind enough to help me find their graves?'

But although we searched, there was only one O'Hara grave, a common grave that had had its last recorded burial in 1913. 'Oh, it will be where they were laid,' the sexton informed me. 'Nothing is surer. Not everybody had their names put on the headstone. I mean, look at it this way if you will, who would be left to put an inscription for two maiden ladies, if all their family was away and gone across the sea?'

I wasn't sure about this. I thought it strange that two women as well educated as my great-aunts appeared from their letters, and so long prepared for their own deaths, would not have made other arrangements. I doubted they would have been happy laid to rest in a common grave, without an inscription. But there were no other O'Haras in that cemetery, nor, it seemed, any left in town. All gone.

The sexton talked easily to me for some time. Some things he told me unbidden rang true. About the police barracks where my grandfather was supposed to have been staying when he met my grandmother and took her away to England. About my father's and my own maiden name being common enough in Ireland.

I walked back to the town and bought a sheaf of chrysanthemums to lay on the grave. They looked incongruous in the long unkempt grass, but perhaps, on Sunday, as the congregation filed past, someone might stop and say the name O'Hara, and remember.

Afterwards, when it was too late, and I had to return to Cork, I learned that there was another newer town cemetery, about three miles out of the town. That is where I believe my great-aunts are buried.

The sexton did, however, point me in the direction of St Patrick's Quay. I walked through winding lanes, with picturesque houses side by side, painted in pretty colours, and all of it felt familiar, as if I had been there before. The quay area by the river had been renamed, but there were the houses that made up Cavendish Square, and there the house where my grandmother was born.

My father had often spoken of this house, of grand rooms and views across the river and rolling hills beyond. In my head, because we were always poor, and because I never knew what truth really meant to my father, I had come to believe that what I would find was some small derelict cottage, like the place at the end of Darwin Road.

I should have known better. Broken-down Irish cottages don't buy farms in New Zealand. Instead I found a substantial and handsome residence, ample and two-storeyed. It was all as my father had described it. This was the house that had rescued us from Darwin Road.

When Ian and I returned to Menton the other night, I felt an odd sense of peace. We had been in Edinburgh at the festival, where I had given a reading with a fellow New Zealand writer, Fiona Farrell, and it was because of the festival that I hadn't been able to stay longer in Ireland. But in a curious way, I had seen enough. My father's stories, and the strange emotional catch he got in his voice when he spoke of Ireland, made sense to me now. We floated high up in our bus from the airport, back around the bays, the mansions and the luxurious boats of the Riviera, coming down from a hill towards the rosy red tiled roofs of Menton, the citrus groves and the scent of flowers, and it was like coming home, in a sense. Or rather, I understood that this journey was nearly complete. That it had almost done its work, of taking me there and back.

There's a lot I haven't said about Menton. About the dinners by moonlight in strange magnificent old gardens, like that of Englishman William Waterfield, or the days spent in the mountain villages where we have become known, or the evenings when we ate in the town square and talked with artists and their friends who came out after dark. Or the music. Or the tango dancing. So much. But that was never the idea.

There is another part to this story, something I have been coming to.

I came to Menton with the intention of writing a different book from this one. The journey I took to Kerikeri last year, the one I wrote about at the beginning, had given me the idea of writing a retrospective account of my life in Kerikeri, alongside what the place is now, and about how the past and the present influence each other. Afterwards, I went backwards and forwards a couple more times, talking to those old timers who were left and scouring through library records. I found, for the first time, the island hideaway of the poet Lawrence Donald, and marvelled at the causeways and bridges that he had built single-handed. An empty mansion belonging to an absent owner stands there now. I visited an elderly woman I had known as a child. She lives down a long dark driveway and her rickety house is still full of the treasures of China. 'Ah,' she said, swinging a rope of pearls in her hand. 'Your father used to *work* for us.' I visited one of the Dalmatian women I went to school with, who has worked in a fish and chip shop all her life. Her olive skin is flawless, and she seemed genuinely pleased to see me. I called on one of the Maori families whose relatives I had gone to school with, and sensed they found my visit intrusive. I phoned another woman I had known when I lived there and asked if we might meet. She was, she said, rather busy making plum jam that day. 'You do rather like to trawl, don't you?' she said, as she ended the conversation.

I talked to some of the many newcomers in the town and in the adjacent bays. Most of them are rich beyond my comprehension, but in a different, more modern way than the old China hands. Nouveau riche, I suppose you would call them. I found the town as impenetrable as I had when I first went there sixty years ago although, on the face of it, the landscape had opened up. Many of the orchards had gone, and great swathes of gum trees had been cut down, giving the town a naked look. When I wondered aloud about the reason, to a man who ran a trendy little gift shop in the town, he shrugged. Dangerous, he said. Branches fall off and kill people. 'They call them widow trees,' he said. I had never heard that expression or, for that matter, that anyone had been killed by falling gum trees up there in the North.

The week before we came away to live here in France, I went for one last quick trip back, to see if I could find the missing key. I stayed away from Darwin Road until the last evening, wanting to keep myself free from the old emotional twang of the heart-strings that I felt every time I drove up that road. To be objective.

As I had done now and then over the years, I knocked on the door of the house that had replaced ours, although it was some time since I had done this. I noticed that extensive herb gardens had been planted and there was still an exotic mass of tropical foliage, a few orange trees, though not a full orchard. But there was something missing that sent a shiver down my spine, although I couldn't at first work out what it was. Something felt wrong.

I was welcomed by the latest owners, who offered to walk me round. I wished that I could walk on my own, but they were friendly and there were things they wanted to ask me about, so we meandered along together. I knew not to expect any sign of the cottage, that it had finally been dismantled. We walked towards the river, and then it hit me. I couldn't believe that I had not picked up this absence straight away. The belt of gum trees, our trees, had been cut down. I was looking at the bare space of paddocks beyond.

I stopped and said foolishly, 'The trees, why did you cut the trees down?'

The owners looked at me in a perplexed way. 'Our neighbours were having theirs done, so we thought we'd have ours done as well. They were no use.'

We walked on a little way in silence. The wife said, 'We found an old stove in the shed. We wondered where it had come from. It looks like an antique. Perhaps you might know?'

So we went into the shed that my father had built, where I learned to milk a cow and earn enough money to buy *Pride and Prejudice.*

'It's quite black. It really needs a coat of boot polish to bring it up,' said the wife, uncovering her treasure.

'It's not black,' I said immediately. 'If you scratch it, you'll find it's green.'

'Ah, so you do know it?'

'It was my mother's range.' I could feel hot embarrassed tears prodding behind my eyelids. That tiny range, the oven not much bigger than a shoebox. As they scratched and marvelled over the green enamelled surface that emerged, I began to say goodbye.

Really, there was nothing left at all.

I hadn't expected things to turn out like this. When I went looking for the end of Darwin Road, I was looking for a story that is no longer there. Instead, I found a town here in France that became the framework for my own story. Or part of it, because this is only the beginning. What followed after I left broadcasting and took charge of my life, when I at last believed that I had earned the right to call myself a writer, is another story again. When Madeleine stepped down from the airport bus at the end of our street in Menton, I saw for the first time that the Darwin Road which has haunted me for so long, is now a place in the imagination. The scent and the sunlight and the orange groves were all here, and so was our long friendship, intact on the other side of the world. I had found the end of Darwin Road, but it was not the end I expected, or where I thought I would find it.

We have known such happiness here in Menton. The rough leaves are falling over the avenue de Verdun. I have collected up my papers in the Katherine Mansfield Room at Garavan, and left a note to welcome the next writer. I have taken a last look at the engraved brass plaques on either side of the door as I closed it for the last time. The right-hand plaque lists the stories that Mansfield wrote at Villa Isola Bella; on the left these words are inscribed:

Katherine Mansfield, née à Wellington Nouvelle-Zélande le 14 Octobre 1888 morte à Fontainebleau le janvier 1923. 'You will find Isola Bella in pokerwork on my heart. Vous trouverez Isola Bella gravé sur mon Coeur.'

That line makes me very emotional because I have an idea that these words are now engraved on my own heart. They say you never get over Menton.

We have been into the mountains to eat dinner with Madame Imbert and Michel and Luc for the last time. They held an impromptu birthday party for Ian, and Madame cooked us pissaladière and ravioli tossed with freshly gathered white Italian truffles. We toasted each other over and again in a mysterious slightly cloudy wine, and we all wept. We have said goodbye to William Rubinstein in Nice, who has looked after us so kindly while we have been here, taken tea with the Waterfields and the Duponts, shaken hands with Monsieur Parabis and his wife, who live in the apartment building. We have shaken hands, too, with all the staff at the little mini-market by the bus station, opposite the end of Montée du Lutetia, and one of the young women cried. You won't be here to see my baby, she said, patting her stomach. *Le bébé.* We have said goodbye to Pepe, the waiter who kept a special plate of hors d'oeuvres for us at six o'clock when we went for a drink under the shaggy umbrellas, ducking through the cars from the café kitchen on the other side of the road. He looked dejected and shook our hands. 'Au revoir, au revoir,' we called as we walked away up the street. At the corner, we turned. He was still standing there. He raised his arm once more, and then he was out of sight.

 I am finishing this account back in Hataitai. A whole year has passed since we set out for Menton. Our grandson is planting an olive tree on the bank below us. The crisp skin of our own autumn sky stretches over us. Beyond us lie the parched bones of bare hills after a late summer drought. While we've been away a mass of wild orange nasturtiums has appeared along the length of the bank beneath the kitchen window. Their sharp peppery scent rises up to meet me as I walk down the stairs to my study. It can take a long time to find your way home.

Works by the author quoted in this volume

Mandarin Summer (Heinemann edition, 1981)

A Needle in the Heart
'All the Way to Summer'

The Best of Fiona Kidman's Short Stories
'Paradise'

'Circling to your Left'

'At the Lake So Blue'

'Nasturtium'

Ricochet Baby

Songs from the Violet Café

Search for Sister Blue (play)

Wakeful Nights: Poems Selected and New (poems)
'Wakeful Nights'

'Taupo Writers School'

'Return to Waipu'

'Carole Something Like a Lombard'

Honey and Bitters (poems)
'On Going Missing for the Wattie Awards'

'Winter Roses'

Other works quoted in this volume

Letter from Henry Eakin to Hugh Eakin, 11 March 1935

'Kerikeri Gold: A Behavioural Investigation of the Process Involved in the Evolution of Spatial Patterning and the 'personality' of Kerikeri, Bay of Islands', Christine Elson-White, master's thesis prepared for Massey University

Towards the Dawn, Lawrence Donald, Wilson & Horton [?], 1942

Dorothy's Little Tribe, Joan White (late nineteenth century children's novel)

Pride of the Lion: Waipu, The People and the Place, Waipu 150 Trust, 2002

An Accidental Life, Phoebe Meikle, AUP, 1994

'Words', Robin Hyde, from *Houses by the Sea,* The Caxton Press, 1952

'Katherine Mansfield', Robin Hyde, from *Houses by the Sea*

'The Mountain', Lauris Edmond, from *New and Selected Poems,* Oxford University Press, 1991

Acknowledgements

Grateful thanks are due to Meridian Energy who sponsored the Katherine Mansfield Fellowship which I held in 2006, and also the Winn-Manson Menton Trust and Creative New Zealand staff who administer the programme. Special thanks are due to Richard Cathie and Gordon Stewart, and also to the French Embassy in Wellington. I truly appreciated the opportunity to work at Villa Isola Bella, where Mansfield once lived, in Menton, France. I thank William Rubinstein, Luc Lanlo, Michel Imbert and Madame Berthe Imbert for their warm friendship during a wonderful year.

Three people make my writing life possible through their support and belief in me. They are Ian Kidman, husband and companion for 48 years, and my editors, Harriet Allan at Random House, and Anna Rogers.

Many people have given a great deal of their time, helping fill gaps in my memory of some events and commenting on my version of others, in the interests of accuracy. In particular, I thank our son Giles Kidman who decided, without being asked, that he wanted a true account of his life recorded. I thank other family members, including our daughter Joanna Kidman, and our niece Christine Kidman for their views on our family history. Thanks, too, are owed to Jennifer Beck, Mary (Agatha) Campbell, Sharon Crosbie, Fergus Dick, Julian Dickon, Frances Edmond, Chris Else, Cath Ferguson of the Procter Library in Kerikeri, and Trevor Ferguson, Maurice Gee, Mrs Nell Graveson, Chris Hampson, Michael Harlow, Sam Hunt, Witi Ihimaera, Madeleine McFadden, Alison Morgan, Adrienne Morgan-Lynch, Rosemary Norman, Catherine Parker, Bob Ross, Don Starr, Kristen Wickens and Niyaz Martin Wilson.

For research material, thanks are due to Jo Boyle of the Royal New Zealand Plunket Society and Claire Benson of the Ministry of Women's Affairs.

www.ingramcontent.com/pod-product-compliance
Ingram Content Group UK Ltd.
Pitfield, Milton Keynes, MK11 3LW, UK
UKHW041208180426
11947UKWH00023B/1940